Powers of the Mind:
Manifesting Success

Swami Vivekananda

GRAPEVINE INDIA

Published by

GRAPEVINE INDIA PUBLISHERS PVT LTD

www.grapevineindia.com

Delhi | Mumbai

email: grapevineindiapublishers@gmail.com

Ordering Information:

Quantity sales: Special discounts are available on quantity purchases by corporations, associations, and others.

For details, reach out to the publisher.

First published by Grapevine India 2024

Printed at Nutech Print Services - India

MAN

Man is the highest being that exists, and this is the greatest world. We can have no conception of God higher than man, so our God is man, and man is God. When we rise and go beyond and find something higher, we have to jump out of the mind, out of body and the imagination and leave this world; when we rise to be the Absolute, we are no longer in this world. Man is the apex of the only world we can ever know. All we know of animals is only by analogy, we judge them by what we do and feel ourselves.

*

According to us, there are three things in the makeup of man. There is the body, there is the mind, and there is the soul.

First let us consider the body, which is the most external thing about man.

First, see how various are the differences with respect to the body. How many varieties of nose, face, hair, height, complexion, breadth, etc., there are!

The modern ethnologists hold that variety of complexion is due to intermixture of blood. Though the hot or cold climate of the place to a certain extent affects the complexion, no doubt, yet the main cause of its change is heredity. Even in the coldest parts of the world, people with dark complexions are seen, and again in the hottest countries white men are seen to live. The complexion of the aboriginal tribes of Canada, in America, and of the Eskimos of the Northern Polar regions, is not white. While islands, such as Borneo, Celebes, etc., situated in the equatorial regions are peopled by white aborigines.

According to the Hindu Shastras, the three Hindu castes, Brahmana, Kshatriya, and Vaishya, and the several nations outside India, to wit, Cheen, Hun, Darad, Pahlava, Yavana, and Khâsh are all Aryas. This Cheen of our Shastras is not the modern Chinaman. Besides, in those days, the Chinamen did not call themselves Cheen at all. There was a distinct, powerful nation, called Cheen, living in the north-eastern parts of Kashmir, and the Darads lived where are now seen the hill-tribes between India and Afghanistan. Some remnants of the ancient Cheen are yet to be found in very small numbers, and Daradisthan is yet in existence. In the Râjatarangini , the history of Kashmir, references are often made to the supremacy of the powerful Darad-Raj. An ancient tribe of Huns reigned for a long period in the north-western parts of India. The Tibetans now call themselves Hun, but this Hun is perhaps "Hune". The fact is, that the Huns referred to in Manu are not the modern Tibetans, but it is quite probable that the modern Tibetans are the product of a mixture of the ancient Aryan Huns and some other Mogul tribes that came to Tibet from Central Asia. According to Prjevalski and the Duc d' Orleans, the Russian and French travellers, there are still found in some parts of Tibet tribes with faces and eyes of the Aryan type. "Yavana" was the name given to the Greeks. There has been much dispute about the origin of this name. Some say that the name Yavana was first used to designate a tribe of Greeks inhabiting the place called "Ionia", and hence, in the Pâli writs of the Emperor Asoka, the Greeks are named "Yonas", and afterwards from this "Yona" the Sanskrit word Yavana, was derived. Again, according to some of our Indian antiquarians, the word Yavana does not stand for the Greeks. But all these views are wrong. The original word is Yavana itself; for not only the Hindus but the ancient Egyptians and the Babylonians as well called the Greeks by that name. By the word Pahlava is meant the ancient Parsees, speaking the Pahlavi tongue. Even now, Khash denotes the semi-civilised Aryan tribes living in mountainous regions and in the Himalayas, and the word is still used in this sense. In that sense, the present Europeans are the descendants of the Khash; in other words, those Aryan tribes that were uncivilised in ancient days are all Khash.

In the opinion of modern savants, the Aryans had reddish-white complexion, black or red hair, straight noses, well-drawn eyes, etc.; and the formation of the skull varied a little according to the colour of the hair. Where the complexion is dark, there the change has come to pass owing to the mixture of the pure Aryan blood with black races. They hold that there are still some tribes to the west of the Himalayan borders who are of pure Aryan blood, and that the rest are all of mixed blood; otherwise, how could they be dark? But the European Pundits ought to know by this time that, in the southern parts of India, many children are born with red hair, which after two or three years changes into black, and that in the Himalayas many have red hair and blue or grey eyes.

Let the Pundits fight among themselves; it is the Hindus who have all along called themselves Aryas. Whether of pure or mixed blood, the Hindus are Aryas; there it rests. If the Europeans do not like us, Aryas, because we are dark, let them take another name for themselves — what is that to us?

Whether black or white, it does not matter; but of all the nations of the world, the Hindus are the handsomest and finest in feature. I am not bragging nor saying anything in exaggeration because they belong to my own nationality, but this fact is known all over the world. Where else can one find a higher percentage of fine-featured men and women than in India? Besides, it has to be taken into consideration how much more is required in our country to make us look handsome than in other countries, because our bodies are so much more exposed. In other countries, the attempt is always to make ugly persons appear beautiful under cover of elaborate dresses and clothes.

Of course, in point of health, the Westerners are far superior to us. In the West, men of forty years and women of fifty years are still young. This is, no doubt, because they take good food, dress well and live in a good climate, and above all, the secret is that they do not marry at an early age. Ask those few strong tribes among ourselves and see what their marriageable age is. Ask the hill tribes, such as, the Goorkhas, the Punjabis, the Jats, and the Afridis, what their marriageable age is. Then read your own Shastras — thirty is the age fixed for the Brahmana, twenty-five for the Kshatriya, and twenty for the Vaishya. In point of longevity and physical and mental strength, there is a great difference between the Westerners and ourselves. As soon as we attain to forty, our hope and physical and mental strength are on the decline. While, at that age, full of youthful vigour and hope, they have only made a start.

*

An intellectual, heartless man never becomes an inspired man. It is always the heart that speaks in the man of love; it discovers a greater instrument than intellect can give you, the instrument of inspiration.

* *

Religious thought is in man's very constitution, so much so that it is impossible for him to give, up religion until he can give up his mind and body, until he can give up thought and life. As long as a man thinks, this struggle must go on, and so long man must have some form of religion. Thus we see various forms of religion in the world. It is a bewildering study; but it is not, as many of us think, a vain speculation. Amidst this chaos there is harmony, throughout these discordant sounds there is a note of concord; and he who is prepared to listen to it will catch the tone.

*

Each man has a mission in life, which is the result of all his infinite past Karma. Each of you was born with a splendid heritage, which is the whole of the infinite past life of your glorious nation. Millions of your ancestors are watching, as it were, every action of yours, so be alert.

And what is the mission with which every Hindu child is born? Have you not read the proud declaration of Manu regarding the Brahmin where he says that the birth of the Brahmin is "for the protection of the treasury of religion"?

I should say that that is the mission not only of the Brahmin, but of every child, whether boy or girl, who is born in this blessed land "for the protection of the treasury of religion". And every other problem in life must be subordinated to that one principal theme. That is also the law of harmony in music.

There may be a nation whose theme of life is political supremacy; religion and everything else must become subordinate to that one great theme of its life. But here is another nation whose great theme of life is spirituality and renunciation, whose one watchword is that this world is all vanity and a delusion of three days, and everything else, whether science or knowledge, enjoyment or powers, wealth, name, or fame, must be subordinated to that one theme.

The secret of a true Hindu's character lies in the subordination of his knowledge of European sciences and learning, of his wealth, position, and name, to that one principal theme which is inborn in every Hindu child — the spirituality and purity of the race. Therefore between these two, the case of the orthodox man who has the whole of that life-spring of the race, spirituality, and the other man whose hands are full of Western imitation jewels but has no hold on the life-giving principle, spirituality — of these, I do not doubt that every one here will agree that we should choose the first, the orthodox, because there is some hope in him — he has the national theme, something to hold to; so he will live, but the other will die.

Just as in the case of individuals, if the principle of life is undisturbed, if the principal function of that individual life is present, any injuries received as regards other functions are not serious, do not kill the individual, so, as long as this principal function of our life is not disturbed, nothing can destroy our nation. But mark you, if you give up that spirituality, leaving it aside to go after the materialising civilisation of the West, the result will be that in three generations you will be an extinct race; because the backbone of the nation will be broken, the foundation upon which the national edifice has been built will be undermined, and the result will be annihilation all round.

*

Each man is perfect by his nature; prophets have manifested this perfection, but it is potential in us. How can we understand that Moses saw God unless we too see Him? If God ever came to anyone, He will come to me. I will go to God direct; let Him talk to me. I cannot take belief as a basis; that is atheism and blasphemy. If God spake to a man in the deserts of Arabia two thousand years ago, He can also speak to me today, else how can I know that He has not died? Come to God any way you can; only come.

*

Each man must begin where he stands, must learn how to control the things that are nearest to him. This body is very near to us, nearer than anything in the external universe, and this mind is the nearest of all. The Prana which is working this mind and body is the nearest to us of all the Prana in this universe. This little wave of the Prana which represents our own energies, mental and physical, is the nearest to us of all the waves of the infinite ocean of Prana. If we can succeed in controlling that little wave, then alone we can hope to control the whole of Prana. The Yogi who has done this gains perfection; no longer is he under any power. He becomes almost almighty, almost all-knowing.

*

The gigantic principles, the scope, the plan of religion were already discovered ages ago when man found the last words, as they are called, of the Vedas — "I am He" — that there is that One in whom this whole universe of matter and mind finds its unity, whom they call God, or Brahman, or Allah, or Jehovah, or any other name. We cannot go beyond that. The grand principle has been already mapped out for us. Our work lies in filling it in, working it out, applying it to every part of our lives. We have to work now so that every one will become a prophet. There is a great work before us.

In old times, many did not understand what a prophet meant. They thought it was something by chance, that just by a fiat of will or some superior intelligence, a man gained superior knowledge.

Every man who, we think, gets something by chance, has been working for it slowly and surely through ages. In modern times, we are prepared to demonstrate that this knowledge is the birthright of every living being, whosoever and wheresoever he be, and that there is no chance in this universe.

And the whole question devolves upon us: "Do we want to be prophets?" If we want, we shall be.

*

In one sense Brahman is known to every human being; he knows, "I am"; but man does not know himself as he is. We all know we are, but not how we are. All lower explanations are partial truths; but the flower, the essence of the Vedas, is that the Self in each of us is Brahman. Every phenomenon is included in birth, growth, and death — appearance, continuance and disappearance. Our own realisation is beyond the Vedas, because even they depend upon that. The highest Vedanta is the philosophy of the Beyond.

*

What we call extraordinary, superconscious inspiration is only the result of a higher development of ordinary consciousness, gained by long and continued effort. The difference between the ordinary and the extraordinary is merely one of degree in manifestation. Conscious efforts lead the way to superconscious illumination.

Infinite perfection is in every man, though unmanifested. Every man has in him the potentiality of attaining to perfect saintliness, Rishihood, or to the most exalted position of an Avatâra, or to the greatness of a hero in material discoveries. It is only a question of time and adequate well-guided investigation, etc., to have this perfection manifested. In a society where once such great men were born, there the possibility of their reappearance is greater. There can be no doubt that a society with the help of such wise guides advances faster than the one without it. But it is equally certain that such guides will rise up in the societies that are now without them and will lead them to equally rapid progress in the future.

*

Man always is perfect, or he never could become so; but he had to realise it. If man were bound by external causes, he could only be mortal. Immortality can only be true of the uncondi tioned. Nothing can act on the Atman — the idea is pure delusion; but man must identify himself with that, not with body or mind. Let him know that he is the witness of the universe, then he can enjoy the beauty of the wonderful panorama passing before him. Let him even tell himself, "I am the universe, I am Brahman." When man really identifies himself with the One, the Atman, everything is possible to him and all matter becomes his servant. As Shri Ramakrishna has said: After the butter is churned, it can be put in water or milk and will never mix with either; so when man has once realised the Self, he can no more be contaminated by the world.

*

Man as Atman is really free; as man he is bound, changed by every physical condition. As man, he is a machine with an idea of freedom; but this human body is the best and the human mind the highest mind there is.

When a man attains to the Atman state, he can take a body, making it to suit himself; he is above law. This is a statement and must be proved. Each one must prove it for himself; we may satisfy ourselves, but we cannot satisfy another.

Râja-Yoga is the only science of religion that can be demonstrated; and only what I myself have proved by experience, do I teach. The full ripeness of reason is intuition, but intuition cannot antagonise reason.

*

Man is an infinite circle whose circumference is nowhere, but the centre is located in one spot; and God is an infinite circle whose circumference is nowhere, but whose centre is everywhere. He works through all hands, sees through all eyes, walks on all feet, breathes through all bodies, lives in all life, speaks through every mouth, and thinks through every brain. Man can become like God and acquire control over the whole universe if he multiplies infinitely his centre of self-consciousness. Consciousness, therefore, is the chief thing to understand. Let us say that here is an infinite line amid darkness. We do not see the line, but on it there is one luminous point which moves on. As it moves along the line, it lights up its different parts in succession, and all that is left behind becomes dark again. Our consciousness; may well be likened to this luminous point. Its past experiences have been replaced by the present, or have become subconscious. We are not aware of their presence in us; but there they are, unconsciously influencing our body and mind. Every movement that is now being made without the help of consciousness was previously conscious. Sufficient impetus has been given to it to work of itself.

*

Morality and an ethical code, derived from religion and spirituality, has the whole of infinite man for its scope. It takes up the individual, but its relations are to the Infinite, and it takes up society also — because society is nothing but numbers of these individuals grouped together; and as it applies to the individual and his eternal relations, it must necessarily apply to the whole of society, in whatever condition it may be at any given time. Thus we see that there is always the necessity of spiritual religion for mankind. Man cannot always think of matter, however pleasurable it may be.

*

It has been said that too much attention to things spiritual disturbs our practical relations in this world. As far back as in the days of the Chinese sage Confucius, it was said, "Let us take care of this world: and then, when we have finished with this world, we will take care of other world." It is very well that we should take care of this world. But if too much attention to the spiritual may affect a little our practical relations, too much attention to the so-called practical hurts us here and hereafter. It makes us materialistic. For man is not to regard nature as his goal, but something higher.

Man is man so long as he is struggling to rise above nature , and this nature is both internal and external. Not only does it comprise the laws that govern the particles of matter outside us and in our bodies, but also the more subtle nature within, which is, in fact, the motive power governing the external. It is good and very grand to conquer external nature, but grander still to conquer our internal nature. It is grand and good to know the laws that govern the stars and planets; it is infinitely grander and better to know the laws that govern the passions, the feelings, the will, of mankind. This conquering of the inner man, understanding the secrets of the subtle workings that are within the human mind, and knowing its wonderful secrets, belong entirely to religion. Human nature — the ordinary human nature, I mean — wants to see big material facts. The ordinary man cannot understand anything that is subtle. Well has it been said that the masses admire the lion that kills a thousand lambs, never for a moment thinking that it is death to the lambs. Although a momentary triumph for the lion; because they find pleasure only in manifestations of physical strength. Thus it is with the ordinary run of mankind. They understand and find pleasure in everything that is external. But in every society there is a section whose pleasures are not in the senses, but beyond, and who now and then catch glimpses of something higher than matter and struggle to reach it. And if we read the history of nations between the lines, we shall always find that the rise of a nation comes with an increase in the number of such men; and the fall begins when this pursuit after the Infinite, however vain Utilitarians may call it, has ceased. That is to say, the mainspring of the strength Of every race lies in its spirituality, and the death of that race begins the day that spirituality wanes and materialism gains ground.

Thus, apart from the solid facts and truths that we may learn from religion, apart from the comforts that we may gain from it, religion, as a science, as a study, is the greatest and healthiest exercise that the human mind can have. This pursuit of the Infinite, this struggle to grasp the Infinite, this effort to get beyond the limitations of the senses — out of matter, as it were — and to evolve the spiritual man — this striving day and night to make the Infinite one with our being — this struggle itself is the grandest and most glorious that man can make.

*

Some persons find the greatest pleasure in eating. We have no right to say that they should not. Others find the greatest pleasure in possessing certain things. We have no right to say that they should not. But they also have no right to say "no" to the man who finds his highest pleasure in spiritual thought. The lower the organisation, the greater the pleasure in the senses. Very few men can eat a meal with the same gusto as a dog or a wolf. But all the pleasures of the dog or the wolf have gone, as it were into the senses. The lower types of humanity in all nations find pleasure in the senses, while the cultured and the educated find it in thought, in philosophy, in arts and sciences. Spirituality is a still higher plane. The subject being infinite, that plane is the highest, and the pleasure there is the highest for those who can appreciate it. So, even on the utilitarian ground that man is to seek for pleasure, he should cultivate religious thought, for it is the highest pleasure that exists. Thus religion, as a study, seems to me to be absolutely necessary.

*

God can only be known in and through man. Vibrations of light are everywhere, even in the darkest corners; but it is only in the lamp that it becomes visible to man. Similarly God, though everywhere, we can only conceive Him as a big man. All ideas of God such as merciful preserver, helper, protector — all these are human ideas, anthropomorphic; and again these must cling to a man, call him a Guru or a Prophet or an Incarnation. Man cannot go beyond his nature, no more than you can jump out of your body. What harm is there in some people worshipping their Guru when that Guru was a hundred times more holy than even your historical prophets all taken together? If there is no harm in worshipping Christ, Krishna, or Buddha, why should there be any in worshipping this man who never did or thought anything unholy, whose intellect only through intuition stands head and shoulders above all the other prophets, because they were all one-sided? It was he that brought first to the world this idea of truth, not in but of every religion, which is gaining ground all over the world, and that without the help of science or philosophy or any other acquirement. *

God comes to those who work hard. God helps them that help themselves. An opposite idea of God weakens our nerves, softens our muscles, makes us dependent. Everything independent is happy; everything dependent is miserable. Man has infinite power within himself, and he can realise it — he can realise himself as the one infinite Self. It can be done; but you do not believe it. You pray to God and keep your powder dry all the time.

*

All religions, without one exception, hold that man is a degeneration of what he was, whether they clothe this in mythological words, or in the clear language of philosophy, or in the beautiful expressions of poetry. This is the one fact that comes out of every scripture and of every mythology that the man that is, is a degeneration of what he was. This is the kernel of truth within the story of Adam's fall in the Jewish scripture. This is again and again repeated in the scriptures of the Hindus; the dream of a period which they call the Age of Truth, when no man died unless he wished to die, when he could keep his body as long as he liked, and his mind was pure and strong. There was no evil and no misery; and the present age is a corruption of that state of perfection.

*

Man is born to conquer nature and not to follow it.

*

Man is guided by the stomach. He walks and the stomach goes first and the head afterwards. Have you not seen that? It will take ages for the head to go first.

*

Knowledge is first objective, the Knower knowing Himself. The Self, the only subject, is in manifestation seeking only to know Itself. The better the mirror, the better reflection it can give; so man is the best mirror, and the purer the man, the more clearly he can reflect God.

Man makes the mistake of separating himself from God and identifying himself with the body. This mistake arises through Maya, which is not exactly delusion but might be said to be seeing the real as something else and not as it is. This identifying of ourselves with the body leads to inequality, which inevitably leads to struggle and jealousy, and so long as we see inequality, we can never know happiness. "Ignorance and inequality are the two sources of all misery", says Jnana.

*

We know as yet but little of man, consequently but little of the universe. When we know more of man, we shall probably know more of the universe. Man is the epitome of all things and all knowledge is in him. Only for the infinitesimal portion of the universe, which comes into sense-perception, are we able to find a reason; never can we give the reason for any fundamental principle. Giving a reason for a thing is simply to classify it and put it in a pigeon-hole of the mind. When we meet a new fact, we at once strive to put it in some existing category and the attempt to do this is to reason. When we succeed in placing the fact, it gives a certain amount of satisfaction, but we can never go beyond the physical plane in this classification. That man can transcend the limits of the senses is the emphatic testimony of all past ages. The Upanishads told 5,000 years ago that the realisation of God could never be had through the senses. So far, modern agnosticism agrees, but the Vedas go further than the negative side and assert in the plainest terms that man can and does transcend this sense-bound, frozen universe. He can, as it were, find a hole in the ice, through which he can pass and reach the whole ocean of life. Only by so transcending the world of sense, can he reach his true Self and realise what he really is.

Man is the greatest being that ever can be. The highest worship there is, is to worship man as Krishna, Buddha, Christ. What you want, you create.

*

The human soul has sojourned in lower and higher forms, migrating from one to another, according to the Samskaras or impressions, but it is only in the highest form as man that it attains to freedom. The man form is higher than even the angel form, and of all forms it is the highest; man is the highest being in creation, because he attains to freedom.

**

All this universe was in Brahman, and it was, as it were, projected out of Him, and has been moving on to go back to the source from which it was projected, like the electricity which comes out of the dynamo, completes the circuit, and returns to it. The same is the case with the soul. Projected from Brahman, it passed through all sorts of vegetable and animal forms, and at last it is in man, and man is the nearest approach to Brahman.

To go back to Brahman from which we have been projected is the great struggle of life. Whether people know it or not does not matter. In the universe, whatever we see of motion, of struggles in minerals or plants or animals is an effort to come back to the centre and be at rest. There was an equilibrium, and that has been destroyed; and all parts and atoms and molecules are struggling to find their lost equilibrium again. In this struggle they are combining and re-forming, giving rise to all the wonderful phenomena of nature. All struggles and competitions in animal life, plant life, and everywhere else, all social struggles and wars are but expressions of that eternal struggle to get back to that equilibrium.

*

Even when the sword was lifted to make all people follow one religion, history tells us that ten religions sprang up in its place. One religion cannot suit all. Man is the product of two forces, action and reaction, which make him think. If such forces did not exercise a man's mind, he would be incapable of thinking. Man is a creature who thinks; Manushya (man) is a being with Manas (mind); and as soon as his thinking power goes, he becomes no better than an animal. Who would like such a man? God forbid that any such state should come upon the people of India.

*

Man never dies, nor is he ever born; bodies die, but he never dies.

*

Man according to the Vedanta philosophy, is the greatest being that is in the universe, and this world of work the best place in it, because only herein is the greatest and the best chance for him to become perfect. Angels or gods, whatever you may call them, have all to become men, if they want to become perfect. This is the great centre, the wonderful poise, and the wonderful opportunity — this human life.

*

Our lives are but a passing from dream to dream. Man the infinite dreamer, dreaming finite dreams!

Oh, the blessedness of it, that nothing external can be eternal! They little know what they mean, whose hearts quake when they hear that nothing in this relative world can be eternal.

I am the infinite blue sky. Over me pass these clouds of various colours, remain a moment, and vanish. I am the same eternal blue. I am the witness, the same eternal witness of all. I see, therefore nature exists. I do not see, therefore she does not. Not one of us could see or speak if this infinite unity were broken for a moment.

*

Only man makes Karma. Karma means work which will produce effect. When a man dies and becomes a Deva, he has only a period of pleasure, and during that time makes no fresh Karma; it is simply a reward for his past good Karma. When the good Karma is worked out, then the remaining Karma begins to take effect, and he comes down to earth. He becomes man again, and if he does very good works, and purifies himself, he goes to Brahmaloka and comes back no more.

*

Nature is conquered by man every day. As a race, man is manifesting his power. Try in imagination to put a limit to this power in man. You admit that man as a race has infinite power, has [an] infinite body. The only question is what you are. Are you the race or one [individual]? The moment you isolate yourself, everything hurts you. The moment you expand and feel for others, you gain help. The selfish man is the most miserable in the world. The happiest is the man who is not at all selfish.

*

All the people that work and toil and labour like machines do not really enjoy life, but it is the wise man who enjoys. A rich man buys a picture at a cost of a hundred thousand dollars perhaps, but it is the man who understands art that enjoys it; and if the rich man is without knowledge of art, it is useless to him, he is only the owner. All over the world, it is the wise man who enjoys the happiness of the world. The ignorant man never enjoys; he has to work for others unconsciously.

*

We should follow reason and also sympathise with those who do not come to any sort of belief, following reason. For it is better that mankind should become atheist by following reason than blindly believe in two hundred millions of gods on the authority of anybody. What we want is progress, development, realisation. No theories ever made men higher. No amount of books can help us to become purer. The only power is in realisation, and that lies in ourselves and comes from thinking. Let men think. A clod of earth never thinks; but it remains only a lump of earth. The glory of man is that he is a thinking being. It is the nature of man to think and therein he differs from animals. I believe in reason and follow reason having seen enough of the evils of authority, for I was born in a country where they have gone to the extreme of authority.

*

This external world is only the world of suggestion. All that we see, we project out of our own minds. A grain of sand gets washed into the shell of an oyster and irritates it. The irritation produces a secretion in the oyster, which covers the grain of sand and the beautiful pearl is the result. Similarly, external things furnish us with suggestions, over which we project our own ideals and make our objects. The wicked see this world as a perfect hell, and the good as a perfect heaven. Lovers see this world as full of love, and haters as full of hatred; fighters see nothing but strife, and the peaceful nothing but peace. The perfect man sees nothing but God. So we always worship our highest ideal, and when we have reached the point, when we love the ideal as the ideal, all arguments and doubts vanish for ever. Who cares whether God can be demonstrated or not? The ideal can never go, because it is a part of my own nature. I shall only question the ideal when I question my own existence, and as I cannot question the one, I cannot question the other. Who cares whether God can be almighty and all-merciful at the same time or not ? Who cares whether He is the rewarder of mankind, whether He looks at us with the eyes of a tyrant or with the eyes of a beneficent monarch?

*

In worshipping God we have been always worshipping our own hidden Self. The worst lie that you ever tell yourself is that you were born a sinner or a wicked man. He alone is a sinner who sees a sinner in another man. Suppose there is a baby here, and you place a bag of gold on the table. Suppose a robber comes and takes the gold away. To the baby it is all the same; because there is no robber inside, there is no robber outside. To sinners and vile men, there is vileness outside, but not to good men. So the wicked see this universe as a hell, and the partially good see it as heaven, while the perfect beings realise it as God Himself. Then alone the veil falls from the eyes, and the man, purified and cleansed, finds his whole vision changed. The bad dreams that have been torturing him for millions of years, all vanish, and he who was thinking of himself either as a man, or a god, or a demon, he who was thinking of himself as living in low places, in high places, on earth, in heaven, and so on, finds that he is really omnipresent; that all time is in him, and that he is not in time; that all the heavens are in him, that he is not in any heaven; and that all the gods that man ever worshipped are in him, and that he is not in any one of those gods. He was the manufacturer of gods and demons, of men and plants and animals and stones, and the real nature of man now stands unfolded to him as being higher than heaven, more perfect than this universe of ours, more infinite than infinite time, more omnipresent than the omnipresent ether. Thus alone man becomes fearless, and becomes free. Then all delusions cease, all miseries vanish, all fears come to an end for ever. Birth goes away and with it death; pains fly, and with them fly away pleasures; earths vanish, and with them vanish heavens; bodies vanish, and with them vanishes the mind also. For that man disappears the whole universe, as it were. This searching, moving, continuous struggle of forces stops for ever, and that which was manifesting itself as force and matter, as struggles of nature, as nature itself, as heavens and earths and plants and animals and men and angels, all that becomes transfigured into one infinite, unbreakable, unchangeable existence, and the knowing man finds that he is one with that existence. "Even as clouds of various colours come before the sky, remain there for a second and then vanish away," even so before this soul are all these visions coming, of earths and heavens, of the moon and the gods, of pleasures and pains; but they all pass away leaving the one infinite, blue, unchangeable sky. The sky never changes; it is the clouds that change. It is a mistake to think that the sky is changed. It is a mistake to think that we are impure, that we are limited, that we are separate. The real man is the one Unit Existence.

*

If man rests content with the present and gives up all search into the beyond, mankind will have to go back to the animal plane again. It is religion, the inquiry into the beyond, that makes the difference between man and an animal. Well has it been said that man is the only animal that naturally looks upwards; every other animal naturally looks down. That looking upward and going upward and seeking perfection are what is called salvation; and the sooner a man begins to go higher, the sooner he raises himself towards this idea of truth as salvation. It does not consist in the amount of money in your pocket, or the dress you wear, or the house you live in, but in the wealth of spiritual thought in your brain. That is what makes for human progress, that is the source of all material and intellectual progress, the motive power behind, the enthusiasm that pushes mankind forward.

INTELLIGENCE, KNOWLEDGE

The Vedanta says that the Soul is in its nature Existence absolute, Knowledge absolute, Bliss absolute. But these are not qualities of the Soul: they are one, not three, the essence of the Soul; and it agrees with the Sankhya in thinking that intelligence belongs to nature, inasmuch as it comes through nature. The Vedanta also shows that what is called intelligence is a compound. For instance, let us examine our perceptions. I see a black-board. How does the knowledge come? What the German philosophers call "the thing-in-itself" of the blackboard is unknown, I can never know it. Let us call it x .

The black-board x acts on my mind, and the mind reacts. The mind is like a lake. Throw a stone in a lake and a reactionary wave comes towards the stone; this wave is not like the stone at all, it is a wave. The black-board x is like a stone which strikes the mind and the mind throws up a wave towards it, and this wave is what we call the black-board.

I see you. You as reality are unknown and unknowable. You are x and you act upon my mind, and the mind throws a wave in the direction from which the impact comes, and that wave is what I call Mr. or Mrs. So-and-so.

There are two elements in the perception, one coming from outside and the other from inside, and the combination of these two, x + mind, is our external universe. All knowledge is by reaction. In the case of a whale it has been determined by calculation how long after its tail is struck, its mind reacts and the whale feels the pain.

Similar is the case with internal perception. The real self within me is also unknown and unknowable. Let us call it y .

When I know myself as so-and-so, it is y + the mind. That y strikes a blow on the mind. So our whole world is x + mind (external), and y + mind (internal), x and y standing for the thing-in-itself behind the external and the internal worlds respectively.

*

According to Vedanta, the three fundamental factors of consciousness are, I exist, I know, and I am blessed The idea that I have no want, that I am restful, peaceful, that nothing can disturb me, which comes from time to time, is the central fact of our being, the basic principle of our life; and when it becomes limited, and becomes a compound, it manifests itself as existence phenomenal, knowledge phenomenal, and love. Every man exists, and every man must know, and every man is mad for love. He cannot help loving. Through all existence, from the lowest to the highest, all must love. The y , the internal thing-in-itself, which, combining with mind, manufactures existence, knowledge, and love, is called by the Vedantists. Existence absolute, Knowledge absolute, Bliss absolute. That real existence is limitless, unmixed, uncombined, knows no change, is the free soul; when it gets mixed up, muddled up, as it were, with the mind, it becomes what we call individual existence. It is plant life, animal life, human life, just as universal space is cut off in a room, in a jar, and so on. And that real knowledge is not what we know, not intuition, nor reason, nor instinct. When that degenerates and is confused, we call it intuition; when it degenerates more, we call it reason; and when it degenerates still more, we call it instinct. That knowledge itself is Vijnâna, neither intuition, nor reason nor instinct. The nearest expression for it is all-knowingness. There is no limit to it, no combination in it. That bliss, when it gets clouded over, we call love, attraction for gross bodies or fine bodies, or for ideas. This is only a distorted manifestation of that blessedness. Absolute Existence, absolute Knowledge, and absolute Blessedness are not qualities of the soul, but the essence; there is no difference between them and the soul. And the three are one; we see the one thing in three different aspects. They are beyond all relative knowledge. That eternal knowledge of the Self percolating through the brain of man becomes his intuition, reason, and so on. Its manifestation varies according to the medium through which it shines. As soul, there is no difference between man and the lowest animal, only the latter's brain is less developed and the manifestation through it which we call instinct is very dull. In a man the brain is much finer, so the manifestation is much clearer, and in the highest man it becomes entirely clear. So with existence; the existence which we know, the limited sphere of existence, is simply a reflection of that real existence which is the nature of the soul. So with bliss; that which we call love or attraction is but the rejection of the eternal blessedness of the Self. With manifestation comes limitation, but the unmanifested, the essential nature of the soul, is unlimited; to that blessedness there is no limit. But in love there is limitation. I love you one day, I hate you the next. My love increases one day and decreases the next, because it is only a manifestation.

*

The first point we will contend with Kapila is his idea of God. Just as the series of modifications of Prakriti, beginning with the individual intellect and ending with the individual body, require a Purusha behind, as the ruler and governor, so, in the Cosmos, the universal intellect, the universal egoism, the universal mind, all universal fine and gross materials, must have a ruler and governor. How will the cosmic series become complete without the universal Purusha behind them all as the ruler and governor? If you deny a universal Purusha behind the cosmic series, we deny your Purusha behind the individual series. If it be true that behind the series of graded, evolved individual manifestations, there stands One that is beyond them all, the Purusha who is not composed of matter, the very same logic will apply to the case of universal manifestations. This Universal Self which is beyond the universal modifications of Prakriti is what is called Ishwara, the Supreme Ruler, God.

Now comes the more important point of difference. Can there be more than one Purusha? The Purusha, we have seen, is omnipresent and infinite. The omnipresent, the infinite, cannot be two. If there are two infinites A and B, the infinite A would limit the infinite B, because the infinite B is not the infinite A, and the infinite A is not the infinite B. Difference in identity means exclusion, and exclusion means limitation. Therefore, A and B, limiting each other, cease to be infinites. Hence, there can be but one infinite, that is, one Purusha.

*

Now we will take up our x and y and show they are one. We have shown how what we call the external world is x + mind, and the internal world y + mind; x and y are both quantities unknown and unknowable. All difference is due to time, space, and causation. These are the constituent elements of the mind. No mentality is possible without them. You can never think without time, you can never imagine anything without space, and you can never have anything without causation. These are the forms of the mind. Take them away, and the mind itself does not exist. All difference is, therefore, due to the mind. According to Vedanta, it is the mind, its forms, that have limited x and y apparently and made them appear as external and internal worlds. But x and y , being both beyond the mind, are without difference and hence one. We cannot attribute any quality to them, because qualities are born of the mind. That which is qualityless must be one; x is without qualities, it only takes qualities of the mind; so does y ; therefore these x and y are one. The whole universe is one. There is only one Self in the universe, only One Existence, and that One Existence, when it passes through the forms of time, space, and causation, is called by different names, Buddhi, fine matter, gross matter, all mental and physical forms. Everything in the universe is that One, appearing in various forms. When a little part of it comes, as it were, into this network of time, space, and causation, it takes forms; take off the network, and it is all one. Therefore in the Advaita philosophy, the whole universe is all one in the Self which is called Brahman. That Self when it appears behind the universe is called God. The same Self when it appears behind this little universe, the body, is the soul. This very soul, therefore, is the Self in man. There is only one Purusha, the Brahman of the Vedanta; God and man, analysed, are one in It. The universe is you yourself, the unbroken you; you are throughout the universe.

"In all hands you work, through all mouths you eat, through all nostrils you breathe through all minds you think." The whole universe is you; the universe is your body; you are the universe both formed and unformed. You are the soul of the universe and its body also. You are God, you are the angels, you are man, you are animals, you are the plants, you are the minerals, you are everything; the manifestation of everything is you. Whatever exists is you. You are the Infinite. The Infinite cannot be divided. It can have no parts, for each part would be infinite, and then the part would be identical with the whole, which is absurd. Therefore the idea that you are Mr. So-and-so can never be true; it is a day-dream. Know this and be free. This is the Advaita conclusion. "I am neither the body, nor the organs, nor am I the mind; I am Existence, Knowledge, and Bliss absolute; I am He." This is true knowledge; all reason and intellect, and everything else is ignorance. Where is knowledge for me, for I am knowledge itself! Where is life for me, for I am life itself! I am sure I live, for I am life, the One Being, and nothing exists except through me, and in me, and as me. I am manifested through the elements, but I am the free One. Who seeks freedom? Nobody. If you think that you are bound, you remain bound; you make your own bondage. If you know that you are free, you are free this moment. This is knowledge, knowledge of freedom. Freedom is the goal of all nature.

MIND

*

The Being of perfect nature, universally appearing to us, is God, is Absolute. The undifferentiated is the perfect condition; all others must be lower and not permanent.

What makes the undifferentiated appear differentiated to mind? This is the same kind of question as what is the origin of evil and free will? The question itself is contradictory and impossible, because the question takes for granted cause and effect. There is no cause and effect in the undifferentiated; the question assumes that the undifferentiated is in the same condition as the differentiated.

"Whys" and "wherefores" are in mind only. The Self is beyond causation, and It alone is free. Its light it is which percolates through every form of mind. With every action I assert I am free, and yet every action proves that I am bound.

The real Self is free, yet when mixed with mind and body, It is not free. The will is the first manifestation of the real Self; the first limitation therefore of this real Self is the will. Will is a compound of Self and mind.

Now, no compound can be permanent, so that when we will to live, we must die. Immortal life is a contradiction in terms, for life, being a compound, cannot be immortal. True Being is undifferentiated and eternal .

*

All that is differentiated is nature. Nature is the quality of the plant, the quality of the animal, and the quality of man. Man's life behaves according to definite methods; so does his mind. Thoughts do not just happen, there is a certain method in their rise, existence and fall. In other words, just as external phenomena are bound by law, internal phenomena, that is to say, the life and mind of man, are also bound by law.

When we consider law in relation to man's mind and existence, it is at once obvious that there can be no such thing as free will and free existence. We know how animal nature is wholly regulated by law. The animal does not appear to exercise any free will. The same is true of man; human nature also is bound by law. The law governing functions of the human mind is called the law of Karma.

Nobody has ever seen anything produced out of nothing; if anything arises in the mind, that also must have been produced from something.

When we speak of free will, we mean the will is not caused by anything.

But that cannot be true, the will is caused; and since it is caused, it cannot be free — it is bound by law. That I am willing to talk to you and you come to listen to me, that is law. Everything that I do or think or feel, every part of my conduct or behaviour, my every movement — all is caused and therefore not free. This regulation of our life and mind — that is the law of Karma.

If such a doctrine had been introduced in olden times into a Western community, it would have produced a tremendous commotion. The Western man does not want to think his mind is governed by law. In India it was accepted as soon as it was propounded by the most ancient Indian system of philosophy. There is no such thing as freedom of the mind; it cannot be.

*

The Vedas are full of passages which prove the existence of a Personal God. The Rishis, who through long devotion saw God, had a peep into the unknown and threw their challenge to the world. It is only presumptuous men, who have not walked in the path described by the Rishis and who have not followed their teachings, that criticise them and oppose them.

No man has yet come forward who would dare to say that he has properly followed their directions and has not seen anything and that these men are liars. There are men who have been under trial at various times and have felt that they have not been forsaken by God. The world is such that if faith in God does not offer us any consolation, it is better to commit suicide.

A pious missionary went out on business. All of a sudden his three sons died of cholera. His wife covered the three dead bodies of her beloved children with a sheet and was awaiting her husband at the gate.

When he returned, she detained him at the gate and put him the question, "My dear husband, some one entrusts something to you and in your absence suddenly takes it back. Will you feel sorry?" He replied, "Certainly I would not."

Then she took him in, removed the sheet and showed the three corpses. He bore this calmly and buried the bodies. Such is the strength of mind of those who hold firm faith in the existence of an all – merciful God who disposes of everything in the universe.

The Absolute can never be thought of. We can have no idea of a thing unless it is finite. God the infinite can only be conceived and worshipped as the finite.

*

All these senses, external and internal, must be under the disciple's control. By hard practice he has to arrive at the stage where he can assert his mind against the senses, against the commands of nature. He should be able to say to his mind, "You are mine; I order you, do not see or hear anything", and the mind will not see or hear anything — no form or sound will react on the mind.

In that state the mind has become free of the domination of the senses, has become separated from them. No longer is it attached to the senses and the body. The external things cannot order the mind now; the mind refuses to attach itself to them. Beautiful fragrance is there.

The disciple says to the mind, "Do not smell", and the mind does not perceive the fragrance. When you have arrived at that point, you are just beginning to be a disciple. That is why when everybody says, "I know the truth", I say, "If you know the truth, you must have self-control; and if you have control of yourself, show it by controlling these organs."

*

Next, the mind must be made to quiet down. It is rushing about. Just as I sit down to meditate, all the vilest subjects in the world come up. The whole thing is nauseating. Why should the mind think thoughts I do not want it to think? I am as it were a slave to the mind. No spiritual knowledge is possible so long as the mind is restless and out of control. The disciple has to learn to control the mind.

Yes, it is the function of the mind to think. But it must not think if the disciple does not want it to; it must stop thinking when he commands it to. To qualify as a disciple, this state of the mind is very necessary.

*

Also, the disciple must have great power of endurance. Life seems comfortable; and you find the mind behaves well when everything is going well with you. But if something goes wrong, your mind loses its balance. That is not good. Bear all evil and misery without one murmur of hurt, without one thought of unhappiness, resistance, remedy, or retaliation. That is true endurance; and that you must acquire.

Good and evil there always are in the world. Many forget there is any evil — at least they try to forget; and when evil comes upon them, they are overwhelmed by it and feel bitter. There are others who deny that there is any evil at all and consider everything good. That also is a weakness; that also proceeds from a fear of evil.

If something is evil-smelling, why sprinkle it with rose water and call it fragrant? Yes, there are good and evil in the world — God has put evil in the world. But you do not have to whitewash Him. Why there is evil is none of your business. Please have faith and keep quiet.

*

Without the "I" there can be no "you" outside. From this some philosophers came to the conclusion that the external world did not exist save in the subject; that the "you" existed only in the "I". Others have argued that the "I" can only be known through the "you" and with equal logic. These two views are partial truths, each wrong in part and each right in part. Thought is as much material and as much in nature as body is. Both matter and mind exist in a third, a unity which divides itself into the two. This unity is the Atman, the real Self.

*

Give up all desire for enjoyment in earth or heaven. Control the organs of the senses and control the mind. Bear every misery without even knowing that you are miserable. Think of nothing but spiritual freedom. Have faith in Guru, in his teachings, and in the surety that you can get free. Say "Soham, Soham" whatever comes. Tell yourself this even in eating, walking, suffering; tell the mind this incessantly — that what we see never existed, that there is only "I". Flash — the dream will break! Think day and night, this universe is zero, only God is. Have intense desire to get free.

*

Before we can control the mind we must study it. We have to seize this unstable mind and drag it from its wanderings and fix it on one idea. Over and over again this must be done. By power of will we must get hold of the mind and make it stop and reflect upon the glory of God.

The easiest way to get hold of the mind is to sit quiet and let it drift where it will for a while. Hold fast to the idea, "I am the witness watching my mind drifting. The mind is not I." Then see it think as if it were a thing entirely apart from yourself. Identify yourself with God, never with matter or with the mind.

Picture the mind as a calm lake stretched before you and the thoughts that come and go as bubbles rising and breaking on its surface. Make no effort to control the thoughts, but watch them and follow them in imagination as they float away. This will gradually lessen the circles. For the mind ranges over wide circles of thought and those circles widen out into ever-increasing circles, as in a pond when we throw a stone into it.

We want to reverse the process and starting with a huge circle make it narrower until at last we can fix the mind on one point and make it stay there. Hold to the idea, "I am not the mind, I see that I am thinking, I am watching my mind act", and each day the identification of yourself with thought and feeling will grow less, until at last you can entirely separate yourself from the mind and actually know it to be apart from yourself.

When this is done, the mind is your servant to control as you will. The first stage of being a Yogi is to go beyond the senses. When the mind is conquered, he has reached the highest stage.

*

"If I know one lump of clay, I know the whole mass of clay." The universe is all built on the same plan. The individual is only a part, like the lump of clay. If we know the human soul—which is one atom—its beginning and general history, we know the whole of nature.

Birth, growth, development, decay, death—this is the sequence in all nature and is the same in the plant and the man. The difference is only in time. The whole cycle may be completed in one case in a day, in the other in three score years and ten; the methods are the same. The only way to reach a sure analysis of the universe is by the analysis of our own minds.

A proper psychology is essential to the understanding of religion. To reach Truth by reason alone is impossible, because imperfect reason cannot study its own fundamental basis. Therefore the only way to study the mind is to get at facts, and then intellect will arrange them and deduce the principles. The intellect has to build the house; but it cannot do so without bricks and it cannot make bricks. Jnana-Yoga is the surest way of arriving at facts.

*

We make a tremendous distinction between matter and mind; we think that the mind is entirely different from matter. Actually, they are but one nature, half of which is continually acting on the other half. Matter is pressing upon the mind in the form of various sensations. These sensations are nothing but force. The force from the outside evokes the force within. From the will to respond to or get away from the outer force, the inner force becomes what we call thought.

Both matter and mind are really nothing but forces; and if you analyse them far enough, you will find that at root they are one. The very fact that the external force can somehow evoke the internal force shows that somewhere they join each other — they must be continuous and, therefore, basically the same force. When you get to the root of things, they become simple and general.

Since the same force appears in one form as matter and in another form as mind, there is no reason to think matter and mind are different. Mind is changed into matter, matter is changed into mind. Thought force becomes nerve force, muscular force; muscular and nerve force become thought force. Nature is all this force, whether expressed as matter or mind.

*

The materialist frightens the idealist by claiming to derive his mind from the elements of the laboratory, while all the time he is struggling to express something higher than all elements and atoms, something of which both the external and the internal phenomena are results, and which he terms matter. The idealist, on the other hand, wants to derive all the elements and atoms of the materialist from his own thought, even while catching glimpses of something which is the cause of both mind and matter, and which he oft-times calls God. That is to say, one party wants to explain the whole universe by a portion of it which is external, the other by another portion which is internal.

Both of these attempts are impossible. Mind and matter cannot explain each other. The only explanation is to be sought for in something which will embrace both matter and mind.

*

Mind is cognised by the Atman, but it is not self-illuminated. The Atman cannot be the cause of anything. How can it be? How can the Purusha join itself to Prakriti (nature)? It does not; it is only illusively thought to do so....

*

The next point is how to use this Prana. We all use it, but how sadly we waste it! The first doctrine in the preparatory stage is that all knowledge is the outcome of experience. Whatever is beyond the five senses must also be experienced in order to become true to us.

Our mind is acting on three planes: the subconscious, conscious, and superconscious. Of men, the Yogi alone is superconscious. The whole theory of Yoga is to go beyond the mind. These three planes can be understood by considering the vibrations of light or sound. There are certain vibrations of light too slow to become visible; then as they get faster, we see them as light; and then they get too fast for us to see them at all. The same with sound.

How to transcend the senses without disturbing the health is what we want to learn. The Western mind has stumbled into acquiring some of the psychic gifts which in them are abnormal and are frequently the sign of disease. The Hindu has studied and made perfect this subject of science, which all may now study without fear or danger.

Mental healing is a fine proof of the superconscious state; for the thought which heals is a sort of vibration in the Prana, and it does not go as a thought but as something higher for which we have no name.

*

Each thought has three states. First, the rising or beginning, of which we are unconscious; second, when the thought rises to the surface; and third, when it goes from us. Thought is like a bubble rising to the surface. When thought is joined to will, we call it power. That which strikes the sick person whom you are trying to help is not thought, but power. The self-man running through it all is called in Sanskrit Sutrâtmâ, the "Thread-self".

The last and highest manifestation of Prana is love. The moment you have succeeded in manufacturing love out of Prana, you are free. It is the hardest and the greatest thing to gain. You must not criticise others; you must criticise yourself . If you see a drunkard, do not criticise him; remember he is you in another shape. He who has not darkness sees no darkness in others. What you have inside you is that you see in others. This is the surest way of reform. If the would-be reformers who criticise and see evil would themselves stop creating evil, the world would be better. Beat this idea into yourself.

*

The modern idea of nature includes only that part of the universe that is manifested on the physical plane. That which is generally understood to be mind is not considered to be nature.

Philosophers endeavouring to prove the freedom of the will have excluded the mind from nature; for as nature is bound and governed by law, strict unbending law, mind, if considered to be in nature, would be bound by law also. Such a claim would destroy the doctrine of free will; for how can that be free which is bound by law?

Law itself is the operation of cause and effect. Certain things happen according to certain other things which have gone before. Every precedent has its consequent. Thus it is in nature. If this operation of law obtains in the mind, the mind is bound and is therefore not free. No, the will is not free. How can it be? But we all know, we all feel, that one are free. Life would have no meaning, it would not be worth living, if we were not free.

The Eastern philosophers accepted this doctrine, or rather propounded it, that the mind and the will are within time, space, and causation, the same as so-called matter; and that they are therefore bound by the law of causation. We think in time; our thoughts are bound by time; all that exists, exists in time and space. All is bound by the law of causation.

That which we call matter and mind are one and the same substance. The only difference is in the degree of vibration. Mind at a very low rate of vibration is what is known as matter. Matter at a high rate of vibration is what is known as mind. Both are the same substance; and therefore, as matter is bound by time and space and causation, mind which is matter at a high rate of vibration is bound by the same law.... Mind becomes matter, and matter in its turn becomes mind, it is simply a question of vibration.

Nature is homogeneous. Differentiation is in manifestation. The Sanskrit word for nature is Prakriti, and means literally differentiation. All is one substance, but it is manifested variously.

Mind becomes matter, and matter in its turn becomes mind, it is simply a question of vibration.

Take a bar of steel and charge it with a force sufficient to cause it to vibrate, and what would happen? If this were done in a dark room, the first thing you would be aware of would be a sound, a humming sound. Increase the force, and the bar of steel would become luminous; increase it still more, and the steel would disappear altogether. It would become mind.

Take another illustration: If I do not eat for ten days, I cannot think. Only a few stray thoughts are in my mind. I am very weak and perhaps do not know my own name. Then I eat some bread, and in a little while I begin to think; my power of mind has returned. The bread has become mind. Similarly, the mind lessens its rate of vibration and manifests itself in the body, becomes matter.

As to which is first — matter or mind, let me illustrate: A hen lays an egg; the egg brings out another hen; that hen lays another egg; that egg brings out another hen, and so on in an endless chain. Now which is first — the egg or the hen? You cannot think of an egg that was not laid by a hen, or a hen that was not hatched out of an egg. It makes no difference which is first. Nearly all our ideas run themselves into the hen and egg business.

The greatest truths have been forgotten because of their very simplicity. Great truths are simple because they are of universal application. Truth itself is always simple. Complexity is due to man's ignorance.

*

The book one must read to learn natural sciences is the book of nature. The book from which to learn religion is your own mind and heart. The sage is often ignorant of physical science, because he reads the wrong book — the book within; and the scientist is too often ignorant of religion, because he too reads the wrong book — the book without.

*

Can you tell me where this "I" exists? How can you speak of anything being killed, which never exists at all? Man only remains hypnotised with the false idea of an ego. When this ghost is off from us, all dreams vanish, and then it is found that the one Self only exists from the highest Being to a blade of grass. This will have to be known, to be realised. All practice or worship is only for taking off this veil. When that will go, you will find that the Sun of Absolute Knowledge is shining in Its own lustre. For the Atman only is self-luminous and has to be realised by Itself.

How can that, which can be experienced only by itself be known with the help of any other thing? Hence the Shruti says, " — Well, through what means is that to be known which is the Knower?"

Whatever you know, you know through the instrumentality of your mind. But mind is something material. It is active only because there is the pure Self behind it. So, how can you know that Self through your mind? But this only becomes known, after all, that the mind cannot reach the pure Self, no, nor even the intellect. Our relative knowledge ends just there. Then, when the mind is free from activity or functioning, it vanishes, and the Self is revealed. This state has been described by the commentator Shankara as supersensuous perception.

*

Between the intellect and the grosser matter outside there is only a difference in degree. The Purusha is the only thing which is immaterial. The mind is an instrument, as it were, in the hands of the soul, through which the soul catches external objects. The mind is constantly changing and vacillating, and can, when perfected, either attach itself to several organs, to one, or to none.

For instance, if I hear the clock with great attention, I will not, perhaps, see anything although my eyes may be open, showing that the mind was not attached to the seeing organ, while it was to the hearing organ. But the perfected mind can be attached to all the organs simultaneously. It has the reflexive power of looking back into its own depths.

This reflexive power is what the Yogi wants to attain; by concentrating the powers of the mind, and turning them inward, he seeks to know what is happening inside. There is in this no question of mere belief; it is the analysis arrived at by certain philosophers.

*

The mind is omnipresent and can be heard and felt anywhere.

*

The science of Raja-Yoga proposes to give us a means of observing the internal states. The instrument is the mind itself. The power of attention, when properly guided, and directed towards the internal world, will analyse the mind, and illumine facts for us.

The powers of the mind are like rays of light dissipated; when they are concentrated, they illumine. This is our only means of knowledge. Everyone is using it, both in the external and the internal world; but, for the psychologist, the same minute observation has to be directed to the internal world, which the scientific man directs to the external; and this requires a great deal of practice.

From our childhood upwards we have been taught only to pay attention to things external, but never to things internal; hence most of us have nearly lost the faculty of observing the internal mechanism. To turn the mind as it were, inside, stop it from going outside, and then to concentrate all its powers, and throw them upon the mind itself, in order that it may know its own nature, analyse itself, is very hard work. Yet that is the only way to anything which will be a scientific approach to the subject.

*

The purer the mind, the easier it is to control. Purity of the mind must be insisted upon if you would control it. Do not think covetously about mere mental powers. Let them go. One who seeks the powers of the mind succumbs to them. Almost all who desire powers become ensnared by them.

Perfect morality is the all in all of complete control over mind. The man who is perfectly moral has nothing more to do; he is free. The man who is perfectly moral cannot possibly hurt anything or anybody. Non-injuring has to be attained by him who would be free. No one is more powerful than he who has attained perfect non-injuring. No one could fight, no one could quarrel, in his presence. Yes, his very presence, and nothing else, means peace, means love wherever he may be. Nobody could be angry or fight in his presence. Even the animals, ferocious animals, would be peaceful before him.

*

I once knew a Yogi, a very old man, who lived in a hole in the ground all by himself. All he had was a pan or two to cook his meals in. He ate very little, and wore scarcely anything, and spent most of his time meditating.

With him all people were alike. He had attained to non-injuring. What he saw in everything, in every person, in every animal, was the Soul, the Lord of the Universe. With him, every person and every animal was "my Lord". He never addressed any person or animal in any other way.

Well, one day a thief came his way and stole one of his pans. He saw him and ran after him. The chase was a long one.

At last the thief from exhaustion had to stop, and the Yogi, running up to him, fell on his knees before him and said, "My Lord, you do me a great honour to come my way. Do me the honour to accept the other pan. It is also yours."

This old man is dead now. He was full of love for everything in the world. He would have died for an ant. Wild animals instinctively knew this old man to be their friend. Snakes and ferocious animals would go into his hole and sleep with him. They all loved him and never fought in his presence.

*

The superconscious is the goal. Then when that state is reached, this very man becomes divine, becomes free. And to the mind thus trained to transcend all, gradually this universe will begin to give up its secrets; the book of nature will be read chapter after chapter, till the goal is attained, and we pass from this valley of life and death to that One, where death and life do not exist, and we know the Real and become the Real.

The first thing necessary is a quiet and peaceable life. If I have to go about the world the whole day to make a living, it is hard for me to attain to anything very high in this life. Perhaps in another life I shall be born under more propitious circumstances. But if I am earnest enough, these very circumstances will change even in this birth.

Was there anything you did not get which you really wanted? It could not be. For it is the want that creates the body. It is the light that has bored the holes, as it were, in your head, called the eyes. If the light had not existed, you would have had no eyes. It is sound that had made the ears. The object of perception existed first, before you made the organ. In a few hundred thousand years or earlier, we may have other organs to perceive electricity and other things.

There is no desire for a peaceful mind. Desire will not come unless there is something outside to fulfil it.

*

This mind is a part of the universal mind. Each mind is connected with every other mind. And each mind, wherever it is located, is in actual communication with the whole world.

*

The mind should always go towards God. No other things have any right to withhold it. It should continuously think of God, though this is a very hard task; yet it can be done by persistent practice. What we are now is the result of our past practice. Again, practice makes us what we shall be. So practice the other way; one sort of turning round has brought us this way, turn the other way and get out of it as soon as you can.

Thinking of the senses has brought us down here — to cry one moment, to rejoice the next, to be at the mercy of every breeze, slave to everything. This is shameful, and yet we call ourselves spirits. Go the other way, think of God; let the mind not think of any physical or mental enjoyment, but of God alone. When it tries to think of anything else, give it a good blow, so that it may turn round and think of God.

As oil poured from one vessel to another falls in an unbroken line, as chimes coming from a distance fall upon the ear as one continuous sound, so should the mind flow towards God in one continuous stream. We should not only impose this practice on the mind, but the senses too should be employed. Instead of hearing foolish things, we must hear about God; instead of talking foolish words, we must talk of God. Instead of reading foolish books, we must read good ones which tell of God.

*

You are not bound by law. That is in your nature. The mind is in nature and is bound by law. All nature is bound by law, the law of its own action; and this law can never be broken. If you could break a law of nature, all nature would come to an end in an instant. There would be no more nature. He who attains freedom breaks the law of nature, and for him nature fades away and has no more power over him. Each one will break the law but once and for ever; and that will end his trouble with nature.

POWERS OF THE MIND

All over the world there has been the belief in the supernatural throughout the ages. All of us have heard of extraordinary happenings, and many of us have had some personal experience of them. I would rather introduce the subject by telling you certain facts which have come within my own experience. I once heard of a man who, if any one went to him with questions in his mind, would answer them immediately; and I was also informed that he foretold events. I was curious and went to see him with a few friends. We each had something in our minds to ask, and, to avoid mistakes, we wrote down our questions and put them in our pockets. As soon as the man saw one of us, he repeated our questions and gave the answers to them. Then he wrote something on paper, which he folded up, asked me to sign on the back, and said, "Don't look at it; put it in your pocket and keep it there till I ask for it again." And so on to each one of us. He next told us about some events that would happen to us in the future. Then he said, "Now, think of a word or a sentence, from any language you like." I thought of a long sentence from Sanskrit, a language of which he was entirely ignorant. "Now, take out the paper from your pocket," he said. The Sanskrit sentence was written there! He had written it an hour before with the remark, "In confirmation of what I have written, this man will think of this sentence." It was correct. Another of us who had been given a similar paper which he had signed and placed in his pocket, was also asked to think of a sentence. He thought of a sentence in Arabic, which it was still less possible for the man to know; it was some passage from the Koran. And my friend found this written down on the paper.

Another of us was a physician. He thought of a sentence from a German medical book. It was written on his paper.

Several days later I went to this man again, thinking possibly I had been deluded somehow before. I took other friends, and on this occasion also he came out wonderfully triumphant.

Another time I was in the city of Hyderabad in India, and I was told of a Brâhmin there who could produce numbers of things from where, nobody knew. This man was in business there; he was a respectable gentleman. And I asked him to show me his tricks. It so happened that this man had a fever, and in India there is a general belief that if a holy man puts his hand on a sick man he would be well. This Brahmin came to me and said, "Sir, put your hand on my head, so that my fever may be cured." I said, "Very good; but you show me your tricks." He promised. I put my hand on his head as desired, and later he came to fulfil his promise. He had only a strip of cloth about his loins, we took off everything else from him. I had a blanket which I gave him to wrap round himself, because it was cold, and made him sit in a corner. Twenty-five pairs of eyes were looking at him. And he said, "Now, look, write down anything you want." We all wrote down names of fruits that never grew in that country, bunches of grapes, oranges, and so on. And we gave him those bits of paper. And there came from under his blanket, bushels of grapes, oranges, and so forth, so much that if all that fruit was weighed, it would have been twice as heavy as the man. He asked us to eat the fruit. Some of us objected, thinking it was hypnotism; but the man began eating himself — so we all ate. It was all right.

He ended by producing a mass of roses. Each flower was perfect, with dew-drops on the petals, not one crushed, not one injured. And masses of them! When I asked the man for an explanation, he said, "It is all sleight of hand."

Whatever it was, it seemed to be impossible that it could be sleight of hand merely. From whence could he have got such large quantities of things?

Well, I saw many things like that. Going about India you find hundreds of similar things in different places. These are in every country. Even in this country you will find some such wonderful things. Of course there is a great deal of fraud, no doubt; but then, whenever you see fraud, you have also to say that fraud is an imitation. There must be some truth somewhere, that is being imitated; you cannot imitate nothing. Imitation must be of something substantially true.

In very remote times in India, thousands of years ago, these facts used to happen even more than they do today. It seems to me that when a country becomes very thickly populated, psychical power deteriorates. Given a vast country thinly inhabited, there will, perhaps, be more of psychical power there. These facts, the Hindus, being analytically minded. took up and investigated. And they came to certain remarkable conclusions; that is, they made a science of it. They found out that all these, though extraordinary, are also natural; there is nothing supernatural. They are under laws just the same as any other physical phenomenon. It is not a freak of nature that a man is born with such powers. They can be systematically studied, practiced, and acquired. This science they call the science of Râja-Yoga. There are thousands of people who cultivate the study of this science, and for the whole nation it has become a part of daily worship.

The conclusion they have reached is that all these extraordinary powers are in the mind of man. This mind is a part of the universal mind. Each mind is connected with every other mind. And each mind, wherever it is located, is in actual communication with the whole world.

Have you ever noticed the phenomenon that is called thought-transference? A man here is thinking something, and that thought is manifested in somebody else, in some other place. With preparations — not by chance — a man wants to send a thought to another mind at a distance, and this other mind knows that a thought is coming, and he receives it exactly as it is sent out. Distance makes no difference. The thought goes and reaches the other man, and he understands it. If your mind were an isolated something here, and my mind were an isolated something there, and there were no connection between the two, how would it be possible for my thought to reach you? In the ordinary cases, it is not my thought that is reaching you direct; but my thought has got to be dissolved into ethereal vibrations and those ethereal vibrations go into your brain, and they have to be resolved again into your own thoughts. Here is a dissolution of thought, and there is a resolution of thought. It is a roundabout process. But in telepathy, there is no such thing; it is direct.

This shows that there is a continuity of mind, as the Yogis call it. The mind is universal. Your mind, my mind, all these little minds, are fragments of that universal mind, little waves in the ocean; and on account of this continuity, we can convey our thoughts directly to one another.

You see what is happening all around us. The world is one of influence. Part of our energy is used up in the preservation of our own bodies. Beyond that, every particle of our energy is day and night being used in influencing others. Our bodies, our virtues, our intellect, and our spirituality, all these are continuously influencing others; and so, conversely, we are being influenced by them This is going on all around us. Now, to take a concrete example. A man comes; you know he is very learned, his language is beautiful, and he speaks to you by the hour; but he does not make any impression. Another man comes, and he speaks a few words, not well arranged, ungrammatical perhaps; all the same, he makes an immense impression. Many of you have seen that. So it is evident that words alone cannot always produce an impression. Words, even thoughts contribute only one-third of the influence in making an impression, the man, two-thirds. What you call the personal magnetism of the man — that is what goes out and impresses you.

In our families there are the heads; some of them are successful, others are not. Why? We complain of others in our failures. The moment I am unsuccessful, I say, so-and-so is the cause of the failure. In failure, one does not like to confess one's own faults and weaknesses. Each person tries to hold himself faultless and lay the blame upon somebody or something else, or even on bad luck. When heads of families fail, they should ask themselves, why it is that some persons manage a family so well and others do not. Then you will find that the difference is owing to the man — his presence, his personality.

Coming to great leaders of mankind, we always find that it was the personality of the man that counted. Now, take all the great authors of the past, the great thinkers. Really speaking, how many thoughts have they thought? Take all the writings that have been left to us by the past leaders of mankind; take each one of their books and appraise them. The real thoughts, new and genuine, that have been thought in this world up to this time, amount to only a handful. Read in their books the thoughts they have left to us. The authors do not appear to be giants to us, and yet we know that they were great giants in their days. What made them so? Not simply the thoughts they thought, neither the books they wrote, nor the speeches they made, it was something else that is now gone, that is their personality. As I have already remarked, the personality of the man is two-thirds, and his intellect, his words, are but one-third. It is the real man, the personality of the man, that runs through us. Our actions are but effects. Actions must come when the man is there; the effect is bound to follow the cause.

The ideal of all education, all training, should be this man-making. But, instead of that, we are always trying to polish up the outside. What use in polishing up the outside when there is no inside? The end and aim of all training is to make the man grow. The man who influences, who throws his magic, as it were, upon his fellow-beings, is a dynamo of power, and when that man is ready, he can do anything and everything he likes; that personality put upon anything will make it work.

Now, we see that though this is a fact, no physical laws that we know of will explain this. How can we explain it by chemical and physical knowledge? How much of oxygen, hydrogen, carbon, how many molecules in different positions, and how many cells, etc., etc. can explain this mysterious personality? And we still see, it is a fact, and not only that, it is the real man; and it is that man that lives and moves and works, it is that man that influences, moves his fellow-beings, and passes out, and his intellect and books and works are but traces left behind. Think of this. Compare the great teachers of religion with the great philosophers. The philosophers scarcely influenced anybody's inner man, and yet they wrote most marvellous books. The religious teachers, on the other hand, moved countries in their lifetime. The difference was made by personality. In the philosopher it is a faint personality that influences; in the great prophets it is tremendous. In the former we touch the intellect, in the latter we touch life. In the one case, it is simply a chemical process, putting certain chemical ingredients together which may gradually combine and under proper circumstances bring out a flash of light or may fail. In the other, it is like a torch that goes round quickly, lighting others.

The science of Yoga claims that it has discovered the laws which develop this personality, and by proper attention to those laws and methods, each one can grow and strengthen his personality. This is one of the great practical things, and this is the secret of all education. This has a universal application. In the life of the householder, in the life of the poor, the rich, the man of business, the spiritual man, in every one's life, it is a great thing, the strengthening of this personality. There are laws, very fine, which are behind the physical laws, as we know. That is to say, there are no such realities as a physical world, a mental world, a spiritual world. Whatever is, is one. Let us say, it is a sort of tapering existence; the thickest part is here, it tapers and becomes finer and finer. The finest is what we call spirit; the grossest, the body. And just as it is here in microcosm, it is exactly the same in the macrocosm. The universe of ours is exactly like that; it is the gross external thickness, and it tapers into something finer and finer until it becomes God.

We also know that the greatest power is lodged in the fine, not in the coarse. We see a man take up a huge weight, we see his muscles swell, and all over his body we see signs of exertion, and we think the muscles are powerful things. But it is the thin thread-like things, the nerves, which bring power to the muscles; the moment one of these threads is cut off from reaching the muscles, they are not able to work at all. These tiny nerves bring the power from something still finer, and that again in its turn brings it from something finer still — thought, and so on. So, it is the fine that is really the seat of power. Of course we can see the movements in the gross; but when fine movements take place, we cannot see them. When a gross thing moves, we catch it, and thus we naturally identify movement with things which are gross. But all the power is really in the fine. We do not see any movement in the fine, perhaps, because the movement is so intense that we cannot perceive it. But if by any science, any investigation, we are helped to get hold of these finer forces which are the cause of the expression, the expression itself will be under control. There is a little bubble coming from the bottom of a lake; we do not see it coming all the time, we see it only when it bursts on the surface; so, we can perceive thoughts only after they develop a great deal, or after they become actions. We constantly complain that we have no control over our actions, over our thoughts. But how can we have it? If we can get control over the fine movements, if we can get hold of thought at the root, before it has become thought, before it has become action, then it would be possible for us to control the whole. Now, if there is a method by which we can analyse, investigate, understand, and finally grapple with those finer powers, the finer causes, then alone is it possible to have control over ourselves, and the man who has control over his own mind assuredly will have control over every other mind. That is why purity and morality have been always the object of religion; a pure, moral man has control of himself. And all minds are the same, different parts of one Mind. He who knows one lump of clay has known all the clay in the universe. He who knows and controls his own mind knows the secret of every mind and has power over every mind

Now, a good deal of our physical evil we can get rid of, if we have control over the fine parts; a good many worries we can throw off, if we have control over the fine movements; a good many failures can be averted, if we have control over these fine powers. So far, is utility. Yet beyond, there is something higher.

Now, I shall tell you a theory, which I will not argue now, but simply place before you the conclusion. Each man in his childhood runs through the stages through which his race has come up; only the race took thousands of years to do it, while the child takes a few years. The child is first the old savage man — and he crushes a butterfly under his feet. The child is at first like the primitive ancestors of his race. As he grows, he passes through different stages until he reaches the development of his race. Only he does it swiftly and quickly. Now, take the whole of humanity as a race, or take the whole of the animal creation, man and the lower animals, as one whole. There is an end towards which the whole is moving. Let us call it perfection. Some men and women are born who anticipate the whole progress of mankind. Instead of waiting and being reborn over and over again for ages until the whole human race has attained to that perfection, they, as it were, rush through them in a few short years of their life. And we know that we can hasten these processes, if we be true to ourselves. If a number of men, without any culture, be left to live upon an island, and are given barely enough food, clothing, and shelter, they will gradually go on and on, evolving higher and higher stages of civilization. We know also, that this growth can be hastened by additional means. We help the growth of trees, do we not? Left to nature they would have grown, only they would have taken a longer time; we help them to grow in a shorter time than they would otherwise have taken. We are doing all the time the same thing, hastening the growth of things by artificial means. Why cannot we hasten the growth of man? We can do that as a race Why are teachers sent to other countries? Because by these means we can hasten the growth of races. Now, can we not hasten the growth of individuals? We can. Can we put a limit to the hastening? We cannot say how much a man can grow in one life. You have no reason to say that this much a man can do and no more. Circumstances can hasten him wonderfully. Can there be any limit then, till you come to perfection? So, what comes of it? — That a perfect man, that is to say, the type that is to come of this race, perhaps millions of years hence, that man can come today. And this is what the Yogis say, that all great incarnations and prophets are such men; that they reached perfection in this one life. We have had such men at all periods of the world's history and at all times. Quite recently, there was such a man who lived the life of the whole human race and reached the end — even in this life. Even this hastening of the growth must be under laws. Suppose we can investigate these laws and understand their secrets and apply them to our own needs; it follows that we grow. We hasten our growth, we hasten our development, and we become perfect, even in this life. This is the higher part of our life, and the science of the study of mind and its powers has this perfection as its real end. Helping others with money and other material things and teaching them how to go on smoothly in their daily life are mere details.

The utility of this science is to bring out the perfect man, and not let him wait and wait for ages, just a plaything in the hands of the physical world, like a log of drift-wood carried from wave to wave and tossing about in the ocean. This science wants you to be strong, to take the work in your own hand, instead of leaving it in the hands of nature, and get beyond this little life. That is the great idea.

Man is growing in knowledge, in power, in happiness. Continuously, we are growing as a race. We see that is true, perfectly true. Is it true of individuals? To a certain extent, yes. But yet, again comes the question: Where do you fix the limit? I can see only at a distance of so many feet. But I have seen a man close his eyes and see what is happening in another room. If you say you do not believe it, perhaps in three weeks that man can make you do the same. It can be taught to anybody. Some persons, in five minutes even, can be made to read what is happening in another man's mind. These facts can be demonstrated.

Now, if these things are true, where can we put a limit? If a man can read what is happening in another's mind in the corner of this room, why not in the next room? Why not anywhere? We cannot say, why not. We dare not say that it is not possible. We can only say, we do not know how it happens. Material scientists have no right to say that things like this are not possible; they can only say, "We do not know." Science has to collect facts, generalise upon them, deduce principles, and state the truth — that is all. But if we begin by denying the facts, how can a science be?

There is no end to the power a man can obtain. This is the peculiarity of the Indian mind, that when anything interests it, it gets absorbed in it and other things are neglected. You know how many sciences had their origin in India. Mathematics began there. You are even today counting 1, 2, 3, etc. to zero, after Sanskrit figures, and you all know that algebra also originated in India, and that gravitation was known to the Indians thousands of years before Newton was born.

You see the peculiarity. At a certain period of Indian history, this one subject of man and his mind absorbed all their interest. And it was so enticing, because it seemed the easiest way to achieve their ends. Now, the Indian mind became so thoroughly persuaded that the mind could do anything and everything according to law, that its powers became the great object of study. Charms, magic, and other powers, and all that were nothing extraordinary, but a regularly taught science, just as the physical sciences they had taught before that. Such a conviction in these things came upon the race that physical sciences nearly died out. It was the one thing that came before them. Different sects of Yogis began to make all sorts of experiments. Some made experiments with light, trying to find out how lights of different colours produced changes in the body. They wore a certain coloured cloth, lived under a certain colour, and ate certain coloured foods. All sorts of experiments were made in this way. Others made experiments in sound by stopping and unstopping their ears. And still others experimented in the sense of smell, and so on.

The whole idea was to get at the basis, to reach the fine parts of the thing. And some of them really showed most marvellous powers. Many of them were trying to float in the air or pass through it. I shall tell you a story which I heard from a great scholar in the West. It was told him by a Governor of Ceylon who saw the performance. A girl was brought forward and seated cross-legged upon a stool made of sticks crossed. After she had been seated for a time, the show-man began to take out, one after another, these cross-bars; and when all were taken out, the girl was left floating in the air. The Governor thought there was some trick, so he drew his sword and violently passed it under the girl; nothing was there. Now, what was this? It was not magic or something extraordinary. That is the peculiarity. No one in India would tell you that things like this do not exist. To the Hindu it is a matter of course. You know what the Hindus would often say when they have to fight their enemies — "Oh, one of our

Yogis will come and drive the whole lot out!" It is the extreme belief of the race. What power is there in the hand or the sword? The power is all in the spirit.

If this is true, it is temptation enough for the mind to exert its highest. But as with every other science it is very difficult to make any great achievement, so also with this, nay much more. Yet most people think that these powers can be easily gained. How many are the years you take to make a fortune? Think of that! First, how many years do you take to learn electrical science or engineering? And then you have to work all the rest of your life.

Again, most of the other sciences deal with things that do not move, that are fixed. You can analyse the chair, the chair does not fly from you. But this science deals with the mind, which moves all the time; the moment you want to study it, it slips. Now the mind is in one mood, the next moment, perhaps, it is different, changing, changing all the time. In the midst of all this change it has to be studied, understood, grasped, and controlled. How much more difficult, then, is this science! It requires rigorous training. People ask me why I do not give them practical lessons. Why, it is no joke. I stand upon this platform talking to you and you go home and find no benefit; nor do I. Then you say, "It is all bosh." It is because you wanted to make a bosh of it. I know very little of this science, but the little that I gained I worked for thirty years of my life, and for six years I have been telling people the little that I know. It took me thirty years to learn it; thirty years of hard struggle. Sometimes I worked at it twenty hours during the twenty-four; sometimes I slept only one hour in the night; sometimes I worked whole nights; sometimes I lived in places where there was hardly a sound, hardly a breath; sometimes I had to live in caves. Think of that. And yet I know little or nothing; I have barely touched the hem of the garment of this science. But I can understand that it is true and vast and wonderful.

Now, if there is any one amongst you who really wants to study this science, he will have to start with that sort of determination, the same as, nay even more than, that which he puts into any business of life.

And what an amount of attention does business require, and what a rigorous taskmaster it is! Even if the father, the mother, the wife, or the child dies, business cannot stop! Even if the heart is breaking, we still have to go to our place of business, when every hour of work is a pang. That is business, and we think that it is just, that it is right.

This science calls for more application than any business can ever require. Many men can succeed in business; very few in this. Because so much depends upon the particular constitution of the person studying it. As in business all may not make a fortune, but everyone can make something, so in the study of this science each one can get a glimpse which will convince him of its truth and of the fact that there have been men who realised it fully.

This is the outline of the science. It stands upon its own feet and in its own light, and challenges comparison with any other science. There have been charlatans, there have been magicians, there have been cheats, and more here than in any other field. Why? For the same reason, that the more profitable the business, the greater the number of charlatans and cheats. But that is no reason why the business should not be good. And one thing more; it may be good intellectual gymnastics to listen to all the arguments and an intellectual satisfaction to hear of wonderful things. But, if any one of you really wants to learn something beyond that, merely attending lectures will not do. That cannot be taught in lectures, for it is life; and life can only convey life. If there are any amongst you who are really determined to learn it, I shall be very glad to help them.

CONTROLLING THE MIND

How hard it is to control the mind! Well has it been compared to the maddened monkey. There was a monkey, restless by his own nature, as all monkeys are. As if that were not enough some one made him drink freely of wine, so that he became still more restless. Then a scorpion stung him. When a man is stung by a scorpion, he jumps about for a whole day; so the poor monkey found his condition worse than ever. To complete his misery a demon entered into him. What language can describe the uncontrollable restlessness of that monkey? The human mind is like that monkey, incessantly active by its own nature; then it becomes drunk with the wine of desire, thus increasing its turbulence. After desire takes possession comes the sting of the scorpion of jealousy at the success of others, and last of all the demon of pride enters the mind, making it think itself of all importance. How hard to control such a mind!

*

The first lesson, then, is to sit for some time and let the mind run on. The mind is bubbling up all the time. It is like that monkey jumping about. Let the monkey jump as much as he can; you simply wait and watch. Knowledge is power, says the proverb, and that is true. Until you know what the mind is doing you cannot control it. Give it the rein; many hideous thoughts may come into it; you will be astonished that it was possible for you to think such thoughts. But you will find that each day the mind's vagaries are becoming less and less violent, that each day it is becoming calmer. In the first few months you will find that the mind will have a great many thoughts, later you will find that they have somewhat decreased, and in a few more months they will be fewer and fewer, until at last the mind will be under perfect control; but we must patiently practice every day. As soon as the steam is turned on, the engine must run, as soon as things are before us we must perceive; so a man, to prove that he is not a machine, must demonstrate that he is under the control of nothing. This controlling of the mind, and not allowing it to join itself to the centres, is Pratyahara. How is this practised? It is a tremendous work, not to be done in a day. Only after a patient, continuous struggle for years can we succeed.

*

After you have practised Pratyahara for a time, take the next step, the Dhâranâ, holding the mind to certain points. What is meant by holding the mind to certain points? Forcing the mind to feel certain parts of the body to the exclusion of others. For instance, try to feel only the hand, to the exclusion of other parts of the body. When the Chitta, or mind-stuff, is confined and limited to a certain place it is Dharana. This Dharana is of various sorts, and along with it, it is better to have a little play of the imagination. For instance, the mind should be made to think of one point in the heart. That is very difficult; an easier way is to imagine a lotus there. That lotus is full of light, effulgent light. Put the mind there. Or think of the lotus in the brain as full of light, or of the different centres in the Sushumna mentioned before.

*

If the mind is not under control, it is no use living in a cave because the same mind will bring all disturbances there. We will find twenty devils in the cave because all the devils are in the mind. If the mind is under control, we can have the cave anywhere, wherever we are.

It is our own mental attitude which makes the world what it is for us. Our thoughts make things beautiful, our thoughts make things ugly. The whole world is in our own minds. Learn to see things in the proper light. First, believe in this world — that there is meaning behind everything. Everything in the world is good, is holy and beautiful. If you see something evil, think that you are not understanding it in the right light. Throw the burden on yourselves! ... Whenever we are tempted to say that the world is going to the dogs, we ought to analyse ourselves, and we shall find that we have lost the faculty of seeing things as they are.

*

The Atman is not to be gained by the weak." If there is no strength in the body and mind, the Atman cannot be realised. First you have to build the body by good nutritious food — then only will the mind be strong. The mind is but the subtle part of the body. You must retain great strength in your mind and words. "I am low, I am low" — repeating these ideas in the mind, man belittles and degrades himself.

*

Despondency is not religion, whatever else it may be. By being pleasant always and smiling, it takes you nearer to God, nearer than any prayer. How can those minds that are gloomy and dull love? If they talk of love, it is false; they want to hurt others. Think of the fanatics; they make the longest faces, and all their religion is to fight against others in word and act. Think of what they have done in the past, and of what they would do now if they were given a free hand. They would deluge the whole world in blood tomorrow if it would bring them power. By worshipping power and making long faces, they lose every bit of love from their hearts. So the man who always feels miserable will never come to God. It is not religion, it is diabolism to say, "I am so miserable." Every man has his own burden to bear. If you are miserable, try to be happy, try to conquer it.

God is not to be reached by the weak. Never be weak. You must be strong; you have infinite strength within you. How else will you conquer anything? How else will you come to God?

*

"This Atman is not to be attained by the weak", says the Shruti. Both physical weakness and mental weakness are meant here. "The strong, the hardy" are the only fit students. What can puny, little, decrepit things do? They will break to pieces whenever the mysterious forces of the body and mind are even slightly awakened by the practice of any of the Yogas. It is "the young, the healthy, the strong" that can score success. Physical strength, therefore, is absolutely necessary. It is the strong body alone that can bear the shock of reaction resulting from the attempt to control the organs. He who wants to become a Bhakta must be strong, must be healthy. When the miserably weak attempt any of the Yogas, they are likely to get some incurable malady, or they weaken their minds. Voluntarily weakening the body is really no prescription for spiritual enlightenment.

The mentally weak also cannot succeed in attaining the Atman. The person who aspires to be a Bhakta must be cheerful. In the Western world the idea of a religious man is that he never smiles, that a dark cloud must always hang over his face, which, again, must be long drawn with the jaws almost collapsed. People with emaciated bodies and long faces are fit subjects for the physician, they are not Yogis. It is the cheerful mind that is persevering. It is the strong mind that hews its way through a thousand difficulties. And this, the hardest task of all, the cutting of our way out of the net of Maya, is the work reserved only for giant wills.

*

Yet at the same time excessive mirth should be avoided (Anuddharsha). A mind in that state never becomes calm; it becomes fickle. Excessive merriment will always be followed by sorrow. Tears and laughter are near kin. People so often run from one extreme to the other. Excessive mirth makes us unfit for serious thought. It also fritters away the energies of the mind in vain. The stronger the will, the less the yielding to the sway of the emotions. Excessive hilarity is quite as objectionable as too much of sad seriousness, and all religious realisation is possible only when the mind is in a steady, peaceful condition of harmonious equilibrium.

Let the mind be cheerful, but calm. Never let it run into excesses, because every excess will be followed by a reaction.

*

The mind uncontrolled and unguided will drag us down, down, for ever—rend us, kill us; and the mind controlled and guided will save us, free us. So it must be controlled, and psychology teaches us how to do it.

To study and analyse any material science, sufficient data are obtained. These facts are studied and analysed and a knowledge of the science is the result. But in the study and analysis of the mind, there are no data, no facts acquired from without, such as are equally at the command of all. The mind is analysed by itself. The greatest science, therefore, is the science of the mind, the science of psychology.

*

If you intend to study the mind, you must have systematic training; you must practice to bring the mind under your control, to attain to that consciousness from which you will be able to study the mind and remain unmoved by any of its wild gyrations. Otherwise the facts observed will not be reliable; they will not apply to all people and therefore will not be truly facts or data at all.

Among that class who have gone deeply into the study of the mind, the facts observed have been the same, no matter in what part of the world such persons may be or what religious belief they may have. The results obtained by all who go deep enough into the mind are the same.

The mind operates by perception and impulsion. For instance, the rays of the light enter by eyes, are carried by the nerves to the brain, and still I do not see the light. The brain then conveys the impulse to the mind, but yet I do not see the light; the mind then reacts, and the light flashes across the mind. The mind's reaction is impulsion, and as a result the eye perceives the object.

To control the mind you must go deep down into the subconscious mind, classify and arrange in order all the different impressions, thoughts, etc., stored up there, and control them. This is the first step. By the control of the subconscious mind you get control over the conscious.

POWER

Accumulate power in silence and become a dynamo of spirituality. What can a beggar give? Only a king can give, and he only when he wants nothing himself.

*

Those who lay the fault of attempting to bring down the supremacy of the priestly class at the door of any particular person or body of persons other than themselves ought to know that, in obedience to the inevitable law of nature, the Brahmin caste is erecting with its own hands its own sepulchre; and this is what ought to be. It is good and appropriate that every caste of high birth and privileged nobility should make it its principal duty to raise its own funeral pyre with its own hands. Accumulation of power is as necessary as its diffusion, or rather more so. The accumulation of blood in the heart is an indispensable condition for life; its non-circulation throughout the body means death. For the welfare of society, it is absolutely necessary at certain times to have all knowledge and power concentrated in certain families or castes to the exclusion of others, but that concentrated power is focussed for the time being, only to be scattered broadcast over the whole of society in future. If this diffusion be withheld, the destruction of that society is, without doubt, near at hand.

*

Man is very short-sighted and impatient. All want power, but few will wait to gain it for themselves. He distributes but will not store up. It takes a long time to earn and but a short time to distribute. Therefore store up your powers as you acquire them and do not dissipate them.

*

I would rather see every one of you rank atheists than superstitious fools, for the atheist is alive and you can make something out of him. But if superstition enters, the brain is gone, the brain is softening, degradation has seized upon the life. Avoid these two. Brave, bold men, these are what we want. What we want is vigour in the blood, strength in the nerves, iron muscles and nerves of steel, not softening namby-pamby ideas. Avoid all these.

*

Power and things like that will come by themselves. Put yourself to work, and you will final such tremendous power coming to you that you will feel it hard to bear. Even the least work done for others awakens the power within; even thinking the least good of others gradually instils into the heart the strength of a lion.

*

Whatever sects have arisen in India, they are all at one in this respect that infinite power is latent in this soul; from the ant to the perfect man there is the same Âtman in all, the difference being only in manifestation. That power manifests as soon as it gets the opportunity and the right place and time. From the highest god to the meanest grass, the same power is present in all — whether manifested or not. We shall have to call forth that power by going from door to door.

*

If one has got power, one must manifest it in action.

*

there is the state called Sattva, serenity, calmness, in which the waves cease, and the water of the mind-lake becomes clear. It is not inactive, but rather intensely active. It is the greatest manifestation of power to be calm. It is easy to be active. Let the reins go, and the horses will run away with you. Anyone can do that, but he who can stop the plunging horses is the strong man. Which requires the greater strength, letting go or restraining? The calm man is not the man who is dull. You must not mistake Sattva for dullness or laziness. The calm man is the one who has control over the mind waves. Activity is the manifestation of inferior strength, calmness, of the superior.

*

The theory of creation is that matter is subject to five conditions: ether, luminous ether, gaseous, liquid, and solid. They are all evoked out of one primal element, which is very finest ether.

The name of the energy in the universe is Prâna, which is the force residing in these elements. Mind is the great instrument for using the Prana. Mind is material. Behind the mind is Âtman which takes hold of the Prana. Prana is the driving power of the world, and can be seen in every manifestation of life. The body is mortal and the mind is mortal; both, being compounds, must die. Behind all is the Atman which never dies. The Atman is pure intelligence controlling and directing Prana. But the intelligence we see around us is always imperfect. When intelligence is perfect, we get the Incarnation — the Christ. Intelligence is always trying to manifest itself, and in order to do this it is creating minds and bodies of different degrees of development. In reality, and at the back of all things, every being is equal.

Mind is very fine matter; it is the instrument for manifesting Prana. Force requires matter for manifestation.

*

The mind acts on the body, and the body in its turn acts upon the mind. They act and react upon each other. Every mental state creates a corresponding state in the body, and every action in the body has its corresponding effect on the mind. It makes no difference whether you think the body and mind are two different entities, or whether you think they are both but one body — the physical body being the gross part and the mind the fine part. They act and react upon each other. The mind is constantly becoming the body. In the training of the mind, it is easier to reach it through the body. The body is easier to grapple with than the mind.

The finer the instrument, the greater the power. The mind is much finer and more powerful than the body.

The power is with the silent ones, who only live and love and then withdraw their personality. They never say "me" and "mine"; they are only blessed in being instruments. Such men are the makers of Christs and Buddhas, ever living fully identified with God, ideal existences, asking nothing, and not consciously doing anything. They are the real movers, the Jivanmuktas, (Literally, free even while living.) absolutely selfless, the little personality entirely blown away, ambition non-existent. They are all principle, no personality.

*

The attention to forms, to formulas, to the everyday details of religion, and to rituals, may sometimes be laughed at; but nevertheless, within them is strength. Many times in the rushing forward we lose much strength. As a fact, the fanatic is stronger than the liberal man. Even the fanatic, therefore, has one great virtue, he conserves energy, a tremendous amount of it. As with the individual so with the race, energy is gathered to be conserved. Hemmed in all around by external enemies, driven to focus in a centre by the Romans, by the Hellenic tendencies in the world of intellect, by waves from Persia, India, and Alexandria — hemmed in physically, mentally, and morally — there stood the race with an inherent, conservative, tremendous strength, which their descendants have not lost even today. And the race was forced to concentrate and focus all its energies upon Jerusalem and Judaism. But all power when once gathered cannot remain collected; it must expend and expand itself. There is no power on earth which can be kept long confined within a narrow limit. It cannot be kept compressed too long to allow of expansion at a subsequent period.

*

This is the one great idea to understand that our power is already ours. Say either that it has become contracted, or say that it has been covered with the veil of Mâyâ, it matters little; the idea is there already; you must have to believe in that, believe in the possibility of everybody — that even in the lowest man there is the same possibility as in the Buddha. This is the doctrine of the Atman.

*

Religious truths need verification by everyone. To see God is the one goal. Power is not the goal. Pure Existence-Knowledge and Love is the goal; and Love is God.

*

"A fool indeed is he who, living on the banks of the Ganga, seeks to dig a little well for water. A fool indeed is the man who, living near a mine of diamonds, spends his life in searching for beads of glass." God is that mine of diamonds. We are fools indeed to give up God for legends of ghosts or flying hobgoblins. It is a disease, a morbid desire. It degenerates the race, weakens the nerves and the brain, living in incessant morbid fear of hobgoblins, or stimulating the hunger for wonders; all these wild stories about them keep the nerves at an unnatural tension — a slow and sure degeneration of the race. It is degeneration to think of giving up God, purity, holiness, and spirituality, to go after all this nonsense! Reading other men's thoughts! If I must read everyone else's thoughts for five minutes at a time I shall go crazy. Be strong and stand up and seek the God of Love. This is the highest strength.

What power is higher than the power of purity? Love and purity govern the world. This love of God cannot be reached by the weak; therefore, be not weak, either physically, mentally, morally or spiritually. The Lord alone is true. Everything else is untrue; everything else should be rejected for the salve of the Lord. Vanity of vanities, all is vanity. Serve the Lord and Him alone.

*

From what does this universe come, in what does it remain, to what does it go back? And the answer is: From love it comes, in love it remains, back it goes unto love. Thus we are in a position to understand that, whether one likes it or not, there is no going back for anyone. Everyone has to get to the centre, however he may struggle to go back. Yet if we struggle consciously, knowingly, it will smooth the passage, it will lessen the jar, and quicken the time.

Another conclusion we naturally arrive at from this is that all knowledge and all power are within and not without. What we call nature is a reflecting glass — that is all the use of nature — and all knowledge is this reflection of the within on this glass of nature. What we call powers, secrets of nature, and force, are all within. In the external world are only a series of changes. In the external world are only a series of changes. There is no knowledge in nature; all knowledge comes from the human soul. Man manifests knowledge, discovers it within himself, which is pre-existing through eternity. Everyone is the embodiment of Knowledge, everyone is the embodiment of eternal Bliss, and eternal Existence. The ethical effect is just the same, as we have seen elsewhere, with regard to equality.

*

Whenever power is used for evil, it becomes diabolical; it must be used for good only. So this accumulated culture of ages of which the Brahmin has been the trustee, he must now give to the people at large, and it was because he did not give it to the people that the Mohammedan invasion was possible. It was because he did not open this treasury to the people from the beginning, that for a thousand years we have been trodden under the heels of every one who chose to come to India. It was through that we have become degraded, and the first task must be to break open the cells that hide the wonderful treasures which our common ancestors accumulated; bring them out and give them to everybody and the Brahmin must be the first to do it.

*

Karma in its effect on character is the most tremendous power that man has to deal with. Man is, as it were, a centre, and is attracting all the powers of the universe towards himself, and in this centre is fusing them all and again sending them off in a big current. Such a centre is the real man — the almighty, the omniscient — and he draws the whole universe towards him. Good and bad, misery and happiness, all are running towards him and clinging round him; and out of them he fashions the mighty stream of tendency called character and throws it outwards. As he has the power of drawing in anything, so has he the power of throwing it out.

All the actions that we see in the world, all the movements in human society, all the works that we have around us, are simply the display of thought, the manifestation of the will of man. Machines or instruments, cities, ships, or men-of-war, all these are simply the manifestation of the will of man; and this will is caused by character, and character is manufactured by Karma. As is Karma, so is the manifestation of the will. The men of mighty will the world has produced have all been tremendous workers — gigantic souls, with wills powerful enough to overturn worlds, wills they got by persistent work, through ages, and ages. Such a gigantic will as that of a Buddha or a Jesus could not be obtained in one life, for we know who their fathers were. It is not known that their fathers ever spoke a word for the good of mankind. Millions and millions of carpenters like Joseph had gone; millions are still living. Millions and millions of petty kings like Buddha's father had been in the world. If it was only a case of hereditary transmission, how do you account for this petty prince, who was not, perhaps, obeyed by his own servants, producing this son, whom half a world worships? How do you explain the gulf between the carpenter and his son, whom millions of human beings worship as God? It cannot be solved by the theory of heredity. The gigantic will which Buddha and Jesus threw over the world, whence did it come? Whence came this accumulation of power? It must have been there through ages and ages, continually growing bigger and bigger, until it burst on society in a Buddha or a Jesus, even rolling down to the present day.

*

According to Karma-Yoga, the action one has done cannot be destroyed until it has borne its fruit; no power in nature can stop it from yielding its results. If I do an evil action, I must suffer for it; there is no power in this universe to stop or stay it. Similarly, if I do a good action, there is no power in the universe which can stop its bearing good results. The cause must have its effect; nothing can prevent or restrain this.

*

The desire to do good is the highest motive power we have, if we know all the time that it is a privilege to help others. Do not stand on a high pedestal and take five cents in your hand and say, "Here, my poor man," but be grateful that the poor man is there, so that by making a gift to him you are able to help yourself. It is not the receiver that is blessed, but it is the giver. Be thankful that you are allowed to exercise your power of benevolence and mercy in the world, and thus become pure and perfect. All good acts tend to make us pure and perfect.

*

Nothing in the universe has power over you until you allow it to exercise such a power. Nothing has power over the Self of man, until the Self becomes a fool and loses independence. So, by non-attachment, you overcome and deny the power of anything to act upon you. It is very easy to say that nothing has the right to act upon you until you allow it to do so; but what is the true sign of the man who really does not allow anything to work upon him, who is neither happy nor unhappy when acted upon by the external world? The sign is that good or ill fortune causes no change in his mind: in all conditions he continues to remain the same.

DISCIPLINE

The Hindu Ideal of life is Nivarti; it means subjugation and conquest of evil passions, of nature of lust, revenge and avarice.

It does not mean conquest of all desire. It means only the annihilation of gross desires.

Every man is bound to love and sympathize with his fellow-creatures. A Sanyasi is one who has vanquished all his selfish passions and vowed to devote his life for the good of others. He loves all.

Sanyasis ought to be fed. They are not like the Christian bishops and Archbishops who must be paid to do their work with thousands of pounds per annum; all whose earnings are spent upon their own luxury — their wife and children.

The Sanyasi wants only a morsel of food, and then he places all his knowledge and services at the disposal of the public. He is a wandering missionary. Individuals and society have to work themselves up from "brute through man, into divine".

Even the lowest of the Hindus, the Pariah, has less of the brute in him than a Briton in a similar social status. This is the result of an old and excellent religious civilization. This evolution to a higher spiritual state is possible only through discipline and education.

*

Sometimes it is a good discipline to be forced to work for work's sake, even to the length of not being allowed to enjoy the fruits of one's labour.

*

Our motherland is a glowing example of the results and consequence of the eternal subjection of the individual to society and forced self-sacrifice by dint of institution and discipline.

In this country men are born according to Shâstric injunctions, they eat and drink by prescribed rules throughout life, they go through marriage and kindred functions in the same way; in short, they even die according to Shastric injunctions. The hard discipline, with the exception of one great good point, is fraught with evil.

The good point is that men can do one or two things well with very little effort, having practiced them every day through generations. The delicious rice and curry which a cook of this country prepares with the aid of three lumps of earth and a few sticks can be had nowhere else. With the simple mechanism of an antediluvian loom, worth one rupee, and the feet put in a pit, it is possible to make kincobs worth twenty rupees a yard, in this country alone.

A torn mat, an earthen lamp, and that fed by castor oil — with the aid of materials such as these, wonderful savants are produced in this country alone. An all-forbearing attachment to an ugly and deformed wife, and a lifelong devotion to a worthless and villainous husband are possible in this country alone. Thus far the bright side.

But all these things are done by people guided like lifeless machines. There is no mental activity, no unfoldment of the heart, no vibration of life, no flux of hope; there is no strong stimulation of the will, no experience of keen pleasure, nor the contact of intense sorrow; there is no stir of inventive genius, no desire for novelty, no appreciation of new things.

Clouds never pass away from this mind; the radiant picture of the morning sun never charms this heart. It never even occurs to this mind if there is any better state than this; where it does, it cannot convince; in the event of conviction, effort is lacking; and even where there is effort, lack of enthusiasm kills it out.

If living by rule alone ensures excellence, if it be virtue to follow strictly the rules and customs handed down through generations, say then, who is more virtuous than a tree, who is a greater devotee, a holier saint, than a railway train? Who has ever seen a piece of stone transgress a natural law? Who has ever known cattle to commit sin?

Again, can that be called society which is formed by an aggregate of men who are like lumps of clay, like lifeless machines, like heaped up pebbles? How can such society fare well? Were good possible, then instead of being slaves for hundreds of years, we would have been the greatest nation on earth, and this soil of India, instead of being a mine of stupidity, would have been the eternal fountain-head of learning.

EDUCATION

You consider a man as educated if only he can pass some examinations and deliver good lectures. The education which does not help the common mass of people to equip themselves for the struggle for life, which does not bring out strength of character, a spirit of philanthropy, and the courage of a lion — is it worth the name?

Real education is that which enables one to stand on one's own legs. The education that you are receiving now in schools and colleges is only making you a race of dyspeptics. You are working like machines merely, and living a jelly-fish existence.

The peasant, the shoemaker, the sweeper, and such other lower classes of India have much greater capacity for work and self-reliance than you. They have been silently working through long ages and producing the entire wealth of the land, without a word of complaint.

Very soon they will get above you in position. Gradually capital is drifting into their hands, and they are not so much troubled with wants as you are. Modern education has changed your fashion, but new avenues of wealth lie yet undiscovered for want of the inventive genius.

You have so long oppressed these forbearing masses; now is the time for their retribution. And you will become extinct in your vain search for employment, making it the be-all and end-all of your life.

*

Coming to great leaders of mankind, we always find that it was the personality of the man that counted. Now, take all the great authors of the past, the great thinkers. Really speaking, how many thoughts have they thought?

Take all the writings that have been left to us by the past leaders of mankind; take each one of their books and appraise them. The real thoughts, new and genuine, that have been thought in this world up to this time, amount to only a handful. Read in their books the thoughts they have left to us.

The authors do not appear to be giants to us, and yet we know that they were great giants in their days. What made them so? Not simply the thoughts they thought, neither the books they wrote, nor the speeches they made, it was something else that is now gone, that is their personality.

As I have already remarked, the personality of the man is two-thirds, and his intellect, his words, are but one-third. It is the real man, the personality of the man, that runs through us. Our actions are but effects. Actions must come when the man is there; the effect is bound to follow the cause.

The ideal of all education, all training, should be this man-making. But, instead of that, we are always trying to polish up the outside. What use in polishing up the outside when there is no inside? The end and aim of all training is to make the man grow. The man who influences, who throws his magic, as it were, upon his fellow-beings, is a dynamo of power, and when that man is ready, he can do anything and everything he likes; that personality put upon anything will make it work.

*

Learning has no place in religion; for the majority learning is a block in the way. A man may have read all the libraries in the world and many not be religious at all, and another, who cannot perhaps write his own name, senses religion and realises it.

The whole of religion is our own inner perception. When I use the words "man-making religion", I do not mean books, nor dogmas, nor theories. I mean the man who has realised, has fully perceived, something of that infinite presence in his own heart.

The man at whose feet I sat all my life — and it is only a few ideas of his that try to teach — could [hardly] write his name at all. All my life I have not seen another man like that, and I have travelled all over the world.

When I think of that man, I feel like a fool, because I want to read books and he never did. He never wanted to lick the plates after other people had eaten. That is why he was his own book. All my life I am repeating what Jack said and John said, and never say anything myself.

Mind you, there is no value in learning. You are all mistaken in learning. The only value of knowledge is in the strengthening, the disciplining, of the mind. By all this eternal swallowing it is a wonder that we are not all dyspeptics.

Let us stop, and burn all the books, and get hold of ourselves and think. You all talk [about] and get distracted over losing your "individuality". You are losing it every moment of your lives by this eternal swallowing.

If any one of you believes what I teach, I will be sorry. I will only be too glad if I can excite in you the power of thinking for yourselves. My ambition is to talk to men and women, not to sheep. By men and women, I mean individuals. You are not little babies to drag all the filthy rags from the street and bind them up into a doll!

"This is a place for learning! That man is placed in the university! He knows all about what Mr. Blank said!" But Mr. Blank said nothing! If I had the choice I would say to the professor, "Get out! You are nobody! " Remember this individualism at any cost! Think wrong if you will, no matter whether you get truth or not. The whole point is to discipline the mind. That truth which you swallow from others will not be yours. You cannot teach truth from my mouth; neither can you learn truth from my mouth. None can teach another. You have to realise truth and work it out for yourself according to your own nature. All must struggle to be individuals — strong, standing on your own feet, thinking your own thoughts, realising your own Self. No use swallowing doctrines others pass on — standing up together like soldiers in jail, sitting down together, all eating the same food, all nodding their heads at the same time. Variation is the sign of life. Sameness is the sign of death.

*

Mere book-learning won't do. We want that education by which character is formed, strength of mind is increased, the intellect is expanded, and by which one can stand on one's own feet.

*

What is education? Is it book-learning? No. Is it diverse knowledge? Not even that. The training by which the current and expression of will are brought under control and become fruitful is called education. Now consider, is that education as a result of which the will, being continuously choked by force through generations, is well-nigh killed out; is that education under whose sway even the old ideas, let alone the new ones, are disappearing one by one; is that education which is slowly making man a machine? It is more blessed, in my opinion, even to go wrong, impelled by one's free will and intelligence than to be good as an automaton.

*

All the wealth of the world cannot help one little Indian village if the people are not taught to help themselves. Our work should be mainly educational , both moral and intellectual.

*

Educate and raise the masses, and thus alone a nation is possible. Our reformers do not see where the wound is, they want to save the nation by marrying the widows; do you think that a nation is saved by the number of husbands its widows get? Nor is our religion to blame, for an idol more or less makes no difference.

The whole defect is here: The real nation who live in cottage have forgotten their manhood, their individuality. Trodden under the foot of the Hindu, Mussulman, or Christian, they have come to think that they are born to be trodden under the foot of everybody who has money enough in his pocket. They are to be given back their lost individuality. They are to be educated.

Whether idols will remain or not, whether widows will have husbands enough or not, whether caste is good or bad, I do not bother myself with such questions. Everyone must work out his own salvation. Our duty is to put the chemicals together, the crystallisation will come through God's laws. Let us put ideas into their heads, and they will do the rest.

Now this means educating the masses. Here are these difficulties. A pauper government cannot, will not, do anything; so no help from that quarter.

*

Education is not filling the mind with a lot of facts. Perfecting the instrument and getting complete mastery of my own mind [is the ideal of education]. Education is the manifestation of the perfection already in man.

*

Life is a series of fights and disillusionments. The secret of life is not enjoyment, but education through experience. But, alas, we are called off the moment we begin really to learn. That seems to be a potent argument for a future existence. Everywhere it is better to have a whirlwind come over the work. That clears the atmosphere and gives us a true insight into the nature of things. It is begun anew, but on adamantine foundations.

EDUCATION IS THE SOLUTION

From the day when education and culture etc. began to spread gradually from patricians to plebeians, grew the distinction between the modern civilisation as of Western countries, and the ancient civilisation as of India, Egypt, Rome, etc. I see it before my eyes, a nation is advanced in proportion as education and intelligence spread among the masses.

The chief cause of India's ruin has been the monopolising of the whole education and intelligence of the land, by dint of pride and royal authority, among a handful of men. If we are to rise again, we shall have to do it in the same way, i.e. by spreading education among the masses.

A great fuss has been made for half a century about social reform. Travelling through various places of India these last ten years, I observed the country full of social reform associations. But I did not find one association for them by sucking whose blood the people known as "gentlemen" have become and continue to be gentlemen!

How many sepoys were brought by the Mussulmans? How many Englishmen are there? Where, except in India, can be had millions of men who will cut the throats of their own fathers and brothers for six rupees? Sixty millions of Mussulmans in seven hundred years of Mohammedan rule, and two millions of Christians in one hundred years of Christian rule — what makes it so?

Why has originality entirely forsaken the country? Why are our deft-fingered artisans daily becoming extinct, unable to compete with the Europeans? By what power again has the German labourer succeeded in shaking the many-century-grounded firm footing of the English labourer?

*

Education, education, education alone! Travelling through many cities of Europe and observing in them the comforts and education of even the poor people, there was brought to my mind the state of our own poor people, and I used to shed tears.

What made the difference? Education was the answer I got.

Through education comes faith in one's own Self, and through faith in one's own Self the inherent Brahman is waking up in them, while the Brahman in us is gradually becoming dormant. In New York I used to observe the Irish colonists come — downtrodden, haggard-looking, destitute of all possessions at home, penniless, and wooden-headed — with their only belongings, a stick and a bundle of rags hanging at the end of it, fright in their steps, alarm in their eyes.

A different spectacle in six months — the man walks upright, his attire is changed! In his eyes and steps there is no more sign of fright. What is the cause?

Our Vedanta says that that Irishman was kept surrounded by contempt in his own country — the whole of nature was telling him with one voice, "Pat, you have no more hope, you are born a slave and will remain so."

Having been thus told from his birth, Pat believed in it and hypnotised himself that he was very low, and the Brahman in him shrank away. While no sooner had he landed in America than he heard the shout going up on all sides, "Pat, you are a man as we are. It is man who has done all, a man like you and me can do everything: have courage!"

Pat raised his head and saw that it was so, the Brahman within woke up. Nature herself spoke, as it were, "Arise, awake, and stop not till the goal is reached" (Katha Upanishad, I. ii. 4.)

*

Likewise the education that our boys receive is very negative. The schoolboy learns nothing, but has everything of his own broken down — want of Shraddhâ is the result. The Shraddha which is the keynote of the Veda and the Vedanta — the Shraddha which emboldened Nachiketâ to face Yama and question him, through which Shraddha this world moves the annihilation of that Shraddha! — "The ignorant, the man devoid of Shraddha, the doubting self runs to ruin."

Therefore are we so near destruction. The remedy now is the spread of education.

*

All other kinds of knowledge are but non-knowledge in comparison with Self-knowledge.

By Self-knowledge, I do not mean thereby, matted hair, staff, Kamandalu, and mountain caves which the word suggests. What do I mean then? Cannot the knowledge, by which is attained even freedom from the bondage of worldly existence, bring ordinary material prosperity? Certainly it can.

Freedom, dispassion, renunciation all these are the very highest ideals, but—"Even a little of this Dharma saves one from the great fear (of birth and death)."

*

Secondly, along with this, education has to be imparted.

That is easy to say, but how to reduce it into practice? There are thousands of unselfish, kind-hearted men in our country who has renounced everything. In the same way as they travel about and give religious instructions without any remuneration, so at least half of them can be trained as teachers or bearers of such education as we need most.

For that, we want first of all a centre in the capital of each Presidency, from whence to spread slowly throughout the whole of India. Two centres have recently been started in Madras and Calcutta; there is hope of more soon.

Then, the greater part of the education to the poor should be given orally, time is not yet ripe for schools. Gradually in these main centres will be taught agriculture, industry, etc., and workshops will be established for the furtherance of arts. To sell the manufactures of those workshops in Europe and America, associations will be started like those already in existence.

It will be necessary to start centres for women, exactly like those for men. But you are aware how difficult that is in this country.

Again, "The snake which bites must take out its own poison" — and that this is going to be is my firm conviction; the money required for these works would have to come from the West. And for that reason, our religion should be preached in Europe and America.

*

We have had a negative education all along from our boyhood. We have only learnt that we are nobodies. Seldom are we given to understand that great men were ever born in our country. Nothing positive has been taught to us. We do not even know how to use our hands and feet!

We master all the facts and figures concerning the ancestors of the English, but we are sadly unmindful about our own. We have learnt only weakness. Being a conquered race, we have brought ourselves to believe that we are weak and have no independence in anything.

The faith in our own selves must be reawakened, and, then only, all the problems which face our country will gradually be solved by ourselves.

WORK

Be perfectly resigned, perfectly unconcerned; then alone can you do any true work. No eyes can see the real forces; we can only see the results. Put out self, forget it; just let God work, it is His business.

*

By work alone men may get to where Buddha got largely by meditation or Christ by prayer. Buddha was a working Jnâni, Christ was a Bhakta, but the same goal was reached by both of them.

*

Do any deserve liberty who are not ready to give it to others? Let us calmly go to work, instead of dissipating our energy in unnecessary fretting and fuming.

*

Each work has to pass through these stages—ridicule, opposition, and then acceptance. Those who think ahead of their time are sure to be misunderstood.

*

Even the greatest fool can accomplish a task if it were after his or her heart. But the intelligent ones are those who can convert every work into one that suits their taste.

No work is petty. Everything in this world is like a banyan-seed, which, though appearing tiny as a mustard-seed, has yet the gigantic banyan tree latent within it. He indeed is intelligent who notices this and succeeds in making all work truly great.

*

Every man who, we think, gets something by chance, has been working for it slowly and surely through ages.

*

In a truly noble work, not to speak of men, even God Himself befriends the doer.

*

It is a good discipline to be forced to work for work's sake, even to the length of not being allowed to enjoy the fruits of one's labour.

*

No foolish talk now, but actual work.

*

Not a work will be lost, no struggle vain. . .

*

On and on, work, work, work.

*

Our great defect in life is that we are so much drawn to the ideal, the goal is so much more enchanting, so much more alluring, so much bigger in our mental horizon, that we lose sight of the details altogether… One of the greatest lessons I have learnt in my life is to pay as much attention to the means of work as to its end. He was a great man from whom I learnt it, and his own life was a practical demonstration of this great principle I have been always learning great lessons from that one principle, and it appears to me that all the secret of success is there; to pay as much attention to the means as to the end.

*

The man who says that he will work when the world has become all good and then he will enjoy bliss is as likely to succeed as the man who sits beside the Ganga and says, "I will ford the river when all the water has run into the ocean."

The result of every work is mixed with good and evil. There is no good work that has not a touch of evil in it. Like smoke round the fire, some evil always clings to work. We should engage in such works as bring the largest amount of good and the smallest measure of evil.

*

The sun = Knowledge. The stormy water = Work. The lotus = Love. The serpent = Yoga. The swan = the Self. The Motto = May the Swan (the Supreme Self) send us that. It is the mind-lake. (Swami Vivekananda's explanation of Ramakrishna Mission's emblem)

*

There are certain works which are, as it were, the aggregate, the sum total, of a large number of smaller works. If we stand near the seashore and hear the waves dashing against the shingle, we think it is such a great noise, and yet we know that one wave is really composed of millions and millions of minute waves. Each one of these is making a noise, and yet we do not catch it; it is only when they become the big aggregate that we hear. Similarly, every pulsation of the heart is work. Certain kinds of work we feel and they become tangible to us;

they are, at the same time, the aggregate of a number of small works. If you really want to judge of the character of a man, look not at his great performances. Every fool may become a hero at one time or another. Watch a man do his most common actions; those are indeed the things which will tell you the real character of a great man. Great occasions rouse even the lowest of human beings to some kind of greatness, but he alone is the really great man whose character is great always, the same wherever he be.

*

This world is not for cowards. Do not try to fly. Look not for success or failure. Join yourself to the perfectly unselfish will and work on. Know that the mind which is born to succeed joins itself to a determined will and perseveres. You have the right to work, but do not become so degenerate as to look for results. Work incessantly, but see something behind the work. Even good deeds can find a man in great bondage. Therefore be not bound by good deeds or by desire for name and fame. Those who know this secret pass beyond this round of birth and death and become immortal.

*

To attain liberation through work, join yourself to work but without desire, looking for no result. Such work leads to knowledge, which in turn brings emancipation. To give up work before you know, leads to misery. Work done for the Self gives no bondage. Neither desire pleasure nor fear pain from work. It is the mind and body that work, not I. Tell yourself this unceasingly and realise it. Try not to know that you work.

To work properly… you have first to give up the idea of attachment. Secondly, do not mix in the fray, hold yourself as a witness and go on working. My master used to say, "Look upon your children as a nurse does." The nurse will take your baby and fondle it and play with it and behave towards it as gently as if it were her own child; but as soon as you give her notice to quit, she is ready to start off bag and baggage from the house. Everything in the shape of attachment is forgotten.

*

We also read this in the Gita and learn that we have to work, constantly work with all our power; to put our whole mind in the work, whatever it be, that we are doing. At the same time, we must not be attached. That is to say, we must not be drawn away from the work by anything else; still, we must be able to quit the work whenever we like.

*

We read in the Bhagavad-Gita again and again that we must all work incessantly. All work is by nature composed of good and evil. We cannot do any work which will not do some good somewhere; there cannot be any work which will not cause some harm somewhere. Every work must necessarily be a mixture of good and evil; yet we are commanded to work incessantly. Good and evil will both have their results, will produce their Karma. Good action will entail upon us good effect; bad action, bad. But good and bad are both bondages of the soul. The solution reached in the Gita in regard to this bondage-producing nature of work is that, if we do not attach ourselves to the work we do, it will not have any binding effect on our soul. We shall try to understand what is meant by this "non-attachment to" to work.

*

When you are doing any work, do not think of anything beyond. Do it as worship.

*

Work and worship are necessary to take away the veil, to lift off the bondage and illusion.

Work for the idea, not the person.

*

Work incessantly, but be not attached to it.

*

Work on, brave hearts, fail not — no saying nay; work on — the Lord is behind the work. Mahâshakti is with you.

*

Work on! Hold on! Be brave! Dare anything and everything!

*

Work on, my brave boys. We shall see the light some day. Let things slowly grow. Rome was not built in a day.

*

Work on with a heart.

*

Work on with energy.

*

Work on with the intrepidity of a lion but, at the same time with the tenderness of a flower.

*

Work out the salvation of this land and of the whole world, each of you thinking that the entire burden is on your shoulders.

*

Work through freedom! Work through love! The word "love" is very difficult to understand; love never comes until there is freedom. There is no true love possible in the slave.

*

Work unto death — I am with you, and when I am gone, my spirit will work with you.

*

Work, work — conquer all by your love!

*

Work, work, for, to work only for the good of others is life.

*

Work, work the idea, the plan, my boys, my brave, noble, good souls — to the wheel, to the wheel put your shoulders!

*

Work, work, work — let this be your motto.

*

Listen to an old story. A lazy tramp sauntering along the road saw an old man sitting at the door of his house and stopped to inquire of him the whereabouts of a certain place. "How far is such and such a village?" he asked. The old man remained silent. The man repeated his query several times. Still there was no answer. Disgusted at this, the traveller turned to go away. The old man then stood up and said, "The village of — is only a mile from here." "What!" said the tramp, "Why did you not speak when I asked you before?" "Because then", said the old man, "you seemed so halting and careless about proceeding, but now you are starting off in good earnest, and you have a right to an answer."

Will you remember this story, my son? Go to work, the rest will come: "Whosoever not trusting in anything else but Me, rests on Me, I supply him with everything he needs" (Gitâ, IX. 22). This is no dream.

Even the lowest forms of work are not to be despised. Let the man, who knows no better, work for selfish ends, for name and fame; but everyone should always try to get towards higher and higher motives and to understand them. "To work we have the right, but not to the fruits thereof:" Leave the fruits alone. Why care for results? If you wish to help a man, never think what that man's attitude should be towards you. If you want to do a great or a good work, do not trouble to think what the result will be.

PATIENCE

Are great things ever done smoothly? Time, patience, and indomitable will must show.

*

Every work has got to pass through hundreds of difficulties before succeeding. Those that persevere will see the light, sooner or later.

*

"Fortune favours the brave and energetic." Don't look back — forward, infinite energy, infinite enthusiasm, infinite daring, and infinite patience — then alone can great deeds be accomplished. We must set the whole world afire.

*

Have fire and spread all over. Work, work. Be the servant while leading, be unselfish, and never listen to one friend in private accusing another. Have infinite patience, and success is yours.

*

Have patience and be faithful unto death. Do not fight among yourselves. Be perfectly pure in money dealings… We will do great things yet… So long as you have faith and honesty and devotion, everything will prosper.

*

Shyness won't do any more.... He who has infinite patience and infinite energy at his back, will alone succeed.

*

Infinite patience, infinite purity, and infinite perseverance are the secret of success in a good cause.

*

The more heart you will be able to manifest, the greater will be the victory you achieve. It is only a few that understand the language of the brain, but everyone from the Creator down to a clump of grass, understands the language that comes from the heart.

But then, in our country, it is a case of rousing men that are, as it were, dead. It will take time, but if you have infinite patience and perseverance, success is bound to come. No mistake in that.

*

Know full well that patience is the best means of succeeds.

*

Know it for certain that without steady devotion for the Guru and unflinching patience and perseverance, nothing is to be achieved.

*

Love conquers in the long run. It won't do to become impatient — wait, wait — patience is bound to give success.

*

Can anything be done unless everybody exerts himself to his utmost? " " etc.— "It is the man of action, the lion-heart, that the Goddess of Wealth resorts to." No need for looking behind. FORWARD! We want infinite energy, infinite zeal, infinite courage, and infinite patience, then only will great things achieved.

*

Nothing else is necessary but these — love, sincerity, and patience.

*

Nothing shall be done in haste. Purity, patience, and perseverance are the three essentials to success and, above all, love. All time is yours, there is no indecent haste. Everything will come right if you are pure and sincere.

*

Persevere on, my brave lads, We have only just begun. Never despond! Never say enough!

*

Purity, perseverance, and energy— these three I want.

*

Purity, patience and perseverance overcome all obstacles. All great things must of necessity be slow.

*

The fruit falls from the tree when it gets ripe. So wait for the time to come. Do not hurry. Moreover, no one has the right to make others miserable by his foolish acts. Wait, have patience, everything will come right in time.

*

Those who really want to be Yogis must give up, once for all, this nibbling at things. Take up one idea. Make that one idea your life — think of it, dream of it, live on that idea. Let the brain, muscles, nerves, every part of your body, be full of that idea, and just leave every other idea alone.

This is the way to success, and this is the way great spiritual giants are produced. Others are mere talking machines. If we really want to be blessed, and make others blessed, we must go deeper.

The first step is not to disturb the mind, not to associate with persons whose ideas are disturbing. All of you know that certain persons, certain places, certain foods, repel you. Avoid them; and those who want to go to the highest, must avoid all company, good or bad.

Practise hard; whether you live or die does not matter. You have to plunge in and work, without thinking of the result. If you are brave enough, in six months you will be a perfect Yogi.

But those who take up just a bit of it and a little of everything else make no progress. It is of no use simply to take a course of lessons. To those who are full of Tamas, ignorant and dull — those whose minds never get fixed on any idea, who only crave for something to amuse them — religion and philosophy are simply objects of entertainment. These are the unpersevering. They hear a talk, think it very nice, and then go home and forget all about it.

To succeed, you must have tremendous perseverance, tremendous will. 'I will drink the ocean', says the persevering soul, 'at my will mountains will crumble up.' Have that sort of energy, that sort of will, work hard, and you will reach the goal.

*

Wait, my child, wait and work on. Patience, patience.

*

Rejoice that you have done so much. When you feel gloomy, think what has been done within the last year. How, rising from nothing, we have the eyes of the world fixed upon us now. Not only India, but the world outside, is expecting great things of us.

*

There was a great god-sage called Narada. Just as there are sages among mankind, great Yogis, so there are great Yogis among the gods. Narada was a good Yogi, and very great. He travelled everywhere.

One day he was passing through a forest, and saw a man who had been meditating until the white ants had built a huge mound round his body — so long had he been sitting in that position. He said to

Narada, "Where are you going?"

Narada replied, "I am going to heaven."

"Then ask God when He will be merciful to me; when I shall attain freedom."

Further on Narada saw another man. He was jumping about, singing, dancing, and said, "Oh, Narada, where are you going?" His voice and his gestures were wild.

Narada said, "I am going to heaven."

"Then, ask when I shall be free."

Narada went on. In the course of time he came again by the same road, and there was the man who had been meditating with the ant-hill round him. He said, "Oh, Narada, did you ask the Lord about me?"

"Oh, yes."

"What did He say?"

"The Lord told me that you would attain freedom in four more births."

Then the man began to weep and wail, and said, "I have meditated until an ant-hill has grown around me, and I have four more births yet!"

Narada went to the other man. "Did you ask my question?"

"Oh, yes. Do you see this tamarind tree? I have to tell you that as many leaves as there are on that tree, so many times, you shall be born, and then you shall attain freedom."

The man began to dance for joy, and said, "I shall have freedom after such a short time!"

A voice came, "My child, you will have freedom this minute."

That was the reward for his perseverance. He was ready to work through all those births, nothing discouraged him. But the first man felt that even four more births were too long. Only perseverance, like that of the man who was willing to wait aeons brings about the highest result.

*

The most horrible thing about competition is that one may conquer the environments, but that where one may conquer, thousands are crowded out. So it is evil at best. That cannot be good which helps only one and hinders the majority. Patanjali says that these struggles remain only through our ignorance, and are not necessary, and are not part of the evolution of man. It is just our impatience which creates them.

We have not the patience to go and work our way out. For instance, there is a fire in a theatre, and only a few escape. The rest in trying to rush out crush one another down. That crush was not necessary for the salvation of the building nor of the two or three who escaped. If all had gone out slowly, not one would have been hurt.

That is the case in life. The doors are open for us, and we can all get out without the competition and struggle; and yet we struggle. The struggle we create through our own ignorance, through impatience; we are in too great a hurry. The highest manifestation of strength is to keep ourselves calm and on our own feet.

*

Freedom of the will — it is as you feel you are free to act. But this freedom is a species of necessity. There is one infinite link before, after, and between the thought and the action, but the latter takes the name of freedom — like a bird flitting through a bright room. We feel the freedom and feel it has no other cause. We cannot go beyond consciousness, therefore we feel we are free. We can trace it no further than consciousness. God alone feels the real freedom. Mahapurushas (saints) feel themselves identified with God; hence they also feel the real freedom.

You may stop the water flowing out of the fountain by closing that part of the stream and gathering it all in the fountain; you have no liberty beyond it. But the source remains unchanged. Everything is predestination — and a part of that predestination is that you shall have such feeling — the feeling of freedom. I am shaping my own action. Responsibility is the feeling of reaction. There is no absolute power.

Power here is the conscious feeling of exercising any faculty which is created by necessity. Man has the feeling "I act"; what he means by power of freedom is the feeling. The power is attended with responsibility. Whatever may be done through us by predestination, we feel the reaction. A ball thrown by one, itself feels the reaction.

But this innate necessity which comes to us as our freedom does not affect also the conscious relations we form with our surroundings. The relativity is not changed. Either everybody is free or everybody is under necessity. That would not matter. The relations would be the same. Vice and virtue would be the same.

If a thief pleads that he was under the necessity of stealing, the magistrate would say that he was under the necessity to punish. We are seated in a room, and the whole room is moving — the relation between us is unchanged.

To get out of this infinite chain of causation is Mukti (freedom). Muktas (free souls) are not actuated by necessity, they are like god. They begin the chain of cause and effect. God is the only free being — the first source of their will — and is always experienced by them as such.

The feeling of want is the real prayer, not the words. But you must have patience to wait and see if your prayers are answered.

*

The Lord is the only One who never changes. His love never fails. Wherever we are and whatever we do, He is ever and ever the same merciful, the same loving heart. He never changes, He is never angry, whatever we do. How can God be angry with us? Your babe does many mischievous things: are you angry with that babe? Does not God know what we are going to be? He knows we are all going to be perfect, sooner or later. He has patience, infinite patience. We must love Him, and everyone that lives — only in and through Him. This is the keynote.

*

You occasionally hear that the prophets and great teachers were rather cowardly, and dared not say and do what they thought was right; but that was not so. Fanatics little understand the infinite power of love in the hearts of these great sages who looked upon the inhabitants of this world as their children.

They were the real fathers, the real gods, filled with infinite sympathy and patience for everyone; they were ready to bear and forbear. They knew how human society should grow, and patiently slowly, surely, went on applying their remedies, not by denouncing and frightening people, but by gently and kindly leading them upwards step by step.

Such were the writers of the Upanishads. They knew full well how the old ideas of God were not reconcilable with the advanced ethical ideas of the time; they knew full well that what the atheists were preaching contained a good deal of truth, nay, great nuggets of truth; but at the same time, they understood that those who wished to sever the thread that bound the beads, who wanted to build a new society in the air, would entirely fail.

*

Beware of compromises. I do not mean that you are to get into antagonism with anybody, but you have to hold on to your own principles in weal or woe and never adjust them to others' "fads" through the greed of getting supporters. Your Âtman is the support of the universe — whose support do you stand in need of? Wait with patience and love and strength; if helpers are not ready now, they will come in time. Why should we be in a hurry? The real working force of all great work is in its almost unperceived beginnings.

*

Do not fight with people; do not antagonise anyone. Why should we mind if Jack and John become Christians? Let them follow whatever religion suits them. Why should you mix in controversies? Bear with the various opinions of everybody. Patience, purity, and perseverance will prevail.

*

Take courage and work on. Patience and steady work — this is the only way. Go on; remember — patience and purity and courage and steady work. . . . So long as you are pure, and true to your principles, you will never fail — Mother will never leave you, and all blessings will be yours.

*

Through the imparting of moral principles, good behaviour, and education we must make the Chandala come up to the level of the Brahmana. They will hear with patience the words of a man they like, however nonsense, and will not listen to anyone they do not like. Think of this and modify your conduct accordingly. Everything will come all right. Be the servant if you will rule. That is the real secret. Your love will tell even if your words be harsh. Instinctively men feel the love clothed in whatever language.

*

Infinite patience, infinite purity, and infinite perseverance are the secret of success in a good cause.

*

No need of looking behind. FORWARD! We want infinite energy, infinite zeal, infinite courage, and infinite patience, then only will great things be achieved.

*

POWER

Accumulate power in silence and become a dynamo of spirituality. What can a beggar give? Only a king can give, and he only when he wants nothing himself.

*

Those who lay the fault of attempting to bring down the supremacy of the priestly class at the door of any particular person or body of persons other than themselves ought to know that, in obedience to the inevitable law of nature, the Brahmin caste is erecting with its own hands its own sepulchre; and this is what ought to be. It is good and appropriate that every caste of high birth and privileged nobility should make it its principal duty to raise its own funeral pyre with its own hands. Accumulation of power is as necessary as its diffusion, or rather more so. The accumulation of blood in the heart is an indispensable condition for life; its non-circulation throughout the body means death. For the welfare of society, it is absolutely necessary at certain times to have all knowledge and power concentrated in certain families or castes to the exclusion of others, but that concentrated power is focussed for the time being, only to be scattered broadcast over the whole of society in future. If this diffusion be withheld, the destruction of that society is, without doubt, near at hand.

*

Man is very short-sighted and impatient. All want power, but few will wait to gain it for themselves. He distributes but will not store up. It takes a long time to earn and but a short time to distribute. Therefore store up your powers as you acquire them and do not dissipate them.

*

I would rather see every one of you rank atheists than superstitious fools, for the atheist is alive and you can make something out of him. But if superstition enters, the brain is gone, the brain is softening, degradation has seized upon the life. Avoid these two. Brave, bold men, these are what we want. What we want is vigour in the blood, strength in the nerves, iron muscles and nerves of steel, not softening namby-pamby ideas. Avoid all these.

*

Power and things like that will come by themselves. Put yourself to work, and you will final such tremendous power coming to you that you will feel it hard to bear. Even the least work done for others awakens the power within; even thinking the least good of others gradually instils into the heart the strength of a lion.

*

Whatever sects have arisen in India, they are all at one in this respect that infinite power is latent in this soul; from the ant to the perfect man there is the same Âtman in all, the difference being only in manifestation. That power manifests as soon as it gets the opportunity and the right place and time. From the highest god to the meanest grass, the same power is present in all — whether manifested or not. We shall have to call forth that power by going from door to door.

*

If one has got power, one must manifest it in action.

*

there is the state called Sattva, serenity, calmness, in which the waves cease, and the water of the mind-lake becomes clear. It is not inactive, but rather intensely active. It is the greatest manifestation of power to be calm. It is easy to be active. Let the reins go, and the horses will run away with you. Anyone can do that, but he who can stop the plunging horses is the strong man. Which requires the greater strength, letting go or restraining? The calm man is not the man who is dull. You must not mistake Sattva for dullness or laziness. The calm man is the one who has control over the mind waves. Activity is the manifestation of inferior strength, calmness, of the superior.

*

The theory of creation is that matter is subject to five conditions: ether, luminous ether, gaseous, liquid, and solid. They are all evoked out of one primal element, which is very finest ether.

The name of the energy in the universe is Prâna, which is the force residing in these elements. Mind is the great instrument for using the Prana. Mind is material. Behind the mind is Âtman which takes hold of the Prana. Prana is the driving power of the world, and can be seen in every manifestation of life. The body is mortal and the mind is mortal; both, being compounds, must die. Behind all is the Atman which never dies. The Atman is pure intelligence controlling and directing Prana. But the intelligence we see around us is always imperfect. When intelligence is perfect, we get the Incarnation — the Christ. Intelligence is always trying to manifest itself, and in order to do this it is creating minds and bodies of different degrees of development. In reality, and at the back of all things, every being is equal.

Mind is very fine matter; it is the instrument for manifesting Prana. Force requires matter for manifestation.

*

The mind acts on the body, and the body in its turn acts upon the mind. They act and react upon each other. Every mental state creates a corresponding state in the body, and every action in the body has its corresponding effect on the mind. It makes no difference whether you think the body and mind are two different entities, or whether you think they are both but one body — the physical body being the gross part and the mind the fine part. They act and react upon each other. The mind is constantly becoming the body. In the training of the mind, it is easier to reach it through the body. The body is easier to grapple with than the mind.

The finer the instrument, the greater the power. The mind is much finer and more powerful than the body.

The power is with the silent ones, who only live and love and then withdraw their personality. They never say "me" and "mine"; they are only blessed in being instruments. Such men are the makers of Christs and Buddhas, ever living fully identified with God, ideal existences, asking nothing, and not consciously doing anything. They are the real movers, the Jivanmuktas, (Literally, free even while living.) absolutely selfless, the little personality entirely blown away, ambition non-existent. They are all principle, no personality.

*

The attention to forms, to formulas, to the everyday details of religion, and to rituals, may sometimes be laughed at; but nevertheless, within them is strength. Many times in the rushing forward we lose much strength. As a fact, the fanatic is stronger than the liberal man. Even the fanatic, therefore, has one great virtue, he conserves energy, a tremendous amount of it. As with the individual so with the race, energy is gathered to be conserved. Hemmed in all around by external enemies, driven to focus in a centre by the Romans, by the Hellenic tendencies in the world of intellect, by waves from Persia, India, and Alexandria — hemmed in physically, mentally, and morally — there stood the race with an inherent, conservative, tremendous strength, which their descendants have not lost even today. And the race was forced to concentrate and focus all its energies upon Jerusalem and Judaism. But all power when once gathered cannot remain collected; it must expend and expand itself. There is no power on earth which can be kept long confined within a narrow limit. It cannot be kept compressed too long to allow of expansion at a subsequent period.

*

This is the one great idea to understand that our power is already ours. Say either that it has become contracted, or say that it has been covered with the veil of Mâyâ, it matters little; the idea is there already; you must have to believe in that, believe in the possibility of everybody — that even in the lowest man there is the same possibility as in the Buddha. This is the doctrine of the Atman.

*

Religious truths need verification by everyone. To see God is the one goal. Power is not the goal. Pure Existence-Knowledge and Love is the goal; and Love is God.

*

"A fool indeed is he who, living on the banks of the Ganga, seeks to dig a little well for water. A fool indeed is the man who, living near a mine of diamonds, spends his life in searching for beads of glass." God is that mine of diamonds. We are fools indeed to give up God for legends of ghosts or flying hobgoblins. It is a disease, a morbid desire. It degenerates the race, weakens the nerves and the brain, living in incessant morbid fear of hobgoblins, or stimulating the hunger for wonders; all these wild stories about them keep the nerves at an unnatural tension — a slow and sure degeneration of the race. It is degeneration to think of giving up God, purity, holiness, and spirituality, to go after all this nonsense! Reading other men's thoughts! If I must read everyone else's thoughts for five minutes at a time I shall go crazy. Be strong and stand up and seek the God of Love. This is the highest strength.

What power is higher than the power of purity? Love and purity govern the world. This love of God cannot be reached by the weak; therefore, be not weak, either physically, mentally, morally or spiritually. The Lord alone is true. Everything else is untrue; everything else should be rejected for the salve of the Lord. Vanity of vanities, all is vanity. Serve the Lord and Him alone.

*

From what does this universe come, in what does it remain, to what does it go back? And the answer is: From love it comes, in love it remains, back it goes unto love. Thus we are in a position to understand that, whether one likes it or not, there is no going back for anyone. Everyone has to get to the centre, however he may struggle to go back. Yet if we struggle consciously, knowingly, it will smooth the passage, it will lessen the jar, and quicken the time.

Another conclusion we naturally arrive at from this is that all knowledge and all power are within and not without. What we call nature is a reflecting glass — that is all the use of nature — and all knowledge is this reflection of the within on this glass of nature. What we call powers, secrets of nature, and force, are all within. In the external world are only a series of changes. In the external world are only a series of changes. There is no knowledge in nature; all knowledge comes from the human soul. Man manifests knowledge, discovers it within himself, which is pre-existing through eternity. Everyone is the embodiment of Knowledge, everyone is the embodiment of eternal Bliss, and eternal Existence. The ethical effect is just the same, as we have seen elsewhere, with regard to equality.

*

Whenever power is used for evil, it becomes diabolical; it must be used for good only. So this accumulated culture of ages of which the Brahmin has been the trustee, he must now give to the people at large, and it was because he did not give it to the people that the Mohammedan invasion was possible. It was because he did not open this treasury to the people from the beginning, that for a thousand years we have been trodden under the heels of every one who chose to come to India. It was through that we have become degraded, and the first task must be to break open the cells that hide the wonderful treasures which our common ancestors accumulated; bring them out and give them to everybody and the Brahmin must be the first to do it.

*

Karma in its effect on character is the most tremendous power that man has to deal with. Man is, as it were, a centre, and is attracting all the powers of the universe towards himself, and in this centre is fusing them all and again sending them off in a big current. Such a centre is the real man — the almighty, the omniscient — and he draws the whole universe towards him. Good and bad, misery and happiness, all are running towards him and clinging round him; and out of them he fashions the mighty stream of tendency called character and throws it outwards. As he has the power of drawing in anything, so has he the power of throwing it out.

All the actions that we see in the world, all the movements in human society, all the works that we have around us, are simply the display of thought, the manifestation of the will of man. Machines or instruments, cities, ships, or men-of-war, all these are simply the manifestation of the will of man; and this will is caused by character, and character is manufactured by Karma. As is Karma, so is the manifestation of the will. The men of mighty will the world has produced have all been tremendous workers — gigantic souls, with wills powerful enough to overturn worlds, wills they got by persistent work, through ages, and ages. Such a gigantic will as that of a Buddha or a Jesus could not be obtained in one life, for we know who their fathers were. It is not known that their fathers ever spoke a word for the good of mankind. Millions and millions of carpenters like Joseph had gone; millions are still living. Millions and millions of petty kings like Buddha's father had been in the world. If it was only a case of hereditary transmission, how do you account for this petty prince, who was not, perhaps, obeyed by his own servants, producing this son, whom half a world worships? How do you explain the gulf between the carpenter and his son, whom millions of human beings worship as God? It cannot be solved by the theory of heredity. The gigantic will which Buddha and Jesus threw over the world, whence did it come? Whence came this accumulation of power? It must have been there through ages and ages, continually growing bigger and bigger, until it burst on society in a Buddha or a Jesus, even rolling down to the present day.

*

According to Karma-Yoga, the action one has done cannot be destroyed until it has borne its fruit; no power in nature can stop it from yielding its results. If I do an evil action, I must suffer for it; there is no power in this universe to stop or stay it. Similarly, if I do a good action, there is no power in the universe which can stop its bearing good results. The cause must have its effect; nothing can prevent or restrain this.

*

The desire to do good is the highest motive power we have, if we know all the time that it is a privilege to help others. Do not stand on a high pedestal and take five cents in your hand and say, "Here, my poor man," but be grateful that the poor man is there, so that by making a gift to him you are able to help yourself. It is not the receiver that is blessed, but it is the giver. Be thankful that you are allowed to exercise your power of benevolence and mercy in the world, and thus become pure and perfect. All good acts tend to make us pure and perfect.

*

Nothing in the universe has power over you until you allow it to exercise such a power. Nothing has power over the Self of man, until the Self becomes a fool and loses independence. So, by non-attachment, you overcome and deny the power of anything to act upon you. It is very easy to say that nothing has the right to act upon you until you allow it to do so; but what is the true sign of the man who really does not allow anything to work upon him, who is neither happy nor unhappy when acted upon by the external world? The sign is that good or ill fortune causes no change in his mind: in all conditions he continues to remain the same.

THE IMPORTANCE OF CONCENTRATION

All knowledge that we have, either of the external or internal world, is obtained through only one method — by the concentration of the mind. No knowledge can be had of any science unless we can concentrate our minds upon the subject. The astronomer concentrates his mind through the telescope and so on. If you want to study your own mind, it will be the same process. You will have to concentrate your mind and turn it back upon itself. The difference in this world between mind and mind is simply the fact of concentration. One, more concentrated than the other, gets more knowledge.

*

Concentration is the essence of all knowledge, nothing can be done without it. Ninety per cent of thought force is wasted by the ordinary human being, and therefore he is constantly committing blunders; the trained man or mind never makes a mistake. Concentration is restraining the mind into smaller and smaller limits.

When the mind is concentrated and turned backward on itself, all within us will be our servants, not our masters. The Greeks applied their concentration to the external world, and the result was perfection in art, literature, etc. The Hindu concentrated on the internal world, upon the unseen realms in the Self, and developed the science of Yoga.

Yoga is controlling the senses, will and mind. The benefit of its study is that we learn to control instead of being controlled.

Mind seems to be layer on layer. Our real goal is to cross all these intervening strata of our being and find God. The end and aim of Yoga is to realise God.

To do this we must go beyond relative knowledge, go beyond the sense-world. The world is awake to the senses, the children of the Lord are asleep on that plane. The world is asleep to the Eternal, the children of the Lord are awake in that realm. These are the sons of God.

There is but one way to control the senses — to see Him who is the Reality in the universe. Then and only then can we really conquer our senses.

*

The more this power of concentration, the more knowledge is acquired, because this is the one and only method of acquiring knowledge. Even the lowest shoeblack, if he gives more concentration, will black shoes better; the cook with concentration will cook a meal all the better.

In making money, or in worshipping God, or in doing anything, the stronger the power of concentration, the better will that thing be done. This is the one call, the one knock, which opens the gates of nature, and lets out floods of light. This, the power of concentration, is the only key to the treasure-house of knowledge.

*

How are we to know that the mind has become concentrated? Because the idea of time will vanish. The more time passes unnoticed the more concentrated we are.

In common life we see that when we are interested in a book we do not note the time at all; and when we leave the book, we are often surprised to find how many hours have passed. All time will have the tendency to come and stand in the one present.

So the definition is given: When the past and present come and stand in one, the mind is said to be concentrated.

*

We read many books, but that does not bring us knowledge. We may read all the Bibles in the world, but that will not give us religion. Theoretical religion is easy enough to get, any one may get that. What we want is practical religion.

The Christian idea of a practical religion is in doing good works — worldly utility.

What good is utility? Judged from a utilitarian standpoint, religion is a failure. Every hospital is a prayer that more people may come there.

What is meant by charity? Charity is not fundamental. It is really helping on the misery of the world, not eradicating it. One looks for name and fame and covers his efforts to obtain them with the enamel of charity and good works. He is working for himself under the pretext of working for others. Every so-called charity is an encouragement of the very evil it claims to operate against.

Men and women go to balls and dance all night in honour of some hospital or other charitable institution then go home, behave like beasts, and bring devils into the world to fill jails, insane asylums, and hospitals. So it goes on, and it is called good works — building hospital etc.

The ideal of good works is to lessen, or eradicate, the misery of the world. The Yogi says, all misery comes from not being able to control the mind. The Yogi's ideal is freedom from nature. Conquest of nature is his standard of work. The Yogi says that all power is in the soul, and by the controlling of the mind and body one conquers nature by the power of the soul.

*

How has all the knowledge in the world been gained but by the concentration of the powers of the mind? The world is ready to give up its secrets if we only know how to knock, how to give it the necessary blow.

The strength and force of the blow come through concentration. There is no limit to the power of the human mind. The more concentrated it is, the more power is brought to bear on one point; that is the secret.

*

It is impossible to find God outside of ourselves. Our own souls contribute all the divinity that is outside of us. We are the greatest temple. The objectification is only a faint imitation of what we see within ourselves.

Concentration of the powers of the mind is our only instrument to help us see God. If you know one soul (your own), you know all souls, past, present, and to come.

The will concentrates the mind, certain things excite and control this will, such as reason, love, devotion, breathing. The concentrated mind is a lamp that shows us every corner of the soul.

*

The main difference between men and the animals is the difference in their power of concentration. All success in any line of work is the result of this.

Everybody knows something about concentration. We see its results every day. High achievements in art, music, etc., are the results of concentration.

An animal has very little power of concentration. Those who have trained animals find much difficulty in the fact that the animal is constantly forgetting what is told him. He cannot concentrate his mind long upon anything at a time. Herein is the difference between man and the animals — man has the greater power of concentration.

The difference in their power of concentration also constitutes the difference between man and man. Compare the lowest with the highest man. The difference is in the degree of concentration. This is the only difference.

Everybody's mind becomes concentrated at times. We all concentrate upon those things we love, and we love those things upon which we concentrate our minds.

What mother is there that does not love the face of her homeliest child? That face is to her the most beautiful in the world. She loves it because she concentrates her mind on it; and if every one could concentrate his mind on that same face, every one would love it. It would be to all the most beautiful face.

We all concentrate our minds upon those things we love. When we hear beautiful music, our minds become fastened upon it, and we cannot take them away. Those who concentrate their minds upon what you call classical music do not like common music, and vice versa. Music in which the notes follow each other in rapid succession holds the mind readily.

A child loves lively music, because the rapidity of the notes gives the mind no chance to wander. A man who likes common music dislikes classical music, because it is more complicated and requires a greater degree of concentration to follow it.

The great trouble with such concentrations is that we do not control the mind; it controls us. Something outside of ourselves, as it were, draws the mind into it and holds it as long as it chooses. We hear melodious tones or see a beautiful painting, and the mind is held fast! We cannot take it away.

If I speak to you well upon a subject you like, your mind becomes concentrated upon what I am saying. I draw your mind away from yourself and hold it upon the subject in spite of yourself. Thus our attention is held, our minds are concentrated upon various things, in spite of ourselves. We cannot help it.

Now the question is: Can this concentration be developed, and can we become masters of it? The Yogis say, yes. The Yogis say that we can get perfect control of the mind.

On the ethical side there is danger in the development of the power of concentration — the danger of concentrating the mind upon an object and then being unable to detach it at will. This state causes great suffering. Almost all our suffering is caused by our not having the power of detachment.

So along with the development of concentration we must develop the power of detachment. We must learn not only to attach the mind to one thing exclusively, but also to detach it at a moment's notice and place it upon something else. These two should be developed together to make it safe.

This is the systematic development of the mind. To me the very essence of education is concentration of mind, not the collecting of facts. If I had to do my education over again, and had any voice in the matter, I would not study facts at all. I would develop the power of concentration and detachment, and then with a perfect instrument I could collect facts at will. Side by side, in the child, should be developed the power of concentration and detachment.

*

In the lives of all great men, past and present, we find this tremendous power of concentration. Those are men of genius, you say. The science of Yoga tells us that we are all geniuses if we try hard to be. Some will come into this life better fitted and will do it quicker perhaps. We can all do the same. The same power is in everyone. The subject of the present lecture is how to concentrate the mind in order to study the mind itself. Yogis have laid down certain rules and this night I am going to give you a sketch of some of these rules.

THE DEVELOPMENT OF CONCENTRATION

Concentration, of course, comes from various sources. Through the senses you can get concentration. Some get it when they hear beautiful music, others when they see beautiful scenery. Some get concentrated by lying upon beds of spikes, sharp iron spikes, others by sitting upon sharp pebbles.

These are extraordinary cases [using] most unscientific procedure. Scientific procedure is gradually training the mind.

One gets concentrated by holding his arm up. Torture gives him the concentration he wants. But all these are extraordinary.

Universal methods have been organised according to different philosophers. Some say the state we want to attain is superconsciousness of the mind — going beyond the limitations the body has made for us.

The value of ethics to the Yogi lies in that it makes the mind pure. The purer the mind, the easier it is to control it. The mind takes every thought that rises and works it out. The grosser the mind, the more difficult [it is] to control [it].

The immoral man will never be able to concentrate his mind to study psychology. He may get a little control as he begins, get a little power of hearing. and even those powers will go from him. The difficulty is that if you study closely, you see how [the] extraordinary power arrived at was not attained by regular scientific training.

The men who, by the power of magic, control serpents will be killed by serpents. The man who attains any extraordinary powers will in the long run succumb to those powers. There are millions [who] receive power through all sorts of ways in India. The vast majority of them die raving lunatics. Quite a number commit suicide, the mind [being] unbalanced.

The study must be put on the safe side: scientific, slow, peaceful. The first requisite is to be moral. Such a man wants the gods to come down, and they will come down and manifest themselves to him. That is our psychology and philosophy in essence, [to be] perfectly moral.

Just think what that means! No injury, perfect purity, perfect austerity! These are absolutely necessary. Just think, if a man can attain all these in perfection! What more do you want? If he is free from all enmity towards any being, all animals will give up their enmity [in his presence].

*

The law of laws is concentration. First, concentrate all the nerve energies and all power lodged in the cells of the body into one force and direct it at will. Then bring the mind, which is thinner matter, into one centre.

The mind has layer after layer. When the nerve force concentrated is made to pass through the spinal column, one layer of the mind is open. When it is concentrated in one bone [plexus, or "lotus"], another part of the world is open.

So from world to world it goes until it touches the pineal gland in the centre of the brain. This is the seat of conservation of potential energy, the source of both activity and passivity.

*

No one method can suit all. Different methods are not steps necessary to be taken one after another. Ceremonials are the lowest form; next God external, and after that God internal.

In some cases gradation may be needed, but in many only one way is required. It would be the height of folly to say to everyone, "You must pass through Karma and Bhakti before you can reach Jnana."

Stick to your reason until you reach something higher; and you will know it to be higher, because it will not jar with reason. The stage beyond consciousness is inspiration (Samâdhi); but never mistake hysterical trances for the real thing.

It is a terrible thing to claim this inspiration falsely, to mistake instinct for inspiration. There is no external test for inspiration, we know it ourselves; our guardian against mistake is negative — the voice of reason. All religion is going beyond reason, but reason is the only guide to get there.

Instinct is like ice, reason is the water, and inspiration is the subtlest form or vapour; one follows the other. Everywhere is this eternal sequence — unconsciousness, consciousness, intelligence — matter, body, mind — and to us it seems as if the chain began with the particular link we first lay hold of.

Arguments on both sides are of equal weight, and both are true. We must reach beyond both, to where there is neither the one nor the other. These successions are all Maya.

*

It is easy to concentrate the mind on external things, the mind naturally goes outwards; but not so in the case of religion, or psychology, or metaphysics, where the subject and the object, are one. The object is internal, the mind itself is the object, and it is necessary to study the mind itself — mind studying mind.

We know that there is the power of the mind called reflection. I am talking to you. At the same time I am standing aside, as it were, a second person, and knowing and hearing what I am talking. You work and think at the same time, while a portion of your mind stands by and sees what you are thinking.

The powers of the mind should be concentrated and turned back upon itself, and as the darkest places reveal their secrets before the penetrating rays of the sun, so will this concentrated mind penetrate its own innermost secrets. Thus will we come to the basis of belief, the real genuine religion. We will perceive for ourselves whether we have souls, whether life is of five minutes or of eternity, whether there is a God in the universe or more. It will all be revealed to us.

This is what Raja-Yoga proposes to teach. The goal of all its teaching is how to concentrate the minds, then, how to discover the innermost recesses of our own minds, then, how to generalise their contents and form our own conclusions from them.

It, therefore, never asks the question what our religion is, whether we are Deists or Atheists, whether Christians, Jews, or Buddhists. We are human beings; that is sufficient. Every human being has the right and the power to seek for religion. Every human being has the right to ask the reason, why, and to have his question answered by himself, if he only takes the trouble.

So far, then, we see that in the study of this Raja-Yoga no faith or belief is necessary. Believe nothing until you find it out for yourself; that is what it teaches us.

*

Do you mean to say that the facts of our awakened state require any dreams or imaginings to prove them? Certainly not. This study of Raja-Yoga takes a long time and constant practice. A part of this practice is physical, but in the main it is mental.

As we proceed we shall find how intimately the mind is connected with the body. If we believe that the mind is simply a finer part of the body, and that mind acts upon the body, then it stands to reason that the body must react upon the mind.

If the body is sick, the mind becomes sick also. If the body is healthy, the mind remains healthy and strong. When one is angry, the mind becomes disturbed. Similarly when the mind is disturbed, the body also becomes disturbed.

With the majority of mankind the mind is greatly under the control of the body, their mind being very little developed. The vast mass of humanity is very little removed from the animals. Not only so, but in many instances, the power of control in them is little higher than that of the lower animals.

We have very little command of our minds. Therefore to bring that command about, to get that control over body and mind, we must take certain physical helps. When the body is sufficiently controlled, we can attempt the manipulation of the mind.

By manipulating the mind, we shall be able to bring it under our control, make it work as we like, and compel it to concentrate its powers as we desire.

SAMADHI (SUPERCONSCIOUSNESS)

All our knowledge which is called rational is referred to consciousness. My consciousness of this table, and of your presence, makes me know that the table and you are here. At the same time, there is a very great part of my existence of which I am not conscious. All the different organs inside the body, the different parts of the brain — nobody is conscious of these.

When I eat food, I do it consciously; when I assimilate it, I do it unconsciously. When the food is manufactured into blood, it is done unconsciously. When out of the blood all the different parts of my body are strengthened, it is done unconsciously.

And yet it is I who am doing all this; there cannot be twenty people in this one body. How do I know that I do it, and nobody else? It may be urged that my business is only in eating and assimilating the food, and that strengthening the body by the food is done for me by somebody else.

That cannot be, because it can be demonstrated that almost every action of which we are now unconscious can be brought up to the plane of consciousness. The heart is beating apparently without our control. None of us here can control the heart; it goes on its own way.

But by practice men can bring even the heart under control, until it will just beat at will, slowly, or quickly, or almost stop. Nearly every part of the body can be brought under control.

*

What does this show? That the functions which are beneath consciousness are also performed by us, only we are doing it unconsciously.

We have, then, two planes in which the human mind works. First is the conscious plane, in which all work is always accompanied with the feeling of egoism. Next comes the unconscious plane, where all work is unaccompanied by the feeling of egoism.

That part of mind-work which is unaccompanied with the feeling of egoism is unconscious work, and that part which is accompanied with the feeling of egoism is conscious work. In the lower animals this unconscious work is called instinct. In higher animals, and in the highest of all animals, man, what is called conscious work prevails.

*

But it does not end here. There is a still higher plane upon which the mind can work. It can go beyond consciousness. Just as unconscious work is beneath consciousness, so there is another work which is above consciousness, and which also is not accompanied with the feeling of egoism.

The feeling of egoism is only on the middle plane. When the mind is above or below that line, there is no feeling of "I", and yet the mind works. When the mind goes beyond this line of self-consciousness, it is called Samâdhi or superconsciousness.

How, for instance, do we know that a man in Samadhi has not gone below consciousness, has not degenerated instead of going higher? In both cases the works are unaccompanied with egoism.

The answer is, by the effects, by the results of the work, we know that which is below, and that which is above. When a man goes into deep sleep, he enters a plane beneath consciousness. He works the body all the time, he breathes, he moves the body, perhaps, in his sleep, without any accompanying feeling of ego; he is unconscious, and when he returns from his sleep, he is the same man who went into it.

The sum total of the knowledge which he had before he went into the sleep remains the same; it does not increase at all. No enlightenment comes. But when a man goes into Samadhi, if he goes into it a fool, he comes out a sage.

What makes the difference? From one state a man comes out the very same man that he went in, and from another state the man comes out enlightened, a sage, a prophet, a saint, his whole character changed, his life changed, illumined. These are the two effects. Now the effects being different, the causes must be different. As this illumination with which a man comes back from Samadhi is much higher than can be got from unconsciousness, or much higher than can be got by reasoning in a conscious state, it must, therefore, be superconsciousness, and Samadhi is called the superconscious state.

*

This, in short, is the idea of Samadhi. What is its application?

The application is here. The field of reason, or of the conscious workings of the mind, is narrow and limited. There is a little circle within which human reason must move. It cannot go beyond. Every attempt to go beyond is impossible, yet it is beyond this circle of reason that there lies all that humanity holds most dear.

All these questions, whether there is an immortal soul, whether there is a God, whether there is any supreme intelligence guiding this universe or not, are beyond the field of reason. Reason can never answer these questions. What does reason say? It says, "I am agnostic; I do not know either yea or nay."

Yet these questions are so important to us. Without a proper answer to them, human life will be purposeless. All our ethical theories, all our moral attitudes, all that is good and great in human nature, have been moulded upon answers that have come from beyond the circle.

It is very important, therefore, that we should have answers to these questions. If life is only a short play, if the universe is only a "fortuitous combination of atoms," then why should I do good to another? Why should there be mercy, justice, or fellow-feeling? The best thing for this world would be to make hay while the sun shines, each man for himself.

If there is no hope, why should I love my brother, and not cut his throat? If there is nothing beyond, if there is no freedom, but only rigorous dead laws, I should only try to make myself happy here.

You will find people saying nowadays that they have utilitarian grounds as the basis of morality. What is this basis? Procuring the greatest amount of happiness to the greatest number. Why should I do this? Why should I not produce the greatest unhappiness to the greatest number, if that serves my purpose? How will utilitarians answer this question? How do you know what is right, or what is wrong?

I am impelled by my desire for happiness, and I fulfil it, and it is in my nature; I know nothing beyond. I have these desires, and must fulfil them; why should you complain? Whence come all these truths about human life, about morality, about the immortal soul, about God, about love and sympathy, about being good, and, above all, about being unselfish?

All ethics, all human action and all human thought, hang upon this one idea of unselfishness. The whole idea of human life can be put into that one word, unselfishness.

Why should we be unselfish? Where is the necessity, the force, the power, of my being unselfish?

You call yourself a rational man, a utilitarian; but if you do not show me a reason for utility, I say you are irrational. Show me the reason why I should not be selfish. To ask one to be unselfish may be good as poetry, but poetry is not reason. Show me a reason.

Why shall I be unselfish, and why be good? Because Mr. and Mrs. So-and-so say so does not weigh with me. Where is the utility of my being unselfish? My utility is to be selfish if utility means the greatest amount of happiness. What is the answer? The utilitarian can never give it.

*

The answer is that this world is only one drop in an infinite ocean, one link in an infinite chain. Where did those that preached unselfishness, and taught it to the human race, get this idea? We know it is not instinctive; the animals, which have instinct, do not know it. Neither is it reason; reason does not know anything about these ideas. Whence then did they come?

We find, in studying history, one fact held in common by all the great teachers of religion the world ever had. They all claim to have got their truths from beyond, only many of them did not know where they got them from.

For instance, one would say that an angel came down in the form of a human being, with wings, and said to him, "Hear, O man, this is the message." Another says that a Deva, a bright being, appeared to him.

A third says he dreamed that his ancestor came and told him certain things. He did not know anything beyond that. But this is common that all claim that this knowledge has come to them from beyond, not through their reasoning power.

What does the science of Yoga teach? It teaches that they were right in claiming that all this knowledge came to them from beyond reasoning, but that it came from within themselves.

The Yogi teaches that the mind itself has a higher state of existence, beyond reason, a superconscious state, and when the mind gets to that higher state, then this knowledge, beyond reasoning, comes to man. Metaphysical and transcendental knowledge comes to that man.

This state of going beyond reason, transcending ordinary human nature, may sometimes come by chance to a man who does not understand its science; he, as it were, stumbles upon it. When he stumbles upon it, he generally interprets it as coming from outside. So this explains why an inspiration, or transcendental knowledge, may be the same in different countries, but in one country it will seem to come through an angel, and in another through a Deva, and in a third through God.

What does it mean? It means that the mind brought the knowledge by its own nature, and that the finding of the knowledge was interpreted according to the belief and education of the person through whom it came. The real fact is that these various men, as it were, stumbled upon this superconscious state.

The Yogi says there is a great danger in stumbling upon this state. In a good many cases there is the danger of the brain being deranged, and, as a rule, you will find that all those men, however great they were, who had stumbled upon this superconscious state without understanding it, groped in the dark, and generally had, along with their knowledge, some quaint superstition. They opened themselves to hallucinations.

Mohammed claimed that the Angel Gabriel came to him in a cave one day and took him on the heavenly horse, Harak, and he visited the heavens. But with all that, Mohammed spoke some wonderful truths. If you read the Koran, you find the most wonderful truths mixed with superstitions.

How will you explain it? That man was inspired, no doubt, but that inspiration was, as it were, stumbled upon. He was not a trained Yogi, and did not know the reason of what he was doing.

Think of the good Mohammed did to the world, and think of the great evil that has been done through his fanaticism! Think of the millions massacred through his teachings, mothers bereft of their children, children made orphans, whole countries destroyed, millions upon millions of people killed!

So we see this danger by studying the lives of great teachers like Mohammed and others. Yet we find, at the same time, that they were all inspired. Whenever a prophet got into the superconscious state by heightening his emotional nature, he brought away from it not only some truths, but some fanaticism also, some superstition which injured the world as much as the greatness of the teaching helped.

To get any reason out of the mass of incongruity we call human life, we have to transcend our reason, but we must do it scientifically, slowly, by regular practice, and we must cast off all superstition. We must take up the study of the superconscious state just as any other science. On reason we must have to lay our foundation, we must follow reason as far as it leads, and when reason fails, reason itself will show us the way to the highest plane.

When you hear a man say, "I am inspired," and then talk irrationally, reject it. Why? Because these three states — instinct, reason, and super-consciousness, or the unconscious, conscious, and superconscious states — belong to one and the same mind. There are not three minds in one man, but one state of it develops into the others. Instinct develops into reason, and reason into the transcendental consciousness; therefore, not one of the states contradicts the others.

Real inspiration never contradicts reason, but fulfils it. Just as you find the great prophets saying, "I come not to destroy but to fulfil," so inspiration always comes to fulfil reason, and is in harmony with it.

*

All the different steps in Yoga are intended to bring us scientifically to the superconscious state, or Samadhi. Furthermore, this is a most vital point to understand, that inspiration is as much in every man's nature as it was in that of the ancient prophets.

These prophets were not unique; they were men as you or I. They were great Yogis. They had gained this super-consciousness, and you and I can get the same. They were not peculiar people. The very fact that one man ever reached that state, proves that it is possible for every man to do so. Not only is it possible, but every man must, eventually, get to that state, and that is religion.

Experience is the only teacher we have. We may talk and reason all our lives, but we shall not understand a word of truth, until we experience it ourselves.

You cannot hope to make a man a surgeon by simply giving him a few books. You cannot satisfy my curiosity to see a country by showing me a map; I must have actual experience. Maps can only create curiosity in us to get more perfect knowledge. Beyond that, they have no value whatever.

Clinging to books only degenerates the human mind. Was there ever a more horrible blasphemy than the statement that all the knowledge of God is confined to this or that book? How dare men call God infinite, and yet try to compress Him within the covers of a little book!

Millions of people have been killed because they did not believe what the books said, because they would not see all the knowledge of God within the covers of a book. Of course, this killing and murdering has gone by, but the world is still tremendously bound up in a belief in books.

*

When the mind has been trained to remain fixed on a certain internal or external location, there comes to it the power of flowing in an unbroken current, as it were, towards that point. This state is called Dhyana.

When one has so intensified the power of Dhyana as to be able to reject the external part of perception and remain meditating only on the internal part, the meaning, that state is called Samadhi.

That is, if the mind can first concentrate upon an object, and then is able to continue in that concentration for a length of time, and then, by continued concentration, to dwell only on the internal part of the perception of which the object was the effect, everything comes under the control of such a mind.

This meditative state is the highest state of existence. So long as there is desire, no real happiness can come. It is only the contemplative, witness-like study of objects that brings to us real enjoyment and happiness. The animal has its happiness in the senses, the man in his intellect, and the god in spiritual contemplation.

It is only to the soul that has attained to this contemplative state that the world really becomes beautiful. To him who desires nothing, and does not mix himself up with them, the manifold changes of nature are one panorama of beauty and sublimity.

NON-ATTACHMENT

Does renunciation demand that we all become ascetics? Who then is to help others? Renunciation is not asceticism. Are all beggars Christ? Poverty is not a synonym for holiness; often the reverse.

Renunciation is of the mind. How does it come? In a desert, when I was thirsty, I saw a lake. It was in the midst of a beautiful landscape. There were trees surrounding it, and their reflections could be seen in the water, upside down. But the whole thing proved to be a mirage.

Then I knew that every day for a month I had seen this; and only that day, being thirsty, I had learnt it to be unreal. Every day for a month I should see it again. But I should never take it to be real.

So, when we reach God, the idea of the universe, the body and so on, will vanish. It will return afterwards. But next time we shall know it to be unreal.

The history of the world is the history of persons like Buddha and Jesus. The passionless and unattached do most for the world.

Picture Jesus in the slums. He sees beyond the misery, "You, my brethren, are all divine." His work is calm. He removes causes. You will be able to work for the good of the world when you know for a fact that this work is all illusion.

The more unconscious this work, the better, because it is then the more superconscious. Our search is not for good or evil; but happiness and good are nearer to truth than their opposites.

A man ran a thorn into his finger, and with another thorn took it out. The first thorn is Evil. The second thorn is Good. The Self is that Peace which passeth beyond both evil and good.

The universe is melting down: man draws nearer to God. For one moment he is real — God. He is re-differentiated — a prophet. Before him, now, the world trembles. A fool sleeps and wakes a fool-a man unconscious; and superconscious, he returns with infinite power, purity, and love — the God-Man. This is the use of the superconscious state.

*

Attachment is the source of all our pleasures now. We are attached to our friends, to our relatives; we are attached to our intellectual and spiritual works; we are attached to external objects, so that we get pleasure from them.

What, again, brings misery but this very attachment? We have to detach ourselves to earn joy. If only we had power to detach ourselves at will, there would not be any misery. That man alone will be able to get the best of nature, who, having the power of attaching himself to a thing with all his energy, has also the power to detach himself when he should do so.

The difficulty is that there must be as much power of attachment as that of detachment. There are men who are never attracted by anything. They can never love, they are hard-hearted and apathetic; they escape most of the miseries of life.

But the wall never feels misery, the wall never loves, is never hurt; but it is the wall, after all. Surely it is better to be attached and caught, than to be a wall. Therefore the man who never loves, who is hard and stony, escaping most of the miseries of life, escapes also its joys.

We do not want that. That is weakness, that is death. That soul has not been awakened that never feels weakness, never feels misery. That is a callous state. We do not want that.

At the same time, we not only want this mighty power of love, this mighty power of attachment, the power of throwing our whole soul upon a single object, losing ourselves and letting ourselves be annihilated, as it were, for other souls — which is the power of the gods — but we want to be higher even than the gods.

The perfect man can put his whole soul upon that one point of love, yet he is unattached. How comes this? There is another secret to learn.

The beggar is never happy. The beggar only gets a dole with pity and scorn behind it, at least with the thought behind that the beggar is a low object. He never really enjoys what he gets.

We are all beggars. Whatever we do, we want a return. We are all traders. We are traders in life, we are traders in virtue, we are traders in religion. And alas! we are also traders in love.

If you come to trade, if it is a question of give-and-take, if it is a question of buy-and-sell, abide by the laws of buying and selling. There is a bad time and there is a good time; there is a rise and a fall in prices: always you expect the blow to come.

It is like looking at the mirrors Your face is reflected: you make a grimace — there is one in the mirror; if you laugh, the mirror laughs. This is buying and selling, giving and taking.

We get caught. How? Not by what we give, but by what we expect. We get misery in return for our love; not from the fact that we love, but from the fact that we want love in return.

There is no misery where there is no want. Desire, want, is the father of all misery. Desires are bound by the laws of success and failure. Desires must bring misery.

*

The great secret of true success, of true happiness, then, is this: the man who asks for no return, the perfectly unselfish man, is the most successful.

It seems to be a paradox. Do we not know that every man who is unselfish in life gets cheated, gets hurt? Apparently, yes. "Christ was unselfish, and yet he was crucified."

True, but we know that his unselfishness is the reason, the cause of a great victory — the crowning of millions upon millions of lives with the blessings of true success.

Ask nothing; want nothing in return. Give what you have to give; it will come back to you — but do not think of that now, it will come back multiplied a thousandfold — but the attention must not be on that. Yet have the power to give: give, and there it ends. Learn that the whole of life is giving, that nature will force you to give.

So, give willingly. Sooner or later you will have to give up. You come into life to accumulate. With clenched hands, you want to take. But nature puts a hand on your throat and makes your hands open.

Whether you will it or not, you have to give. The moment you say, "I will not", the blow comes; you are hurt. None is there but will be compelled, in the long run, to give up everything. And the more one struggles against this law, the more miserable one feels.

It is because we dare not give, because we are not resigned enough to accede to this grand demand of nature, that we are miserable. The forest is gone, but we get heat in return. The sun is taking up water from the ocean, to return it in showers. You are a machine for taking and giving: you take, in order to give.

Ask, therefore, nothing in return; but the more you give, the more will come to you. The quicker you can empty the air out of this room, the quicker it will be filled up by the external air; and if you close all the doors and every aperture, that which is within will remain, but that which is outside will never come in, and that which is within will stagnate, degenerate, and become poisoned.

A river is continually emptying itself into the ocean and is continually filling up again. Bar not the exit into the ocean. The moment you do that, death seizes you.

*

Be, therefore, not a beggar; be unattached.

This is the most terrible task of life! You do not calculate the dangers on the path. Even by intellectually recognising the difficulties, we really do not know them until we feel them. From a distance we may get a general view of a park: well, what of that? We feel and really know it when we are in it. Even if our every attempt is a failure, and we bleed and are torn asunder, yet, through all this, we have to preserve our heart — we must assert our Godhead in the midst of all these difficulties.

Nature wants us to react, to return blow for blow, cheating for cheating, lie for lie, to hit back with all our might. Then it requires a superdivine power not to hit back, to keep control, to be unattached.

Every day we renew our determination to be unattached. We cast our eyes back and look at the past objects of our love and attachment, and feel how every one of them made us miserable. We went down into the depths of despondency because of our "love"! We found ourselves mere slaves in the hands of others, we were dragged down and down!

And we make a fresh determination: "Henceforth, I will be master of myself; henceforth, I will have control over myself." But the time comes, and the same story once more! Again the soul is caught and cannot get out. The bird is in a net, struggling and fluttering. This is our life.

I know the difficulties. Tremendous they are, and ninety per cent of us become discouraged and lose heart, and in our turn, often become pessimists and cease to believe in sincerity, love, and all that is grand and noble.

So, we find men who in the freshness of their lives have been forgiving, kind, simple, and guileless, become in old age lying masks of men. Their minds are a mass of intricacy.

There may be a good deal of external policy, possibly. They are not hot-headed, they do not speak, but it would be better for them to do so; their hearts are dead and, therefore, they do not speak. They do not curse, not become angry; but it would be better for them to be able to be angry, a thousand times better, to be able to curse. They cannot. There is death in the heart, for cold hands have seized upon it, and it can no more act, even to utter a curse, even to use a harsh word.

All this we have to avoid: therefore I say, we require superdivine power. Superhuman power is not strong enough. Superdivine strength is the only way, the one way out. By it alone we can pass through all these intricacies, through these showers of miseries, unscathed. We may be cut to pieces, torn asunder, yet our hearts must grow nobler and nobler all the time.

It is very difficult, but we can overcome the difficulty by constant practice. We must learn that nothing can happen to us, unless we make ourselves susceptible to it.

*

I have just said, no disease can come to me until the body is ready; it does not depend alone on the germs, but upon a certain predisposition which is already in the body. We get only that for which we are fitted.

Let us give up our pride and understand this, that never is misery undeserved. There never has been a blow undeserved: there never has been an evil for which I did not pave the way with my own hands. We ought to know that.

Analyse yourselves and you will find that every blow you have received, came to you because you prepared yourselves for it. You did half, and the external world did the other half: that is how the blow came. That will sober us down.

At the same time, from this very analysis will come a note of hope, and the note of hope is: "I have no control of the external world, but that which is in me and nearer unto me, my own world, is in my control. If the two together are required to make a failure, if the two together are necessary to give me a blow, I will not contribute the one which is in my keeping; and how then can the blow come? If I get real control of myself, the blow will never come."

*

By non-attachment and practice, meditation is perfected.

*

"I cannot tell anything about Thee except that Thou art my love. Thou art beautiful, Oh, Thou art beautiful! Thou art beauty itself." What is after all really required of us in this Yoga is that our thirst after the beautiful should be directed to God.

What is the beauty in the human face, in the sky, in the stars, and in the moon? It is only the partial apprehension of the real all-embracing Divine Beauty. "He shining, everything shines. It is through His light that all things shine."

Take this high position of Bhakti which makes you forget at once all your little personalities. Take yourself away from all the world's little selfish clingings. Do not look upon humanity as the centre of all your human and higher interests. Stand as a witness, as a student, and observe the phenomena of nature. Have the feeling of personal non-attachment with regard to man, and see how this mighty feeling of love is working itself out in the world.

Sometimes a little friction is produced, but that is only in the course of the struggle to attain the higher real love. Sometimes there is a little fight or a little fall; but it is all only by the way.

Stand aside, and freely let these frictions come. You feel the frictions only when you are in the current of the world, but when you are outside of it simply as a witness and as a student, you will be able to see that there are millions and millions of channels in which God is manifesting Himself as Love.

*

The Bhakti-Yogi knows the meaning of life's struggles; he understands it. He has passed through a long series of these struggles and knows what they mean and earnestly desires to be free from the friction thereof; he wants to avoid the clash and go direct to the centre of all attraction, the great Hari.

This is the renunciation of the Bhakta. This mighty attraction in the direction of God makes all other attractions vanish for him. This mighty infinite love of God which enters his heart leaves no place for any other love to live there.

How can it be otherwise? Bhakti fills his heart with the divine waters of the ocean of love, which is God Himself; there is no place there for little loves. That is to say, the Bhakta's renunciation is that Vairâgya or non-attachment for all things that are not God which results from Anurâga or great attachment to God.

*

Whenever we say a thing is "mine", misery will immediately come. Do not even say "my child" in your mind. Possess the child, but do not say "mine". If you do, then will come the misery.

Do not say "my house," do not say "my body". The whole difficulty is there. The body is neither yours, nor mine, nor anybody's. These bodies are coming and going by the laws of nature, but we are free, standing as witness.

This body is no more free than a picture or a wall. Why should we be attached so much to a body? If somebody paints a picture, he does it and passes on. Do not project that tentacle of selfishness, "I must possess it". As soon as that is projected, misery will begin.

So Karma-Yoga says, first destroy the tendency to project this tentacle of selfishness, and when you have the power of checking it, hold it in and do not allow the mind to get into the ways of selfishness. Then you may go out into the world and work as much as you can. Mix everywhere, go where you please; you will never be contaminated with evil. There is the lotus leaf in the water; the water cannot touch and adhere to it; so will you be in the world. This is called "Vairâgya", dispassion or non-attachment.

I believe I have told you that without non-attachment there cannot be any kind of Yoga. Non-attachment is the basis of all the Yogas. The man who gives up living in houses, wearing fine clothes, and eating good food, and goes into the desert, may be a most attached person. His only possession, his own body, may become everything to him; and as he lives he will be simply struggling for the sake of his body.

Non-attachment does not mean anything that we may do in relation to our external body, it is all in the mind. The binding link of "I and mine" is in the mind. If we have not this link with the body and with the things of the senses, we are non-attached, wherever and whatever we may be. A man may be on a throne and perfectly non-attached; another man may be in rags and still very much attached.

First, we have to attain this state of non-attachment and then to work incessantly. Karma-Yoga gives us the method that will help us in giving up all attachment, though it is indeed very hard.

*

The body is our enemy, and yet is our friend. Which of you can bear the sight of misery? And which of you cannot do so when you see it only as a painting? Because it is unreal, we do not identify ourselves with it, eve know it is only a painting; it cannot bless us, it cannot hurt us.

The most terrible misery painted upon a price of canvas, we may even enjoy; we praise the technique of the artist, we wonder at his marvellous genius, even though the scene he paints is most horrible. That is the secret; that non-attachment. Be the Witness.

*

Since I was a child I have heard about Krishna's life. I take it for granted there must have been a man called Krishna, and his Gita shows he has [left] a wonderful book.

I told you, you can understand the character of a man by analysing the fables about him. The fables have the nature [of decorations]. You must find they are all polished and manipulated to fit into the character.

For instance, take Buddha. The central idea [is] sacrifice. There are thousands of folklore, but in every case the sacrifice must have been kept up.

There are thousands of stories about Lincoln, about some characteristic of that great man. You take all the fables and find the general idea and [know] that that was the central character of the man.

You find in Krishna that non-attachment is the central idea. He does not need anything. He does not want anything. He works for work's sake. "Work for work's sake. Worship for worship's sake. Do good because it is good to do good. Ask no more."

That must have been the character of the man. Otherwise these fables could not be brought down to the one idea of non-attachment.

*

The purer the body and mind, the quicker the desired result will be obtained. You must be perfectly pure. Do not think of evil things, such thoughts will surely drag you down.

If you are perfectly pure and practice faithfully, your mind can finally be made a searchlight of infinite power. There is no limit to its scope.

But there must be constant practice and non-attachment to the world. When a man reaches the superconscious state, all feeling of body melts away. Then alone does he become free and immortal.

MEDITATION

We are at the beck and call of nature. If there is sound outside, I have to hear it. If something is going on, I have to see it. Like monkeys. We are two thousand monkeys concentrated, each one of us.

Monkeys are very curious. So we cannot help ourselves, and call this "enjoying". Wonderful this language! We are enjoying the world! We cannot help enjoying it. Nature wants us to do it. A beautiful sound: I am hearing it. As if I could choose to hear it or not!

Nature says, "Go down to the depths of misery." I become miserable in a moment. We talk about pleasures [of the senses] and possessions.

One man thinks me very learned. Another thinks, "He is a fool." This degradation, this slavery, without knowing anything! In the dark room we are knocking our heads against each other.

What is meditation? Meditation is the power which enables us to resist all this.

Nature may call us, "Look there is a beautiful thing!" I do not look. Now she says, "There is a beautiful smell; smell it! " I say to my nose, "Do not smell it", and the nose doesn't. "Eyes, do not see!"

Nature does such an awful thing - kills one of my children, and says, "Now, rascal, sit down and weep! Go to the depths!" I say, "I don't have to." I jump up. I must be free.

Try it sometimes. [In meditation], for a moment, you can change this nature. Now, if you had that power in yourself, would not that be heaven, freedom? That is the power of meditation.

*

Always think that this body is only an inert instrument. And the self-contained Purusha within is your real nature. The adjunct of mind is His first and subtle covering, then, there is this body which is His gross, outer covering. The indivisible changeless, self-effulgent Purusha is lying hidden under these delusive veils, therefore your real nature is unknown to you.

The direction of the mind which always runs after the senses has to be turned within. The mind has to be killed. The body is but gross — it dies and dissolves into the five elements.

But the bundle of mental impressions, which is the mind, does not die soon. It remains for some time in seed-form and then sprouts and grows in the form of a tree — it takes on another physical body and goes the round of birth and death, until Self-knowledge arises.

Therefore I say, by meditation and concentration and by the power of philosophical discrimination plunge this mind in the Ocean of Existence-Knowledge-Bliss Absolute. When the mind dies, all limiting adjuncts vanish and you are established in Brahman.

*

First, meditation should be of a negative nature. Think away everything. Analyse everything that comes in the mind by the sheer action of the will.

Next, assert what we really are — existence, knowledge and bliss — being, knowing, and loving.

Meditation is the means of unification of the subject and object. Meditate:

Above, it is full of me; below, it is full of me; in the middle, it is full of me. I am in all beings, and all beings are in me. Om Tat Sat, I am It. I am existence above mind. I am the one Spirit of the universe. I am neither pleasure nor pain.

The body drinks, eats, and so on. I am not the body. I am not mind. I am He.

I am the witness. I look on. When health comes I am the witness When disease comes I am the witness.

I am Existence, Knowledge, Bliss.

I am the essence and nectar of knowledge. Through eternity I change not. I am calm, resplendent, and unchanging.

*

Be like the pearl oyster. There is a pretty Indian fable to the effect that if it rains when the star Svâti is in the ascendant, and a drop of rain falls into an oyster, that drop becomes a pearl.

The oysters know this, so they come to the surface when that star shines, and wait to catch the precious raindrop. When a drop falls into them, quickly the oysters close their shells and dive down to the bottom of the sea, there to patiently develop the drop into the pearl.

We should be like that. First hear, then understand, and then, leaving all distractions, shut your minds to outside influences, and devote yourselves to developing the truth within you.

There is the danger of frittering away your energies by taking up an idea only for its novelty, and then giving it up for another that is newer. Take one thing up and do it, and see the end of it, and before you have seen the end, do not give it up.

He who can become mad with an idea, he alone sees light. Those that only take a nibble here and a nibble there will never attain anything. They may titillate their nerves for a moment, but there it will end. They will be slaves in the hands of nature, and will never get beyond the senses.

*

Those who really want to be Yogis must give up, once for all, this nibbling at things. Take up one idea. Make that one idea your life — think of it, dream of it, live on that idea. Let the brain, muscles, nerves, every part of your body, be full of that idea, and just leave every other idea alone.

This is the way to success, and this is the way great spiritual giants are produced. Others are mere talking machines. If we really want to be blessed, and make others blessed, we must go deeper.

The first step is not to disturb the mind, not to associate with persons whose ideas are disturbing. All of you know that certain persons, certain places, certain foods, repel you. Avoid them; and those who want to go to the highest, must avoid all company, good or bad.

Practise hard; whether you live or die does not matter. You have to plunge in and work, without thinking of the result. If you are brave enough, in six months you will be a perfect Yogi.

But those who take up just a bit of it and a little of everything else make no progress. It is of no use simply to take a course of lessons. To those who are full of Tamas, ignorant and dull — those whose minds never get fixed on any idea, who only crave for something to amuse them — religion and philosophy are simply objects of entertainment. These are the unpersevering. They hear a talk, think it very nice, and then go home and forget all about it.

To succeed, you must have tremendous perseverance, tremendous will. "I will drink the ocean," says the persevering soul, "at my will mountains will crumble up." Have that sort of energy, that sort of will, work hard, and you will reach the goal.

*

There is one soul which is the greatest of all. This is Ishvara, Lord of Yoga [God as Creator, with attributes]. He is the individual. He is omnipotent. He resides in every heart.

There is no body. He does not need a body. All you get by the practice of meditation etc., you can get by meditation upon Ishvara, Lord of Yogis.

The same can be attained by meditating upon a great soul; or upon the harmony of life. These are called objective meditations.

So, you begin to meditate upon certain external things, objective things, either outside or inside. If you take a long sentence, that is no meditation at all. That is simply trying to get the mind collected by repetition.

Meditation means the mind is turned back upon itself. The mind stops all the [thought-waves] and the world stops. Your consciousness expands. Every time you meditate you will keep your growth.

Work a little harder, more and more, and meditation comes. You do not feel the body or anything else. When you come out of it after the hour, you have had the most beautiful rest you ever had in your life. That is the only way you ever give rest to your system. Not even the deepest sleep will give you such rest as that.

The mind goes on jumping even in deepest sleep. Just those few minutes [in meditation] your brain has almost stopped. Just a little vitality is kept up.

You may be cut to pieces and not feel it at all. You feel such pleasure in it. You become so light. This perfect rest we will get in meditation.

*

Meditation is a sort of prayer and prayer is meditation. The highest meditation is to think of nothing. If you can remain one moment without thought, great power will come. The whole secret of knowledge is concentration.

Soul best develops itself by loving God with all the heart. Soul is the thinking principle in man, of which mind is a function. Soul is only the conduit from Spirit to mind.

*

These ideas have to be understood in Dhyana, or meditation. We hear a sound. First, there is the external vibration; second, the nerve motion that carries it to the mind; third, the reaction from the mind, along with which flashes the knowledge of the object which was the external cause of these different changes from the ethereal vibrations to the mental reactions.

These three are called in Yoga, Shabda (sound), Artha (meaning), and Jnâna (knowledge). In the language of physics and physiology they are called the ethereal vibration, the motion in the nerve and brain, and the mental reaction.

Now these, though distinct processes, have become mixed up in such a fashion as to become quite indistinct. In fact, we cannot now perceive any of these, we only perceive their combined effect, what we call the external object. Every act of perception includes these three, and there is no reason why we should not be able to distinguish them.

*

When, by the previous preparations, it becomes strong and controlled, and has the power of finer perception, the mind should be employed in meditation. This meditation must begin with gross objects and slowly rise to finer and finer, until it becomes objectless.

The mind should first be employed in perceiving the external causes of sensations, then the internal motions, and then its own reaction. When it has succeeded in perceiving the external causes of sensations by themselves, the mind will acquire the power of perceiving all fine material existences, all fine bodies and forms.

When it can succeed in perceiving the motions inside by themselves, it will gain the control of all mental waves, in itself or in others, even before they have translated themselves into physical energy; and when he will be able to perceive the mental reaction by itself, the Yogi will acquire the knowledge of everything, as every sensible object, and every thought is the result of this reaction. Then will he have seen the very foundations of his mind, and it will be under his perfect control.

Different powers will come to the Yogi, and if he yields to the temptations of any one of these, the road to his further progress will be barred. Such is the evil of running after enjoyments. But if he is strong enough to reject even these miraculous powers, he will attain to the goal of Yoga, the complete suppression of the waves in the ocean of the mind.

Then the glory of the soul, undisturbed by the distractions of the mind, or motions of the body, will shine in its full effulgence; and the Yogi will find himself as he is and as he always was, the essence of knowledge, the immortal, the all-pervading.

*

The power of meditation gets us everything. If you want to get power over nature, [you can have it through meditation].

It is through the power of meditation all scientific facts are discovered today. They study the subject and forget everything, their own identity and everything, and then the great fact comes like a flash. Some people think that is inspiration. There is no more inspiration than there is expiration; and never was anything got for nothing.

*

"By constant repetition of the syllable Om and by meditating on its meaning, everything can be obtained"; "All sins are washed away by uttering the name of the Lord"; "He gets all, who resigns himself to the Will of God" — yes, these words of the Shastras and the sages are, no doubt, true.

But, do you see, thousands of us are, for our whole life, meditating on Om, are getting ecstatic in devotion in the name of the Lord, and are crying, "Thy Will be done, I am fully resigned to Thee! " — and what are they actually getting in return? Absolutely nothing!

How do you account for this? The reason lies here, and it must be fully understood.

Whose meditation is real and effective? Who can really resign himself to the Will of God? Who can utter with power irresistible, like that of a thunderbolt, the name of the Lord?

It is he who has earned Chitta-shuddhi, that is, whose mind has been purified by work, or in other words, he who is the Dharmika.

*

When [the mind] is doubtful that is not its great state. Its great state is meditation. It looks upon things and sees things, not identifying itself with anything else. As long as I feel pain, I have identified myself with the body. When I feel joy or pleasure, I have identified myself with the body.

But the high state will look with the same pleasure or blissfulness upon pleasure or upon pain. Every meditation is direct superconsciousness. In perfect concentration the soul becomes actually free from the bonds of the gross body and knows itself as it is.

Whatever one wants, that comes to him. Power and knowledge are already there. The soul identifies itself with that which is powerless matter and thus weeps. It identifies itself with mortal shapes. But if that free soul wants to exercise any power, it will have it.

If it does not, it does not come. He who has known God has become God. There is nothing impossible to such a free soul. No more birth and death for him. He is free for ever.

*

The greatest help to spiritual life is meditation (Dhyâna). In meditation we divest ourselves of all material conditions and feel our divine nature. We do not depend upon any external help in meditation. The touch of the soul can paint the brightest colour even in the dingiest places; it can cast a fragrance over the vilest thing; it can make the wicked divine — and all enmity, all selfishness is effaced.

The less the thought of the body, the better. For it is the body that drags us down. It is attachment, identification, which makes us miserable.

That is the secret: To think that I am the spirit and not the body, and that the whole of this universe with all its relations, with all its good and all its evil, is but as a series of paintings — scenes on a canvas — of which I am the witness.

*

How is it to be attained? In a dozen different ways. Each temperament has its own way. But this is the general principle: get hold of the mind.

The mind is like a lake, and every stone that drops into it raises waves. These waves do not let us see what we are. The full moon is reflected in the water of the lake, but the surface is so disturbed that we do not see the reflection clearly.

Let it be calm. Do not let nature raise the wave. Keep quiet, and then after a little while she will give you up. Then we know what we are.

God is there already, but the mind is so agitated, always running after the senses. You close the senses and [yet] you whirl and whirl about. Just this moment I think I am all right and I will meditate upon God, and then my mind goes to London in one minute. And if I pull it away from there, it goes to New York to think about the things I have done there in the past.

These [waves] are to be stopped by the power of meditation. Slowly and gradually we are to train ourselves. It is no joke — not a question of a day, or years, or maybe of births.

Never mind! The pull must go on. Knowingly, voluntarily, the pull must go on. Inch by inch we will gain ground. We will begin to feel and get real possessions, which no one can take away from us — the wealth that no man can take, the wealth that nobody can destroy, the joy that no misery can hurt any more.

All these years we have depended upon others. If I have a little pleasure and that person goes away, my pleasure is gone. See the folly of man: he depends for happiness upon men! All separations are misery. Naturally. Depending upon wealth for happiness? There is fluctuation of wealth. Depending upon health or upon anything except the unchangeable spirit must bring misery today or tomorrow.

Excepting the infinite spirit, everything else is changing. There is the whirl of change. Permanence is nowhere except in yourself. There is the infinite joy, unchanging.

Meditation is the gate that opens that to us. Prayers, ceremonials, and all the other forms of worship are simply kindergartens of meditation. You pray, you offer something.

A certain theory existed that everything raised one's spiritual power. The use of certain words, flowers, images, temples, ceremonials like the waving of lights brings the mind to that attitude, but that attitude is always in the human soul, nowhere else. [People] are all doing it; but what they do without knowing it, do knowingly.

That is the power of meditation. All knowledge you have — how did it come? From the power of meditation. The soul churned the knowledge out of its own depths.

What knowledge was there ever outside of it? In the long run this power of meditation separates ourselves from the body, and then the soul knows itself as it is — the unborn, the deathless, and birthless being. No more is there any misery, no more births upon this earth, no more evolution. [The soul knows itself as having] ever been perfect and free.

THE POWER OF MEDITATION

The practice of meditationMeditation has been laid stress upon by all religions. The meditative state of mind is declared by the Yogis to be the highest state in which the mind exists. When the mind is studying the external object, it gets identified with it, loses itself. To use the simile of the old Indian philosopher: the soul of man is like a piece of crystal, but it takes the colour of whatever is near it. Whatever the soul touches it has to take its colour. That is the difficulty. That constitutes the bondage. The colour is so strong, the crystal forgets itself and identifies itself with the colour. Suppose a red flower is near the crystal and the crystal takes the colour and forgets itself, thinks it is red. We have taken the colour of the body and have forgotten what we are. All the difficulties that follow come from that one dead body. All our fears, all worries, anxieties, troubles, mistakes, weakness, evil, are front that one great blunder — that we are bodies. This is the ordinary person. It is the person taking the colour of the flower near to it. We are no more bodies than the crystal is the red flower.

The practice of meditation is pursued. The crystal knows what it is, takes its own colour. It is meditation that brings us nearer to truth than anything else.

*

In India two persons meet. In English they say, "How do you do?" The Indian greeting is, "Are you upon yourself?"

The moment you stand upon something else, you run the risk of being miserable. This is what I mean by meditation — the soul trying to stand upon itself.

That state must surely be the healthiest state of the soul, when it is thinking of itself, residing in its own glory. No, all the other methods that we have — by exciting emotions, prayers, and all that — really have that one end in view. In deep emotional excitement the soul tries to stand upon itself. Although the emotion may arise from anything external, there is concentration of mind.

*

There are three stages in meditation. The first is what is called [Dhâranâ], concentrating the mind upon an object. I try to concentrate my mind upon this glass, excluding every other object from my mind except this glass. But the mind is wavering.

When it has become strong and does not waver so much, it is called [Dhyâna], meditation.

And then there is a still higher state when the differentiation between the glass and myself is lost — [Samâdhi or absorption]. The mind and the glass are identical. I do not see any difference.

All the senses stop and all powers that have been working through other channels of other senses [are focused in the mind]. Then this glass is under the power of the mind entirely. This is to be realised. It is a tremendous play played by the Yogis.

*

Take for granted, the external object exists. Then that which is really outside of us is not what we see. The glass that I see is not the external object certainly. That external something which is the glass I do not know and will never know.

Something produces an impression upon me. Immediately I send the reaction towards that, and the glass is the result of the combination of these two. Action from outside — X. Action from inside — Y. The glass is XY.

When you look at X, call it external world — at Y, internal world If you try to distinguish which is your mind and which is the world — there is no such distinction. The world is the combination of you and something else.

Let us take another example. You are dropping stones upon the smooth surface of a lake. Every stone you drop is followed by a reaction. The stone is covered by the little waves in the lake.

Similarly, external things are like the stones dropping into the lake of the mind. So we do not really see the external . . .; we see the wave only.

These waves that rise in the mind have caused many things outside. We are not discussing the [merits of] idealism and realism. We take for granted that things exist outside, but what we see is different from things that exist outside, as we see what exists outside plus ourselves.

Suppose I take my contribution out of the glass. What remains? Almost nothing. The glass will disappear.

If I take my contribution from the table, what would remain of the table? Certainly not this table, because it was a mixture of the outside plus my contribution. The poor lake has got to throw the wave towards the stone whenever [the stone] is thrown in it. The mind must create the wave towards any sensation.

Suppose we can withhold the mind. At once we are masters. We refuse to contribute our share to all these phenomena. If I do not contribute my share, it has got to stop.

*

You are creating this bondage all the time. How? By putting in your share. We are all making our own beds, forging our own chains.

When the identifying ceases between this external object and myself, then I will be able to take my contribution off, and this thing will disappear. Then I will say, "Here is the glass", and then take my mind off, and it disappears.

If you can take away your share, you can walk upon water. Why should it drown you any more? What of poison? No more difficulties. In every phenomenon in nature you contribute at least half, and nature brings half. If your half is taken off, the thing must stop.

To every action there is equal reaction. If a man strikes me and wounds me it is that man's actions and my body's reaction. Suppose I have so much power over the body that I can resist even that automatic action.

Can such power be attained? The books say it can. If you stumble on [it], it is a miracle. If you learn it scientifically, it is Yoga.

I have seen people healed by the power of mind. There is the miracle worker. We say he prays and the man is healed. Another man says, "Not at all. It is just the power of the mind. The man is scientific. He knows what he is about."

*

The power of meditation gets us everything. If you want to get power over nature, [you can have it through meditation]. It is through the power of meditation all scientific facts are discovered today. They study the subject and forget everything, their own identity and everything, and then the great fact comes like a flash. Some people think that is inspiration. There is no more inspiration than there is expiration; and never was anything got for nothing.

The highest so-called inspiration was the work of Jesus. He worked hard for ages in previous births. That was the result of his previous work — hard work. It is all nonsense to talk about inspiration. Had it been, it would have fallen like rain.

Inspired people in any line of thought only come among nations who have general education and [culture]. There is no inspiration. Whatever passes for inspiration is the result that comes from causes already in the mind. One day, flash comes the result! Their past work was the [cause].

Therein also you see the power of meditation — intensity of thought. These men churn up their own souls. Great truths come to the surface and become manifest.

Therefore the practice of meditation is the great scientific method of knowledge. There is no knowledge without the power of meditation. From ignorance, superstition, etc. we can get cured by meditation for the time being and no more.

[Suppose] a man has told me that if you drink such a poison you will be killed, and another man comes in the night and says, "Go drink the poison!" and I am not killed, [what happens is this:] my mind cut out from the meditation the identity between the poison and myself just for the time being. In another case of [drinking] the poison, I will be killed.

If I know the reason and scientifically raise myself up to that [state of meditation], I can save anyone. That is what the books say; but how far it is correct you must appraise.

*

I am asked, "Why do you Indian people not conquer these things? You claim all the time to be superior to all other people. You practice Yoga and do it quicker than anybody else. You are fitter. Carry it out! If you are a great people, you ought to have a great system. You will have to say good-bye to all the gods. Let them go to sleep as you take up the great philosophers.

"You are mere babies, as superstitious as the rest of the world. And all your claims are failures. If you have the claims, stand up and be bold, and all the heaven that ever existed is yours. There is the musk deer with fragrance inside, and he does not know where the fragrance [comes from]. Then after days and days he finds it in himself. All these gods and demons are within them. Find out, by the powers of reason, education, and culture that it is all in yourself. No more gods and superstitions. You want to be rational, to be Yogis, really spiritual."

[My reply is: With you too] everything is material. What is more material than God sitting on a throne? You look down upon the poor man who is worshipping the image. You are no better.

And you, gold worshippers, what are you? The image worshipper worships his god, something that he can see. But you do not even do that. You do not worship the spirit nor something that you can understand.

Word worshippers! "God is spirit!" God is spirit and should be worshipped in spirit and faith. Where does the spirit reside? On a tree? On a cloud?

What do you mean by God being ours? You are the spirit. That is the first fundamental belief you must never give up. I am the spiritual being. It is there. All this skill of Yoga and this system of meditation and everything is just to find Him there.

*

Why am I saying all this just now? Until you fix the location, you cannot talk. You fix it up in heaven and all the world ever except in the right place. I am spirit, and therefore the spirit of all spirits must be in my soul. Those who think it anywhere else are ignorant.

Therefore it is to be sought here in this heaven; all the heaven that ever existed [is within myself]. There are some sages who, knowing this, turn their eyes inward and find the spirit of all spirits in their own spirit. That is the scope of meditation. Find out the truth about God and about your own soul and thus attain to liberation.

You are all running after life, and we find that is foolishness. There is something much higher than life even. This life is inferior, material. Why should I live at all? I am something higher than life. Living is always slavery. We always get mixed up. Everything is a continuous chain of slavery.

You get something, and no man can teach another. It is through experience [we learn]. That young man cannot be persuaded that there are any difficulties in life. You cannot persuade the old man that life is all smooth. He has had many experiences. That is the difference.

By the power of meditation we have got to control, step by step, all these things. We have seen philosophically that all these differentiations — spirit, mind, matter, etc. — [have no real existences. Whatever exists is one. There cannot be many.

That is what is meant by science and knowledge. Ignorance sees manifold. Knowledge realises one. Reducing the many into one is science. The whole of the universe has been demonstrated into one. That science is called the science of Vedanta. The whole universe is one. The one runs through all this seeming variety.

We have all these variations now and we see them — what we call the five elements: solid, liquid, gaseous, luminous, ethereal. After that the state of existence is mental and beyond that spiritual.

Not that spirit is one and mind is another, ether another, and so on. It is the one existence appearing in all these variations. To go back, the solid must become liquid. The way [the elements evolved] they must go back. The solids will become liquid, etherised. This is the idea of the macrocosm — and universal. There is the external universe and universal spirit, mind, ether, gas, luminosity, liquid, solid.

The same with the mind. I am just exactly the same in the microcosm. I am the spirit; I am mind; I am the ether, solid, liquid, gas. What I want to do is to go back to my spiritual state. It is for the individual to live the life of the universe in one short life. Thus man can be free in this life. He in his own short lifetime shall have the power to live the whole extent of life.

We all struggle. If we cannot reach the Absolute, we will get somewhere, and it will be better than we are now.

Meditation consists in this practice [of dissolving every thing into the ultimate Reality — spirit]. The solid melts into liquid, that into gas, gas into ether, then mind, and mind will melt away. All is spirit.

Some of the Yogis claim that this body will become liquid etc. You will be able to do any thing with it — make it little, or gas pass through this wall — they claim. I do not know. I have never seen anybody do it. But it is in the books. We have no reason to disbelieve the books.

Possibly, some of us will be able to do it in this life. Like a flash it comes, as the result of our past work. Who knows but some here are old Yogis with just a little to do to finish the whole work. Practice!

Meditation, you know, comes by a process imagination. You go through all these processes purification of the elements — making the one melt the other, that into the next higher, that into mind, that into spirit, and then you are spirit. [14]

Spirit is always free, omnipotent, omniscient. Of course, under God. There cannot be many Gods. These liberated souls are wonderfully powerful, almost omnipotent. [But] none can be as powerful as God. If one [liberated soul] said, "I will make this planet go this way", and another said, "I will make it go that way", [there would be confusion].

Don't you make this mistake! When I say in English, "I am God!" it is because I have no better word. In Sanskrit, God means absolute existence, knowledge, and wisdom, infinite self-luminous consciousness. No person. It is impersonal.

I am never Râma [never one with Ishvara, the personal aspect of God], but I am [one with Brahman, the impersonal, all-pervading existence].

Here is a huge mass of clay. Out of that clay I made a little [mouse] and you made a little [elephant]. Both are clay. Melt both down. They are essentially one. "I and my Father are one." [But the clay mouse can never be one with the clay elephant.]

I stop somewhere; I have a little knowledge. You a little more; you stop somewhere. There is one soul which is the greatest of all. This is Ishvara, Lord of Yoga [God as Creator, with attributes]. He is the individual. He is omnipotent. He resides in every heart. There is no body. He does not need a body. All you get by the practice of meditation etc., you can get by meditation upon Ishvara, Lord of Yogis.

*

Thousands of divine beings are standing about you. You do not see them because our world is determined by our senses. We can only see this outside. Let us call it X. We see that X according to our mental state.

Let us take the tree standing outside. A thief came and what did he see in the stump? A policeman. The child saw a huge ghost. The young man was waiting for his sweetheart, and what did he see? His sweetheart.

But the stump of the tree had not changed. It remained the same. This is God Himself, and with our foolishness we see Him to be man, to be dust, to be dumb, miserable.

Those who are similarly constituted will group together naturally and live in the same world. Otherwise stated, you live in the same place. All the heavens and all the hells are right here.

For example: [take planes in the form of] big circles cutting each other at certain points. On this plane in one circle we can be in touch with a certain point in another [circle]. If the mind gets to the centre, you begin to be conscious on all planes.

In meditation sometimes you touch another plane, and you see other beings, disembodied spirits, and so on. You get there by the power of meditation. This power is changing our senses, you see, refining our senses.

If you begin to practise meditation five days, you will feel the pain from within these centres [of conciousness] and hearing [becomes finer]. That is why all the Indian gods have three eyes. That is the psychic eye that opens out and shows you spiritual things.

As this power of Kundalini rises from one centre to the other in the spine, it changes the senses and you begin to see this world another. It is heaven. You cannot talk.

Then the Kundalini goes down to the lower centres. You are again man until the Kundalini reaches the brain, all the centres have been passed, and the whole vision vanishes and you [perceive] nothing but the one existence. You are God. All heavens you make out of Him, all worlds out of Him. He is the one existence. Nothing else exists.

Meditation has been laid stress upon by all religions. The meditative state of mind is declared by the Yogis to be the highest state in which the mind exists. When the mind is studying the external object, it gets identified with it, loses itself. To use the simile of the old Indian philosopher: the soul of man is like a piece of crystal, but it takes the colour of whatever is near it. Whatever the soul touches ... it has to take its colour. That is the difficulty. That constitutes the bondage. The colour is so strong, the crystal forgets itself and identifies itself with the colour. Suppose a red flower is near the crystal and the crystal takes the colour and forgets itself, thinks it is red. We have taken the colour of the body and have forgotten what we are. All the difficulties that follow come from that one dead body. All our fears, all worries, anxieties, troubles, mistakes, weakness, evil, are front that one great blunder — that we are bodies. This is the ordinary person. It is the person taking the colour of the flower near to it. We are no more bodies than the crystal is the red flower.

The practice of meditation is pursued. The crystal knows what it is, takes its own colour. It is meditation that brings us nearer to truth than anything else. ...

In India two persons meet. In English they say, "How do you do?" The Indian greeting is, "Are you upon yourself?" The moment you stand upon something else, you run the risk of being miserable. This is what I mean by meditation — the soul trying to stand upon itself. That state must surely be the healthiest state of the soul, when it is thinking of itself, residing in its own glory. No, all the other methods that we have — by exciting emotions, prayers, and all that — really have that one end in view. In deep emotional excitement the soul tries to stand upon itself. Although the emotion may arise from anything external, there is concentration of mind.

There are three stages in meditation. The first is what is called [Dhâranâ], concentrating the mind upon an object. I try to concentrate my mind upon this glass, excluding every other object from my mind except this glass. But the mind is wavering . . . When it has become strong and does not waver so much, it is called [Dhyâna], meditation. And then there is a still higher state when the differentiation between the glass and myself is lost — [Samâdhi or absorption]. The mind and the glass are identical. I do not see any difference. All the senses stop and all powers that have been working through other channels of other senses [are focused in the mind]. Then this glass is under the power of the mind entirely. This is to be realised. It is a tremendous play played by the Yogis. ... Take for granted, the external object exists. Then that which is really outside of us is not what we see. The glass that I see is not the external object certainly. That external something which is the glass I do not know and will never know.

Something produces an impression upon me. Immediately I send the reaction towards that, and the glass is the result of the combination of these two. Action from outside — X. Action from inside — Y. The glass is XY. When you look at X, call it external world — at Y, internal world . . . If you try to distinguish which is your mind and which is the world — there is no such distinction. The world is the combination of you and something else. ...

Let us take another example. You are dropping stones upon the smooth surface of a lake. Every stone you drop is followed by a reaction. The stone is covered by the little waves in the lake. Similarly, external things are like the stones dropping into the lake of the mind. So we do not really see the external . . .; we see the wave only. . . .

These waves that rise in the mind have caused many things outside. We are not discussing the [merits of] idealism and realism. We take for granted that things exist outside, but what we see is different from things that exist outside, as we see what exists outside plus ourselves.

Suppose I take my contribution out of the glass. What remains? Almost nothing. The glass will disappear. If I take my contribution from the table, what would remain of the table? Certainly not this table, because it was a mixture of the outside plus my contribution. The poor lake has got to throw the wave towards the stone whenever [the stone] is thrown in it. The mind must create the wave towards any sensation. Suppose . . . we can withhold the mind. At once we are masters. We refuse to contribute our share to all these phenomena.... If I do not contribute my share, it has got to stop.

You are creating this bondage all the time. How? By putting in your share. We are all making our own beds, forging our own chains.... When the identifying ceases between this external object and myself, then I will be able to take my contribution off, and this thing will disappear. Then I will say, "Here is the glass", and then take my mind off, and it disappears.... If you can take away your share, you can walk upon water. Why should it drown you any more? What of poison? No more difficulties. In every phenomenon in nature you contribute at least half, and nature brings half. If your half is taken off, the thing must stop.

... To every action there is equal reaction.... If a man strikes me and wounds me it is that man's actions and my body's reaction. ... Suppose I have so much power over the body that I can resist even that automatic action. Can such power be attained? The books say it can. ... If you stumble on [it], it is a miracle. If you learn it scientifically, it is Yoga.

I have seen people healed by the power of mind. There is the miracle worker. We say he prays and the man is healed. Another man says, "Not at all. It is just the power of the mind. The man is scientific. He knows what he is about."

The power of meditation gets us everything. If you want to get power over nature, [you can have it through meditation]. It is through the power of meditation all scientific facts are discovered today. They study the subject and forget everything, their own identity and everything, and then the great fact comes like a flash. Some people think that is inspiration. There is no more inspiration than there is expiration; and never was anything got for nothing.

The highest so-called inspiration was the work of Jesus. He worked hard for ages in previous births. That was the result of his previous work — hard work. ... It is all nonsense to talk about inspiration. Had it been, it would have fallen like rain. Inspired people in any line of thought only come among nations who have general education and [culture]. There is no inspiration. . . . Whatever passes for inspiration is the result that comes from causes already in the mind. One day, flash comes the result! Their past work was the [cause].

Therein also you see the power of meditation — intensity of thought. These men churn up their own souls. Great truths come to the surface and become manifest. Therefore the practice of meditation is the great scientific method of knowledge. There is no knowledge without the power of meditation. From ignorance, superstition, etc. we can get cured by meditation for the time being and no more. [Suppose] a man has told me that if you drink such a poison you will be killed, and another man comes in the night and says, "Go drink the poison!" and I am not killed, [what happens is this:] my mind cut out from the meditation the identity between the poison and myself just for the time being. In another case of [drinking] the poison, I will be killed.

If I know the reason and scientifically raise myself up to that [state of meditation], I can save anyone. That is what the books say; but how far it is correct you must appraise.

I am asked, "Why do you Indian people not conquer these things? You claim all the time to be superior to all other people. You practice Yoga and do it quicker than anybody else. You are fitter. Carry it out! If you are a great people, you ought to have a great system. You will have to say good-bye to all the gods. Let them go to sleep as you take up the great philosophers. You are mere babies, as superstitious as the rest of the world. And all your claims are failures. If you have the claims, stand up and be bold, and all the heaven that ever existed is yours. There is the musk deer with fragrance inside, and he does not know where the fragrance [comes from]. Then after days and days he finds it in himself. All these gods and demons are within them. Find out, by the powers of reason, education, and culture that it is all in yourself. No more gods and superstitions. You want to be rational, to be Yogis, really spiritual."

[My reply is: With you too] everything is material What is more material than God sitting on a throne? You look down upon the poor man who is worshipping the image. You are no better. And you, gold worshippers, what are you? The image worshipper worships his god, something that he can see. But you do not even do that. You do not worship the spirit nor something that you can understand. ... Word worshippers! "God is spirit!" God is spirit and should be worshipped in spirit and faith. Where does the spirit reside? On a tree? On a cloud? What do you mean by God being ours ? You are the spirit. That is the first fundamental belief you must never give up. I am the spiritual being. It is there. All this skill of Yoga and this system of meditation and everything is just to find Him there.

Why am I saying all this just now? Until you fix the location, you cannot talk. You fix it up in heaven and all the world ever except in the right place. I am spirit, and therefore the spirit of all spirits must be in my soul. Those who think it anywhere else are ignorant. Therefore it is to be sought here in this heaven; all the heaven that ever existed [is within myself]. There are some sages who, knowing this, turn their eyes inward and find the spirit of all spirits in their own spirit. That is the scope of meditation. Find out the truth about God and about your own soul and thus attain to liberation. ...

You are all running after life, and we find that is foolishness. There is something much higher than life even. This life is inferior, material. Why should I live at all? I am something higher than life. Living is always slavery. We always get mixed up. ... Everything is a continuous chain of slavery.

You get something, and no man can teach another. It is through experience [we learn]. ... That young man cannot be persuaded that there are any difficulties in life. You cannot persuade the old man that life is all smooth. He has had many experiences. That is the difference.

By the power of meditation we have got to control, step by step, all these things. We have seen philosophically that all these differentiations — spirit, mind, matter, etc. — [have no real existences. ... Whatever exists is one. There cannot be many. That is what is meant by science and knowledge. Ignorance sees manifold. Knowledge realises one. ... Reducing the many into one is science. ... The whole of the universe has been demonstrated into one. That science is called the science of Vedanta. The whole universe is one. The one runs through all this seeming variety. ...

We have all these variations now and we see them — what we call the five elements: solid, liquid, gaseous, luminous, ethereal. After that the state of existence is mental and beyond that spiritual. Not that spirit is one and mind is another, ether another, and so on. It is the one existence appearing in all these variations. To go back, the solid must become liquid. The way [the elements evolved] they must go back. The solids will become liquid, etherised. This is the idea of the macrocosm — and universal. There is the external universe and universal spirit, mind, ether, gas, luminosity, liquid, solid.

The same with the mind. I am just exactly the same in the microcosm. I am the spirit; I am mind; I am the ether, solid, liquid, gas. What I want to do is to go back to my spiritual state. It is for the individual to live the life of the universe in one short life. Thus man can be free in this life. He in his own short lifetime shall have the power to live the whole extent of life....

We all struggle. . . . If we cannot reach the Absolute, we will get somewhere, and it will be better than we are now.

Meditation consists in this practice [of dissolving every thing into the ultimate Reality — spirit]. The solid melts into liquid, that into gas, gas into ether, then mind, and mind will melt away. All is spirit.

Some of the Yogis claim that this body will become liquid etc. You will be able to do any thing with it — make it little, or gas pass through this wall — they claim. I do not know. I have never seen anybody do it. But it is in the books. We have no reason to disbelieve the books.

Possibly, some of us will be able to do it in this life. Like a flash it comes, as the result of our past work. Who knows but some here are old Yogis with just a little to do to finish the whole work. Practice!

Meditation, you know, comes by a process imagination. You go through all these processes purification of the elements — making the one melt the other, that into the next higher, that into mind, that into spirit, and then you are spirit. [14]

Spirit is always free, omnipotent, omniscient. Of course, under God.

There cannot be many Gods. These liberated souls are wonderfully powerful, almost omnipotent. [But] none can be as powerful as God. If one [liberated soul] said, "I will make this planet go this way", and another said, "I will make it go that way", [there would be confusion].

Don't you make this mistake! When I say in English, "I am God!" it is because I have no better word. In Sanskrit, God means absolute existence, knowledge, and wisdom, infinite self-luminous consciousness. No person. It is impersonal. ...

I am never Râma [never one with Ishvara, the personal aspect of God], but I am [one with Brahman, the impersonal, all-pervading existence]. Here is a huge mass of clay. Out of that clay I made a little [mouse] and you made a little [elephant]. Both are clay. Melt both down They are essentially one. "I and my Father are one." [But the clay mouse can never be one with the clay elephant.]

I stop somewhere; I have a little knowledge. You a little more; you stop somewhere. There is one soul which is the greatest of all. This is Ishvara, Lord of Yoga [God as Creator, with attributes]. He is the individual. He is omnipotent. He resides in every heart. There is no body. He does not need a body. All you get by the practice of meditation etc., you can get by meditation upon Ishvara, Lord of Yogis. ...

The same can be attained by meditating upon a great soul; or upon the harmony of life. These are called objective meditations. So you begin to meditate upon certain external things, objective things, either outside or inside. If you take a long sentence, that is no meditation at all. That is simply trying to get the mind collected by repetition. Meditation means the mind is turned back upon itself. The mind stops all the [thought-waves] and the world stops. Your consciousness expands. Every time you meditate you will keep your growth. ... Work a little harder, more and more, and meditation comes. You do not feel the body or anything else. When you come out of it after the hour, you have had the most beautiful rest you ever had in your life. That is the only way you ever give rest to your system. Not even the deepest sleep will give you such rest as that. The mind goes on jumping even in deepest sleep. Just those few minutes [in meditation] your brain has almost stopped. Just a little vitality is kept up. You forget the body. You may be cut to pieces and not feel it at all. You feel such pleasure in it. You become so light. This perfect rest we will get in meditation.

Then, meditation upon different objects. There are meditations upon different centres of the spine. [According to the Yogis, there are two nerves in the spinal column, called Idâ and Pingalâ.They are the main channels through which the afferent and efferent currents travel.] The hollow [canal called Sushumnâ] runs through the middle of the spinal column. The Yogis claim this cord is closed, but by the power of meditation it has to be opened. The energy has to be sent down to [the base of the spine], and the Kundalini rises. The world will be changed. ... (See Complete Works , Vol. I, The Psychic Prana)

Thousands of divine beings are standing about you. You do not see them because our world is determined by our senses. We can only see this outside. Let us call it X. We see that X according to our mental state. Let us take the tree standing outside. A thief came and what did he see in the stump? A policeman. The child saw a huge ghost. The young man was waiting for his sweetheart, and what did he see? His sweetheart. But the stump of the tree had not changed. It remained the same. This is God Himself, and with our foolishness we see Him to be man, to be dust, to be dumb, miserable.

Those who are similarly constituted will group together naturally and live in the same world. Otherwise stated, you live in the same place. All the heavens and all the hells are right here. For example: [take planes in the form of] big circles cutting each other at certain points. . . . On this plane in one circle we can be in touch with a certain point in another [circle]. If the mind gets to the centre, you begin to be conscious on all planes. In meditation sometimes you touch another plane, and you see other beings, disembodied spirits, and so on. You get there by the power of meditation. This power is changing our senses, you see, refining our senses. If you begin to practise meditation five days, you will feel the pain from within these centres [of conciousness] and hearing [becomes finer]. ... (See Complete Works , Vol. I, Pratyahara and Dharana). That is why all the Indian gods have three eyes. That is the psychic eye that opens out and shows you spiritual things.

As this power of Kundalini rises from one centre to the other in the spine, it changes the senses and you begin to see this world another. It is heaven. You cannot talk. Then the Kundalini goes down to the lower centres. You are again man until the Kundalini reaches the brain, all the centres have been passed, and the whole vision vanishes and you [perceive] . . . nothing but the one existence. You are God. All heavens you make out of Him, all worlds out of Him. He is the one existence. Nothing else exists.

THE PRACTICE OF MEDITATION

Yoga has essentially to do with the meditative side of religion, rather than the ethical side, though, of necessity, a little of the latter has to be considered. Men and women are growing to desire more than mere revelation, so called. They want facts in their own consciousness.

Only through experience can there be any reality in religion. Spiritual facts are to be gathered mostly from the superconscious state of mind.

Let us put ourselves into the same condition as did those who claim to have had special experiences; then if we have similar experiences, they become facts for us. We can see all that another has seen; a thing that happened once can happen again, nay, must, under the same circumstances.

Raja-Yoga teaches us how to reach the superconscious state. All the great religions recognise this state in some form; but in India, special attention is paid to this side of religion.

In the beginning, some mechanical means may help us to acquire this state; but mechanical means alone can never accomplish much. Certain positions, certain modes of breathing, help to harmonise and concentrate the mind, but with these must go purity and strong desire for God, or realisation.

The attempt to sit down and fix the mind on one idea and hold it there will prove to most people that there is some need for help to enable them to do this successfully. The mind has to be gradually and systematically brought under control. The will has to be strengthened by slow, continuous, and persevering drill.

This is no child's play, no fad to be tried one day and discarded the next. It is a life's work; and the end to be attained is well worth all that it can cost us to reach it; being nothing less than the realisation of our absolute oneness with the Divine. Surely, with this end in view, and with the knowledge that we can certainly succeed, no price can be too great to pay.

*

No amount of reasoning which I can give you will be proof to you, until you have demonstrated it for yourselves. As soon as you begin to feel these currents in motion all over you, doubts will vanish, but it requires hard practice every day.

You must practice at least twice every day, and the best times are towards the morning and the evening. When night passes into day, and day into night, a state of relative calmness ensues. The early morning and the early evening are the two periods of calmness.

Your body will have a like tendency to become calm at those times. We should take advantage of that natural condition and begin then to practice. Make it a rule not to eat until you have practiced; if you do this, the sheer force of hunger will break your laziness.

In India they teach children never to eat until they have practiced or worshipped, and it becomes natural to them after a time; a boy will not feel hungry until he has bathed and practiced.

Sit in a straight posture, and the first thing to do is to send a current of holy thought to all creation. Mentally repeat, "Let all beings be happy; let all beings be peaceful; let all beings be blissful." So do to the east, south, north and west.

The more you do that the better you will feel yourself. You will find at last that the easiest way to make ourselves healthy is to see that others are healthy, and the easiest way to make ourselves happy is to see that others are happy.

After doing that, those who believe in God should pray — not for money, not for health, nor for heaven; pray for knowledge and light; every other prayer is selfish.

Then the next thing to do is to think of your own body, and see that it is strong and healthy; it is the best instrument you have. Think of it as being as strong as adamant, and that with the help of this body you will cross the ocean of life.

Freedom is never to be reached by the weak. Throw away all weakness. Tell your body that it is strong, tell your mind that it is strong, and have unbounded faith and hope in yourself.

*

The greater part of the practical lessons which the Yogi gives us is in the mind, the power of concentration and meditation. We have become so materialistic. When we think of ourselves, we find only the body. The body has become the ideal, nothing else. Therefore a little physical help is necessary.

First, to sit in the posture in which you can sit still for a long time. All the nerve currents which are working pass along the spine. The spine is not intended to support the weight of the body.

Therefore the posture must be such that the weight of the body is not on the spine. Let it be free from all pressure.

*

There are some other preliminary things. There is the great question of food and exercise.

The food must be simple and taken several times [a day] instead of once or twice. Never get very hungry. "He who eats too much cannot be a Yogi. He who fasts too much cannot be a Yogi. He who sleeps too much cannot be a Yogi, nor he who keeps awake too much." (Gita, VI. 16.)

He who does not do any work and he who works too hard cannot succeed. Proper food, proper exercise, proper sleep, proper wakefulness — these are necessary for any success.

What the proper food is, what kind, we have to determine ourselves. Nobody can determine that [for us].

As a general practice, we have to shun exciting food. We do not know how to vary our diet with our occupation. We always forget that it is the food out of which we manufacture everything we have. So the amount and kind of energy that we want, the food must determine.

Violent exercises are not all necessary. If you want to be muscular, Yoga is not for you. You have to manufacture a finer organism than you have now.

Violent exercises are positively hurtful. Live amongst those who do not take too much exercise. If you do not take violent exercise, you will live longer. You do not want to burn out your lamp in muscles! People who work with their brains are the longest-lived people.

Do not burn the lamp quickly. Let it burn slowly and gently. Every anxiety, every violent exercise — physical and mental — [means] you are burning the lamp.

The proper diet means, generally, simply do not eat highly spiced foods. There are three sorts of mind, says the Yogi, according to the elements of nature. One is the dull mind, which covers the luminosity of the soul. Then there is that which makes people active, and lastly, that which makes them calm and peaceful.

Now there are persons born with the tendency to sleep all the time. Their taste will be towards that type of food which is rotting — crawling cheese. They will eat cheese that fairly jumps off the table. It is a natural tendency with them.

Then active people. Their taste is for everything hot and pungent, strong alcohol.

Sâttvika people are very thoughtful, quiet, and patient. They take food in small quantities, and never anything bad.

*

"He who hates none, who is the friend of all, who is merciful to all, who has nothing of his own, who is free from egoism, who is even-minded in pain and pleasure, who is forbearing, who is always satisfied, who works always in Yoga, whose self has become controlled, whose will is firm, whose mind and intellect are given up unto Me, such a one is My beloved Bhakta.

"From whom comes no disturbance, who cannot be disturbed by others, who is free from joy, anger, fear, and anxiety, such a one is My beloved.

"He who does not depend on anything, who is pure and active, who does not care whether good comes or evil, and never becomes miserable, who has given up all efforts for himself; who is the same in praise or in blame, with a silent, thoughtful mind, blessed with what little comes in his way, homeless, for the whole world is his home, and who is steady in his ideas, such a one is My beloved Bhakta."

Such alone become Yogis.

*

Meditate every day alone. Everything will open up of itself. Now the Divine Mother — the embodiment of illumination — is sleeping within, hence you do not understand this. She is the Kundalini.

When, before meditating, you proceed to "purify the nerves", you must mentally strike hard on the Kundalini in the Muladhara (sacral plexus), and repeat, "Arise, Mother, arise!" One must practise these slowly.

During meditation, suppress the emotional side altogether. This is a great source of danger. Those that are very emotional no doubt have their Kundalini rushing quickly upwards, but it is as quick to come down as to go up. And when it does come down, it leaves the devotee in a state of utter ruin.

It is for this reason that Kirtanas and other auxiliaries to emotional development have a great drawback. It is true that by dancing and jumping, etc. through a momentary impulse, that power is made to course upwards, but it is never enduring. On the contrary when it traces back its course, it rouses violent lust in the individual.

Listening to my lectures in America, through temporary excitement many among the audience used to get into an ecstatic state, and some would even become motionless like statues. But on inquiry I afterwards found that many of them had an excess of the carnal instinct immediately after that state. But this happens simply owing to a lack of steady practice in meditation and concentration.

*

You yourself will be the object of your meditation. Think and meditate that you are the omnipresent Atman. "I am neither the body, nor the mind, nor the Buddhi (determinative faculty), neither the gross nor the subtle body"– by this process of elimination, immerse your mind in the transcendent knowledge which is your real nature.

Kill the mind by thus plunging it repeatedly in this. Then only you will realise the Essence of Intelligence, or be established in your real nature. Knower and known, meditator and the object meditated upon will then become one, and the cessation of all phenomenal superimpositions will follow.

This is styled in the Shastras as the transcendence of the triad or relative knowledge (Triputibheda). There is no relative or conditioned knowledge in this state. When the Atman is the only knower, by what means can you possibly know It? The Atman is Knowledge, the Atman is Intelligence, the Atman is Sachchidananda.

It is through the inscrutable power of Maya, which cannot be indicated as either existent or non – existent, that the relative consciousness has come upon the Jiva who is none other than Brahman. This is generally known as the conscious state.

And the state in which this duality of relative existence becomes one in the pure Brahman is called in the scriptures the superconscious state and described in such words as, "it is like an ocean perfectly at rest and without a name" (Vivekachudamani, 410).

*

There is another way in which this idea of mercy and selfless charity can be put into practice; that is, by looking upon work as "worship" in case we believe in a Personal God. Here we give up all the fruits our work unto the Lord, and worshipping Him thus, we have no right to expect anything from mankind for the work we do.

The Lord Himself works incessantly and is ever without attachment. Just as water cannot wet the lotus leaf, so work cannot bind the unselfish man by giving rise to attachment to results. The selfless and unattached man may live in the very heart of a crowded and sinful city; he will not be touched by sin.

*

This idea of complete self-sacrifice is illustrated in the following story: After the battle of Kurukshetra the five Pândava brothers performed a great sacrifice and made very large gifts to the poor. All people expressed amazement at the greatness and richness of the sacrifice, and said that such a sacrifice the world had never seen before.

But, after the ceremony, there came a little mongoose, half of whose body was golden, and the other half brown; and he began to roll on the floor of the sacrificial hall. He said to those around, "You are all liars; this is no sacrifice."

"What!" they exclaimed, "you say this is no sacrifice; do you not know how money and jewels were poured out to the poor and every one became rich and happy? This was the most wonderful sacrifice any man ever performed."

But the mongoose said, "There was once a little village, and in it there dwelt a poor Brahmin with his wife, his son, and his son's wife. They were very poor and lived on small gifts made to them for preaching and teaching. There came in that land a three years' famine, and the poor Brahmin suffered more than ever. At last when the family had starved for days, the father brought home one morning a little barley flour, which he had been fortunate enough to obtain, and he divided it into four parts, one for each member of the family. They prepared it for their meal, and just as they were about to eat, there was a knock at the door. The father opened it, and there stood a guest. Now in India a guest is a sacred person; he is as a god for the time being, and must be treated as such. So the poor Brahmin said, 'Come in, sir; you are welcome,' He set before the guest his own portion of the food, which the guest quickly ate and said, 'Oh, sir, you have killed me; I have been starving for ten days, and this little bit has but increased my hunger.' Then the wife said to her husband, 'Give him my share,' but the husband said, 'Not so.' The wife however insisted, saying, 'Here is a poor man, and it is our duty as householders to see that he is fed, and it is my duty as a wife to give him my portion, seeing that you have no more to offer him.' Then she gave her share to the guest, which he ate, and said he was still burning with hunger. So the son said, 'Take my portion also; it is the duty of a son to help his father to fulfil his obligations.' The guest ate that, but remained still unsatisfied; so the son's wife gave him her portion also. That was sufficient, and the guest departed, blessing them. That night those four people died of starvation. A few granules of that flour had fallen on the floor; and when I rolled my body on them, half of it became golden, as you see. Since then I have been travelling all over the world, hoping to find another sacrifice like that, but nowhere have I found one; nowhere else has the other half of my body been turned into gold. That is why I say this is no sacrifice."

*

We are all struggling day and night to get rid of misery. We cannot do it by work. Work will produce more work. It is only possible if there is someone who is free himself and lends us a hand. "Hear, ye children of immortality, all those that reside in this plane and all those that reside in the heavens above, I have found the secret", says the great sage. "I have found Him who is beyond all darkness. Through His mercy alone we cross this ocean of life."

*

Think of a space in your heart, and in the midst of that space think that a flame is burning. Think of that flame as your own soul and inside the flame is another effulgent light, and that is the Soul of your soul, God. Meditate upon that in the heart.

Chastity, non-injury, forgiving even the greatest enemy, truth, faith in the Lord, these are all different Vrittis. Be not afraid if you are not perfect in all of these; work, they will come.

He who has given up all attachment, all fear, and all anger, he whose whole soul has gone unto the Lord, he who has taken refuge in the Lord, whose heart has become purified, with whatsoever desire he comes to the Lord, He will grant that to him. Therefore worship Him through knowledge, love, or renunciation.

RELIGION AS A PRACTICE

We read many books, many scriptures. We get various ideas from our childhood, and change them every now and then. We understand what is meant by theoretical religion. We think we understand what is meant by practical religion. Now I am going to present to you my idea of practical religion.

We hear all around us about practical religion, and analysing all that, we find that it can be brought down to one conception — charity to our fellow beings. Is that all of religion? Every day we hear in this country about practical Christianity — that a man has done some good to his fellow beings. Is that all?

What is the goal of life? Is this world the goal of life? Nothing more? Are we to be just what we are, nothing more? Is man to be a machine which runs smoothly without a hitch anywhere? Are all the sufferings he experiences today all he can have, and doesn't he want anything more?

*

The highest dream of many religions is the world. The vast majority of people are dreaming of the time when there will be no more disease, sickness, poverty, or misery of any kind. They will have a good time all around. Practical religion, therefore, simply means. "Clean the streets! Make it nice!" We see how all enjoy it.

Is enjoyment the goal of life? Were it so, it would be a tremendous mistake to become a man at all. What man can enjoy a meal with more gusto than the dog or the cat? Go to a menagerie and see the [wild animals] tearing the flesh from the bone. Go back and become a bird! What a mistake then to become a man! Vain have been my years — hundreds of years — of struggle only to become the man of sense-enjoyments.

*

Mark, therefore, the ordinary theory of practical religion, what it leads to. Charity is great, but the moment you say it is all, you run the risk of running into materialism. It is not religion. It is no better than atheism - a little less.

You Christians, have you found nothing else in the Bible than working for fellow creatures, building hospitals? Here stands a shopkeeper and says how Jesus would have kept the shop! Jesus would neither have kept a saloon, nor a shop, nor have edited a newspaper. That sort of practical religion is good, not bad; but it is just kindergarten religion. It leads nowhere.

If you believe in God, if you are Christians and repeat everyday, "Thy will be done", just think what it means! You say every moment, "Thy will be done", really meaning, "My will be done by Thee, O God." The Infinite is working His own plans out. Even He has made mistakes, and you and I are going to remedy that! The Architect of the universe is going to be taught by the carpenters! He has left the world a dirty hole, and you are going to make it a beautiful place!

What is the goal of it all? Can senses ever be the goal? Can enjoyment of pleasure ever be the goal? Can this life ever be the goal of the soul? If it is, better die this moment; do not want this life! If that is the fate of man, that he is going to be only the perfected machine, it would just mean that we go back to being trees and stones and things like that. Did you ever hear a cow tell a lie or see a tree steal? They are perfect machines. They do not make mistakes. They live in a world where everything is finished.

*

What is the ideal of religion, then, if this cannot be practical [religion]? And it certainly cannot be. What are we here for? We are here for freedom, for knowledge. We want to know in order to make ourselves free. That is our life: one universal cry for freedom.

What is the reason the plant grows from the seed, overturning the ground and raising itself up to the skies? What is the offering for the earth from the sun? What is your life? The same struggle for freedom. Nature is trying all around to suppress us, and the soul wants to express itself.

The struggle with nature is going on. Many things will be crushed and broken in this struggle for freedom. That is your real misery. Large masses of dust and dirt must be raised on the battlefield. Nature says, "I will conquer." The soul says, "I must be the conqueror."

Nature says, "Wait! I will give you a little enjoyment to keep you quiet." The soul enjoys a little, becomes deluded a moment, but the next moment it [cries for freedom again].

Have you marked the eternal cry going on through the ages in every breast? We are deceived by poverty. We become wealthy and are deceived with wealth. We are ignorant. We read and learn and are deceived with knowledge. No man is ever satisfied.

That is the cause of misery, but it is also the cause of all blessing. That is the sure sign. How can you be satisfied with this world? If tomorrow this world becomes heaven, we will say, "Take this away. Give us something else."

*

The infinite human soul can never be satisfied but by the Infinite itself .Infinite desire can only be satisfied by infinite knowledge — nothing short of that.

Worlds will come and go. What of that? The soul lives and for ever expands. Worlds must come into the soul. Worlds must disappear in the soul like drops in the ocean.

And this world to become the goal of the soul! If we have common sense, we cannot he satisfied, though this has been the theme of the poets in all the ages, always telling us to be satisfied. And nobody has been satisfied yet!

Millions of prophets have told us, "Be satisfied with your lot"; poets sing. We have told ourselves to be quiet and satisfied, yet we are not. It is the design of the Eternal that there is nothing in this world to satisfy my soul, nothing in the heavens above, and nothing beneath.

Before the desire of my soul, the stars and the worlds, upper and lower, the whole universe, is but a hateful disease, nothing but that. That is the meaning. Everything is an evil unless that is the meaning. Every desire is evil unless that is the meaning, unless you understand its true importance, its goal. All nature is crying through all the atoms for one thing — its perfect freedom.

*

What is practical religion, then? To get to that state — freedom, the attainment of freedom. And this world, if it helps us on to that goal, [is] all right; if not — if it begins to bind one more layer on the thousands already there, it becomes an evil.

Possessions, learning, beauty, everything else — as long as they help us to that goal, they are of practical value. When they have ceased helping us on to that goal of freedom, they are a positive danger.

What is practical religion, then? Utilise the things of this world and the next just for one goal — the attainment of freedom. Every enjoyment, every ounce of pleasure is to be bought by the expenditure of the infinite heart and mind combined.

Look at the sum total of good and evil in this world. Has it changed? Ages have passed, and practical religion has worked for ages. The world thought that each time the problem would be solved.

It is always the same problem. At best it changes its form. It trades consumption and nerve disease for twenty thousand shops. It is like old rheumatism: Drive it from one place, it goes to another.

A hundred years ago man walked on foot or bought horses. Now he is happy because he rides the railroad; but he is unhappy because he has to work more and earn more. Every machine that saves labour puts more stress upon labour.

This universe, nature, or whatever you call it, must be limited; it can never be unlimited. The Absolute, to become nature, must be limited by time, space, and causation.

The energy [at our disposal] is limited. You can spend it in one place, losing it in another. The sum total is always the same. Wherever there is a wave in one place, there is a hollow in another. If one nation becomes rich, others become poor. Good balances evil. The person for the moment on top of the wave thinks all is good; the person at the bottom says the world is [all evil].

But the man who stands aside sees the divine play going on. Some weep and others laugh. The latter will weep in their turn and the others laugh. What can we do ? We know we cannot do anything.

*

Which of us do anything because we want to do good? How few! They can be counted on the fingers. The rest of us also do good, but because we are forced to do so. We cannot stop. Onward we go, knocked about from place to place.

What can we do? The world will be the same world, the earth the same. It will be changed from blue to brown and from brown to blue. One language translated into another, one set of evils changed into another set of evils — that is what is going on. Six of one, half a dozen of the other.

The American Indian in the forest cannot attend a lecture on metaphysics as you can, but he can digest his meal. You cut him to pieces, and the next moment he is all right. You and I, if we get scratched, we have to go to the hospital for six months.

*

The lower the organism, the greater is its pleasure in the senses. Think of the lowest animals and the power of touch. Everything is touch. When you come to man, you will see that the lower the civilization of the man, the greater is the power of the senses. The higher the organism, the lesser is the pleasure of the senses.

A dog can eat a meal, but cannot understand the exquisite pleasure of thinking about metaphysics. He is deprived of the wonderful pleasure which you get through the intellect. The pleasures of the senses are great.

Greater than those is the pleasure of the intellect. When you attend the fine fifty-course dinner in Paris, that is pleasure indeed. But in the observatory, looking at the stars, seeing worlds coming and developing — think of that!

It must be greater, for I know you forget all about eating. That pleasure must be greater than what you get from worldly things. You forget all about wives, children, husbands, and everything; you forget all about the sense-plane.

That is intellectual pleasure. It is common sense that it must be greater than sense pleasure. It is always for greater joy that you give up the lesser. This is practical religion — the attainment of freedom, renunciation. Renounce!

*

Renounce the lower so that you may get the higher. What is the foundation of society? Morality, ethics, laws.

Renounce. Renounce all temptation to take your neighbour's property, to put hands upon your neighbour, all the pleasure of tyrannising over the weak, all the pleasure of cheating others by telling lies.

Is not morality the foundation of society? What is marriage but the renunciation of unchastity? The savage does not marry. Man marries because he renounces. So on and on.

Renounce! Renounce! Sacrifice! Give up! Not for zero. Not for nothing. But to get the higher.

But who can do this? You cannot, until you have got the higher. You may talk. You may struggle. You may try to do many things. But renunciation comes by itself when you have got the higher. Then the lesser falls away by itself.

*

This is practical religion. What else? Cleaning streets and building hospitals? Their value consists only in this renunciation. And there is no end to renunciation. The difficulty is they try to put a limit to it — thus far and no farther. But there is no limit to this renunciation.

Where God is, there is no other. Where the world is, there is no God. These two will never unite. [Like] light and darkness. That is what I have understood from Christianity and the life of the Teacher.

Is not that Buddhism? Is not that Hinduism? Is not that Mohammedanism? Is not that the teaching of all the great sages and teachers? What is the world that is to be given up? It is here. I am carrying it all with me. My own body. It is all for this body that I put my hand voluntarily upon my fellow man, just to keep it nice and give it a little pleasure; [all for this body] that I injure others and make mistakes.

*

Great men have died. Weak men have died. Gods have died. Death — death everywhere. This world is a graveyard of the infinite past, yet we cling to this [body]: "I am never going to die".

Knowing for sure [that the body must die] and yet clinging to it. There is meaning in that too [because in a sense we do not die]. The mistake is that we cling to the body when it is the spirit that is really immortal.

You are all materialists, because you believe that you are the body. If a man gives me a hard punch, I would say I am punched. If he strikes me, I would say I am struck.

If I am not the body, why should I say so? It makes no difference if I say I am the spirit. I am the body just now. I have converted myself into matter. That is why I am to renounce the body, to go back to what I really am.

I am the spirit — the soul no instrument can pierce, no sword can cut asunder, no fire can burn, no air can dry. Unborn and uncreated, without beginning and without end, deathless, birthless and omnipresent — that is what I am; and all misery comes just because I think this little lump of clay is myself. I am identifying myself with matter and taking all the consequences.

*

Practical religion is identifying myself with my Self. Stop this wrong identification! How far are you advanced in that? You may have built two thousand hospitals, built fifty thousand roads, and yet what of that, if you, have not realised that you are the spirit? You die a dog's; death, with the same feelings that the dog does. The dog howls and weeps because he knows that he is only matter and he is going to be dissolved.

There is death, you know, inevitable death, in water, in air, in the palace, in the prison - death everywhere. What makes you fearless? When you have realised what you are — that infinite spirit, deathless, birthless.

Him no fire can burn, no instrument kill, no poison hurt. Not theory, mind you. Not reading books. [Not parroting.] My old Master used to say, "It is all very good to teach the parrot to say, 'Lord, Lord, Lord' all the time; but let the cat come and take hold of its neck, it forgets all about it."

[You may] pray all the time, read all the scriptures in the world, and worship all the gods there are, [but] unless you realise the soul there is no freedom. Not talking, theorising, argumentation, but realisation. That I call practical religion.

*

This truth about the soul is first to be heard. If you have heard it, think about it. Once you have done that, meditate upon it. No more vain arguments! Satisfy yourself once that you are the infinite spirit. If that is true, it must be nonsense that you are the body.

You are the Self, and that must be realised. Spirit must see itself as spirit. Now the spirit is seeing itself as body. That must stop. The moment you begin to realise that, you are released.

You see this glass, and you know it is simply an illusion. Some scientists tell you it is light and vibration. Seeing the spirit must be infinitely more real: than that, must be the only true state, the only true sensation, the only true vision.

All these [objects you see], are but dreams. You know that now. Not the old idealists alone, but modern physicists also tell you that light is there. A little more vibration makes all the difference.

*

You must see God. The spirit must be realised, and that is practical religion. It is not what Christ preached that you call practical religion: "Blessed are the poor in spirit for theirs is the Kingdom of Heaven."

Was it a joke? What is the practical religion you are thinking, of? Lord help us!

"Blessed are the pure in heart, for they shall see God." That means street-cleaning, hospital-building, and all that? Good works, when you do them with a pure mind.

Don't give the man twenty dollars and buy all the papers in San Francisco to see your name! Don't you read in your own books how no man will help you? Serve as worship of the Lord Himself in the poor, the miserable, the weak. That done, the result is secondary. That sort of work, done without any thought of gain, benefits the soul. And even of such is the Kingdom of Heaven.

*

The Kingdom of Heaven is within us. He is there. He is the soul of all souls. See Him in your own soul. That is practical religion. That is freedom.

Let us ask each other how much we are advanced in that: how much we are worshippers of the body, or real believers in God, the spirit; how much we believe ourselves to be spirit. That is selfless. That is freedom. That is real worship.

Realise yourself. That is all there is to do. Know yourself as you are — infinite spirit. That is practical religion. Everything else is impractical, for everything else will vanish. That alone will never vanish. It Is eternal.

Hospitals will tumble down. Railroad givers will all die. This earth will be blown to pieces, suns wiped out. The soul endureth for ever.

Which is higher, running after these things which perish or. worshipping that which never changes?

Which is more practical, spending all the energies of life in getting things, and before you have got them death comes and you have to leave them all? — like the great [ruler] who conquered all, [who when] death came, said, "Spread out all the jars of things before me."

He said "Bring me that big diamond." And he placed it on his breast and wept. Thus weeping, he died the same as the dog dies.

Man says, "I live." He knows not that it is [the fear of] death that makes him cling slavishly to life. He says "I enjoy." He never dreams that nature has enslaved him.

*

Nature grinds all of us. Keep count of the ounce of pleasure you get. In the long run, nature did her work through you, and when you die your body will make other plants grow. Yet we think all the time that we are getting pleasure ourselves. Thus the wheel goes round.

To realise the spirit as spirit is practical religion. Everything else is good so far as it leads to this one grand idea. That [realization] is to be attained by renunciation, by meditation — renunciation of all the senses, cutting the knots, the chains that bind us down to matter.

CONTROLLING THE MIND

How hard it is to control the mind! Well has it been compared to the maddened monkey. There was a monkey, restless by his own nature, as all monkeys are. As if that were not enough some one made him drink freely of wine, so that he became still more restless.

Then a scorpion stung him. When a man is stung by a scorpion, he jumps about for a whole day; so the poor monkey found his condition worse than ever. To complete his misery a demon entered into him. What language can describe the uncontrollable restlessness of that monkey?

The human mind is like that monkey, incessantly active by its own nature; then it becomes drunk with the wine of desire, thus increasing its turbulence. After desire takes possession comes the sting of the scorpion of jealousy at the success of others, and last of all the demon of pride enters the mind, making it think itself of all importance. How hard to control such a mind!

*

The first lesson, then, is to sit for some time and let the mind run on. The mind is bubbling up all the time. It is like that monkey jumping about. Let the monkey jump as much as he can; you simply wait and watch.

Knowledge is power, says the proverb, and that is true. Until you know what the mind is doing you cannot control it. Give it the rein; many hideous thoughts may come into it; you will be astonished that it was possible for you to think such thoughts.

But you will find that each day the mind's vagaries are becoming less and less violent, that each day it is becoming calmer. In the first few months you will find that the mind will have a great many thoughts, later you will find that they have somewhat decreased, and in a few more months they will be fewer and fewer, until at last the mind will be under perfect control; but we must patiently practice every day.

As soon as the steam is turned on, the engine must run; as soon as things are before us we must perceive; so a man, to prove that he is not a machine, must demonstrate that he is under the control of nothing.

This controlling of the mind, and not allowing it to join itself to the centres, is Pratyahara. How is this practised? It is a tremendous work, not to be done in a day. Only after a patient, continuous struggle for years can we succeed.

*

After you have practised Pratyahara for a time, take the next step, the Dhâranâ, holding the mind to certain points. What is meant by holding the mind to certain points? Forcing the mind to feel certain parts of the body to the exclusion of others.

For instance, try to feel only the hand, to the exclusion of other parts of the body. When the Chitta, or mind-stuff, is confined and limited to a certain place it is Dharana. This Dharana is of various sorts, and along with it, it is better to have a little play of the imagination.

For instance, the mind should be made to think of one point in the heart. That is very difficult; an easier way is to imagine a lotus there. That lotus is full of light, effulgent light. Put the mind there. Or think of the lotus in the brain as full of light, or of the different centres in the Sushumna mentioned before.

*

If the mind is not under control, it is no use living in a cave because the same mind will bring all disturbances there. We will find twenty devils in the cave because all the devils are in the mind. If the mind is under control, we can have the cave anywhere, wherever we are.

It is our own mental attitude which makes the world what it is for us. Our thoughts make things beautiful, our thoughts make things ugly. The whole world is in our own minds.

Learn to see things in the proper light. First, believe in this world — that there is meaning behind everything. Everything in the world is good, is holy and beautiful.

If you see something evil, think that you are not understanding it in the right light. Throw the burden on yourselves! Whenever we are tempted to say that the world is going to the dogs, we ought to analyse ourselves, and we shall find that we have lost the faculty of seeing things as they are.

*

The Atman is not to be gained by the weak." If there is no strength in the body and mind, the Atman cannot be realised.

First you have to build the body by good nutritious food — then only will the mind be strong. The mind is but the subtle part of the body. You must retain great strength in your mind and words.

"I am low, I am low" — repeating these ideas in the mind, man belittles and degrades himself.

*

Despondency is not religion, whatever else it may be. By being pleasant always and smiling, it takes you nearer to God, nearer than any prayer. How can those minds that are gloomy and dull love? If they talk of love, it is false; they want to hurt others.

Think of the fanatics; they make the longest faces, and all their religion is to fight against others in word and act. Think of what they have done in the past, and of what they would do now if they were given a free hand. They would deluge the whole world in blood tomorrow if it would bring them power. By worshipping power and making long faces, they lose every bit of love from their hearts.

So the man who always feels miserable will never come to God. It is not religion, it is diabolism to say, "I am so miserable." Every man has his own burden to bear. If you are miserable, try to be happy, try to conquer it.

God is not to be reached by the weak. Never be weak. You must be strong; you have infinite strength within you. How else will you conquer anything? How else will you come to God?

*

"This Atman is not to be attained by the weak", says the Shruti.

Both physical weakness and mental weakness are meant here. "The strong, the hardy" are the only fit students. What can puny, little, decrepit things do? They will break to pieces whenever the mysterious forces of the body and mind are even slightly awakened by the practice of any of the Yogas.

It is "the young, the healthy, the strong" that can score success. Physical strength, therefore, is absolutely necessary. It is the strong body alone that can bear the shock of reaction resulting from the attempt to control the organs.

He who wants to become a Bhakta must be strong, must be healthy. When the miserably weak attempt any of the Yogas, they are likely to get some incurable malady, or they weaken their minds. Voluntarily weakening the body is really no prescription for spiritual enlightenment.

The mentally weak also cannot succeed in attaining the Atman. The person who aspires to be a Bhakta must be cheerful. In the Western world the idea of a religious man is that he never smiles, that a dark cloud must always hang over his face, which, again, must be long drawn with the jaws almost collapsed.

People with emaciated bodies and long faces are fit subjects for the physician, they are not Yogis. It is the cheerful mind that is persevering.

It is the strong mind that hews its way through a thousand difficulties. And this, the hardest task of all, the cutting of our way out of the net of Maya, is the work reserved only for giant wills.

*

Yet at the same time excessive mirth should be avoided (Anuddharsha). A mind in that state never becomes calm; it becomes fickle. Excessive merriment will always be followed by sorrow. Tears and laughter are near kin. People so often run from one extreme to the other. Excessive mirth makes us unfit for serious thought. It also fritters away the energies of the mind in vain.

The stronger the will, the less the yielding to the sway of the emotions. Excessive hilarity is quite as objectionable as too much of sad seriousness, and all religious realisation is possible only when the mind is in a steady, peaceful condition of harmonious equilibrium.

Let the mind be cheerful, but calm. Never let it run into excesses, because every excess will be followed by a reaction.

*

The mind uncontrolled and unguided will drag us down, down, for ever—rend us, kill us; and the mind controlled and guided will save us, free us. So it must be controlled, and psychology teaches us how to do it.

To study and analyse any material science, sufficient data are obtained. These facts are studied and analysed and a knowledge of the science is the result. But in the study and analysis of the mind, there are no data, no facts acquired from without, such as are equally at the command of all.

The mind is analysed by itself. The greatest science, therefore, is the science of the mind, the science of psychology.

*

If you intend to study the mind, you must have systematic training; you must practice to bring the mind under your control, to attain to that consciousness from which you will be able to study the mind and remain unmoved by any of its wild gyrations. Otherwise the facts observed will not be reliable; they will not apply to all people and therefore will not be truly facts or data at all.

Among that class who have gone deeply into the study of the mind, the facts observed have been the same, no matter in what part of the world such persons may be or what religious belief they may have. The results obtained by all who go deep enough into the mind are the same.

The mind operates by perception and impulsion. For instance, the rays of the light enter by eyes, are carried by the nerves to the brain, and still I do not see the light. The brain then conveys the impulse to the mind, but yet I do not see the light; the mind then reacts, and the light flashes across the mind. The mind's reaction is impulsion, and as a result the eye perceives the object.

To control the mind, you must go deep down into the subconscious mind, classify and arrange in order all the different impressions, thoughts, etc., stored up there, and control them. This is the first step. By the control of the subconscious mind you get control over the conscious.

FREEDOM

The idea of happiness without misery, or of life without death, is very good for school-boys and children; but the thinker sees that it is all a contradiction in terms and gives up both. Seek no praise, no reward, for anything you do.

No sooner do we perform a good action than we begin to desire credit for it. No sooner do we give money to some charity than we want to see our names blazoned in the papers. Misery must come as the result of such desires.

The greatest men in the world have passed away unknown. The Buddhas and the Christs that we know are but second-rate heroes in comparison with the greatest men of whom the world knows nothing.

Hundreds of these unknown heroes have lived in every country working silently. Silently they live and silently they pass away; and in time their thoughts find expression in Buddhas or Christs, and it is these latter that become known to us.

The highest men do not seek to get any name or fame from their knowledge. They leave their ideas to the world; they put forth no claims for themselves and establish no schools or systems in their name. Their whole nature shrinks from such a thing.

*

Supposing that freedom is not your nature, by no manner of means can you become free. Supposing you were free and, in some way, you lost that freedom, that shows that you were not free to begin with.

Had you been free, what could have made you lose it? The independent can never be made dependent; if it is really dependent, its independence was a hallucination.

You cannot establish the immortality of the soul, unless you grant that it is by its nature free, or in other words, that it cannot be acted upon by anything outside. For death is an effect produced by some outside cause. I drink poison and I die, thus showing that my body can be acted upon by something outside that is called poison.

But if it be true that the soul is free, it naturally follows that nothing can affect it, and it can never die. Freedom, immortality, blessedness, all depend upon the soul being beyond the law of causation, beyond this Maya.

Of these two which will you take? Either make the first a delusion, or make the second a delusion. Certainly I will make the second a delusion. It is more consonant with all my feelings and aspirations. I am perfectly aware that I am free by nature, and I will not admit that this bondage is true and my freedom a delusion.

*

If you dare declare that you are free, free you are this moment. If you say you are bound, bound you will remain. This is what Advaita boldly declares. I have told you the ideas of the dualists. You can take whichever you like.

*

Slavery is slavery. The chain of gold is quite as bad as the chain of iron. Is there a way out?

It is only the question of memory [of your true nature], not salvation by work. Do you get salvation? You are [already] free.

Go on saying, "I am free". Never mind if the next moment delusion comes and says, "I am bound." Dehypnotise the whole thing.

[This truth] is first to be heard. Hear it first. Think on it day and night. Fill the mind [with it] day and night: "I am It. I am the Lord of the universe. Never was there any delusion. "

Meditate upon it with all the strength of the mind till you actually see these walls, houses, everything, melt away — [until] body, everything, vanishes. "I will stand alone. I am the One."

Struggle on! "Who cares! We want to be free; [we] do not want any powers. Worlds we renounce; heavens we renounce; hells we renounce. What do I care about all these powers, and this and that! What do I care if the mind is controlled or uncontrolled! Let it run on. What of that! I am not the mind, Let it go on!"

*

When we free ourselves from name and form, especially from a body — when we need no body, good or bad — then only do we escape from bondage. Eternal progression is eternal bondage; annihilation of form is to be preferred. We must get free from any body, even a "god-body". God is the only real existence, there cannot be two. There is but One Soul, and I am That.

*

All nature is crying through all the atoms for one thing — its perfect freedom. However mistaken we may be as to the method, all our struggle is really for freedom We seek neither misery nor happiness, but freedom, freedom alone. This one aim is the secret of the insatiable thirst of man.

*

Freedom in all matters, i.e. advance towards Mukti is the worthiest gain of man. To advance oneself towards freedom — physical, mental, and spiritual — and help others to do so, is the supreme prize of man.

Those social rules which stand in the way of the unfoldment of this freedom are injurious, and steps should be taken to destroy them speedily. Those institutions should be encouraged by which men advance in the path of freedom.

*

Freedom is inseparably connected with immortality. To be free one must be above the laws of nature. Law exists so long as we are ignorant. When knowledge comes, then we find that law nothing but freedom in ourselves.

The will can never be free, because it is the slave of cause and effect. But the "I" behind the will is free; and this is the Self. "I am free" — that is the basis on which to build and live. And freedom means immortality.

*

Work is inevitable, it must be so; but we should work to the highest purpose. Karma-Yoga makes us admit that this world is a world of five minutes, that it is a something we have to pass through; and that freedom is not here, but is only to be found beyond.

To find the way out of the bondages of the world we have to go through it slowly and surely. There may be those exceptional persons about whom I just spoke, those who can stand aside and give up the world, as a snake casts off its skin and stands aside and looks at it. There are no doubt these exceptional beings; but the rest of mankind have to go slowly through the world of work. Karma-Yoga shows the process, the secret, and the method of doing it to the best advantage.

What does it say? "Work incessantly, but give up all attachment to work."

*

Freedom is of the nature of the soul, it is its birthright: that real freedom of the soul shines through veils of matter in the form of the apparent freedom of man.

Every moment of your life you feel that you are free. We cannot live, talk, or breathe for a moment without feeling that we are free; but, at the same time, a little thought shows us that we are like machines and not free.

What is true then? Is this idea of freedom a delusion? One party holds that the idea of freedom is a delusion; another says that the idea of bondage is a delusion.

How does this happen? Man is really free, the real man cannot but be free. It is when he comes into the world of Maya, into name and form, that he becomes bound.

Free will is a misnomer. Will can never be free. How can it be? It is only when the real man has become bound that his will comes into existence, and not before. The will of man is bound, but that which is the foundation of that will is eternally free.

So, even in the state of bondage which we call human life or god-life, on earth or in heaven, there yet remains to us that recollection of the freedom which is ours by divine right. And consciously or unconsciously we are all struggling towards it. When a man has attained his own freedom, how can he be bound by any law? No law in this universe can bind him, for this universe itself is his.

*

I was once travelling in the desert in India. I travelled for over a month and always found the most beautiful landscapes before me, beautiful lakes and all that.

One day I was very thirsty and I wanted to have a drink at one of these lakes; but when I approached that lake it vanished. Immediately with a blow came into my brain the idea that this was a mirage about which I had read all my life; and then I remembered and smiled at my folly, that for the last month all the beautiful landscapes and lakes I had been seeing were this mirage, but I could not distinguish them then.

The next morning I again began my march; there was the lake and the landscape, but with it immediately came the idea, "This is a mirage."

Once known it had lost its power of illusion. So this illusion of the universe will break one day. The whole of this will vanish, melt away. This is realisation.

*

According to the Advaita philosophy, then, this differentiation of matter, these phenomena, are, as it were, for a time, hiding the real nature of man; but the latter really has not been changed at all. In the lowest worm, as well as in the highest human being, the same divine nature is present.

The worm form is the lower form in which the divinity has been more overshadowed by Maya; that is the highest form in which it has been least overshadowed. Behind everything the same divinity is existing, and out of this comes the basis of morality.

Do not injure another. Love everyone as your own self, because the whole universe is one. In injuring another, I am injuring myself; in loving another, I am loving myself.

From this also springs that principle of Advaita morality which has been summed up in one word — self-abnegation. The Advaitist says, this little personalised self is the cause of all my misery.

This individualised self, which makes me different from all other beings, brings hatred and jealousy and misery, struggle and all other evils. o this is to be given up. We must always hold ourselves ready, even to give up our lives for the lowest beings.

When a man has become ready even to give up his life for a little insect, he has reached the perfection which the Advaitist wants to attain; and at that moment when he has become thus ready, the veil of ignorance falls away from him, and he will feel his own nature.

Even in this life, he will feel that he is one with the universe. For a time, as it were, the whole of this phenomenal world will disappear for him, and he will realise what he is. But so long as the Karma of this body remains, he will have to live.

This state, when the veil has vanished and yet the body remains for some time, is what the Vedantists call the Jivanmukti, the living freedom.

*

The mind is not the body, though it is matter in a finer form. It is not eternally bound by the body. This is proved as we get occasionally loosened from it. We can learn to do this at will by controlling the senses.

When we can do that fully, we shall control the universe, because our world is only what the senses bring us. Freedom is the test of the higher being. Spiritual life begins when you have loosened yourself from the control of the senses. He whose senses rule him is worldly — is a slave.

If we could entirely stop our mind-stuff from breaking into waves, it would put an end to our bodies. For millions of years we have worked so hard to manufacture these bodies that in the struggle we have forgotten our real purpose in getting them, which was to become perfect.

We have grown to think that body-making is the end of our efforts. This is Mâyâ. We must break this delusion and return to our original aim and realise we are not the body, it is our servant.

*

Freedom of the will — it is as you feel you are free to act. But this freedom is a species of necessity. There is one infinite link before, after, and between the thought and the action, but the latter takes the name of freedom — like a bird flitting through a bright room. We feel the freedom and feel it has no other cause.

We cannot go beyond consciousness, therefore we feel we are free. We can trace it no further than consciousness. God alone feels the real freedom. Mahapurushas (saints) feel themselves identified with God; hence they also feel the real freedom.

You may stop the water flowing out of the fountain by closing that part of the stream and gathering it all in the fountain; you have no liberty beyond it. But the source remains unchanged.

Everything is predestination — and a part of that predestination is that you shall have such feeling — the feeling of freedom. I am shaping my own action. Responsibility is the feeling of reaction. There is no absolute power. Power here is the conscious feeling of exercising any faculty which is created by necessity.

Man has the feeling "I act"; what he means by power of freedom is the feeling. The power is attended with responsibility. Whatever may be done through us by predestination, we feel the reaction. A ball thrown by one, itself feels the reaction.

But this innate necessity which comes to us as our freedom does not affect also the conscious relations we form with our surroundings. The relativity is not changed. Either everybody is free or everybody is under necessity. That would not matter. The relations would be the same. Vice and virtue would be the same.

If a thief pleads that he was under the necessity of stealing, the magistrate would say that he was under the necessity to punish. We are seated in a room, and the whole room is moving — the relation between us is unchanged.

To get out of this infinite chain of causation is Mukti (freedom). Muktas (free souls) are not actuated by necessity, they are like god. They begin the chain of cause and effect. God is the only free being

— the first source of their will — and is always experienced by them as such.

The feeling of want is the real prayer, not the words. But you must have patience to wait and see if your prayers are answered.

*

We have a place for struggle in the Vedanta, but not for fear. All fears will vanish when you begin to assert your own nature. If you think that you are bound, bound you will remain. If you think you are free, free you will be.

That sort of freedom which we can feel when we are yet in the phenomenal is a glimpse of the real but not yet the real.

I disagree with the idea that freedom is obedience to the laws of nature. I do not understand what it means. According to the history of human progress, it is disobedience to nature that has constituted that progress.

It may be said that the conquest of lower laws was through the higher. But even there, the conquering mind was only trying to be free; and as soon as it found that the struggle was also through law, it wanted to conquer that also. So the ideal was freedom in every case.

The trees never disobey law. I never saw a cow steal. An oyster never told a lie. Yet they are not greater than man. This life is a tremendous assertion of freedom; and this obedience to law, carried far enough, would make us simply matter — either in society, or in politics, or in religion.

Too many laws are a sure sign of death. Wherever in any society there are too many laws, it is a sure sign that that society will soon die. If you study the characteristics of India, you will find that no nation possesses so many laws as the Hindus, and national death is the result.

But the Hindus had one peculiar idea — they never made any doctrines or dogmas in religion; and the latter has had the greatest growth. Eternal law cannot be freedom, because to say that the eternal is inside law is to limit it.

*

The atmosphere of a room may be hypnotised so that everybody who enters it will see all sorts of things — men and objects flying through the air.

Everybody is hypnotised already. The work of attaining freedom, of realising one's real nature, consists in de-hypnotisation.

One thing to be remembered is that we are not gaining powers at all. We have them already. The whole process of growth is de-hypnotisation.

*

Only freedom can produce true morality. If there were only an endless chain of cause and effect, Nirvâna could not be. It is extinction of the seeming self, bound by this chain. That is what constitutes freedom, to get beyond causality.

*

Everything that we perceive around us is struggling towards freedom, from the atom to the man, from the insentient, lifeless particle of matter to the highest existence on earth, the human soul. The whole universe is in fact the result of this struggle for freedom.

In all combinations every particle is trying to go on its own way, to fly from the other particles; but the others are holding it in check. Our earth is trying to fly away from the sun, and the moon from the earth.

Everything has a tendency to infinite dispersion. All that we see in the universe has for its basis this one struggle towards freedom; it is under the impulse of this tendency that the saint prays and the robber robs. When the line of action taken is not a proper one, we call it evil; and when the manifestation of it is proper and high, we call it good.

But the impulse is the same, the struggle towards freedom. The saint is oppressed with the knowledge of his condition of bondage, and he wants to get rid of it; so he worships God. The thief is oppressed with the idea that he does not possess certain things, and he tries to get rid of that want, to obtain freedom from it; so he steals.

Freedom is the one goal of all nature, sentient or insentient; and consciously or unconsciously, everything is struggling towards that goal. The freedom which the saint seeks is very different from that which the robber seeks; the freedom loved by the saint leads him to the enjoyment of infinite, unspeakable bliss, while that on which the robber has set his heart only forges other bonds for his soul.

*

Bondage and liberty, light and shadow, good and evil must be there, but the very fact of the bondage shows also this freedom hidden there. If one is a fact, the other is equally a fact. There must be this idea of freedom.

While now we cannot see that this idea of bondage, in uncultivated man, is his struggle for freedom, yet the idea of freedom is there.

The bondage of sin and impurity in the uncultivated savage is to his consciousness very small, for his nature is only a little higher than the animal's. What he struggles against is the bondage of physical nature, the lack of physical gratification, but out of this lower consciousness grows and broadens the higher conception of a mental or moral bondage and a longing for spiritual freedom.

Here we see the divine dimly shining through the veil of ignorance. The veil is very dense at first and the light may be almost obscured, but it is there, ever pure and undimmed — the radiant fire of freedom and perfection. Man personifies this as the Ruler of the Universe, the One Free Being. He does not yet know that the universe is all one, that the difference is only in degree, in the concept.

FREEDOM IS THE GOAL

Our main problem is to be free. It is evident then that until we realise ourselves as the Absolute, we cannot attain to deliverance.

Yet there are various ways of attaining to this realisation. These methods have the generic name of Yoga (to join, to join ourselves to our reality). These Yogas, though divided into various groups, can principally be classed into four; and as each is only a method leading indirectly to the realisation of the Absolute, they are suited to different temperaments.

Now it must be remembered that it is not that the assumed man becomes the real man or Absolute. There is no becoming with the Absolute. It is ever free, ever perfect; but the ignorance that has covered Its nature for a time is to be removed.

Therefore the whole scope of all systems of Yoga (and each religion represents one) is to clear up this ignorance and allow the Âtman to restore its own nature. The chief helps in this liberation are Abhyâsa and Vairâgya. Vairagya is non-attachment to life, because it is the will to enjoy that brings all this bondage in its train; and Abhyasa is constant practice of any one of the Yogas.

*

Love is God, freedom is God; and everything that is bondage is not God.

Man has freedom already, but he will have to discover it. He has it, but every moment forgets it. That discovering, consciously or unconsciously, is the whole life of every one.

But the difference between the sage and the ignorant man is that one does it consciously and the other unconsciously. Every one is struggling for freedom — from the atom to the star. The ignorant man is satisfied if he can get freedom within a certain limit — if he can get rid of the bondage of hunger or of being thirsty.

But that sage feels that there is a stronger bondage which has to be thrown off. He would not consider the freedom of the Red Indian as freedom at all.

*

According to our philosophers, freedom is the goal. Knowledge cannot be the goal, because knowledge is a compound. It is a compound of power and freedom, and it is freedom alone that is desirable. That is what men struggle after.

Simply the possession of power would not be knowledge. For instance, a scientist can send an electric shock to a distance of some miles; but nature can send it to an unlimited distance.

Why do we not build statues to nature then? It is not law that we want but ability to break law. We want to be outlaws. If you are bound by laws, you will be a lump of clay. Whether you are beyond law or not is not the question; but the thought that we are beyond law — upon that is based the whole history of humanity.

For instance, a man lives in a forest, and never has had any education or knowledge. He sees a stone falling down — a natural phenomenon happening — and he thinks it is freedom. He thinks it has a soul, and the central idea in that is freedom.

But as soon as he knows that it must fall, he calls it nature — dead, mechanical action. I may or may not go into the street. In that is my glory as a man. If I am sure that I must go there, I give myself up and become a machine. Nature with its infinite power is only a machine; freedom alone constitutes sentient life.

The Vedanta says that the idea of the man in the forest is the right one; his glimpse is right, but the explanation is wrong. He holds to this nature as freedom and not as governed by law.

Uniformity of action is what we call law. This uniformity of my actions, I find, is broken into very short periods, and so I do not call my actions under law. I work through freedom. I walk for five minutes; but before those five minutes of walking, which are uniform, there was the action of the will, which gave the impulse to walk.

Therefore man says he is free, because all his actions can be cut up into small periods; and although there is sameness in the small periods, beyond the period there is not the same sameness. In this perception of non-uniformity is the idea of freedom.

In nature we see only very large periods of uniformity; but the beginning and end must be free impulses. The impulse of freedom was given just at the beginning, and that has rolled on; but this, compared with our periods, is much longer.

We find by analysis on philosophic grounds that we are not free. But there will remain this factor, this consciousness that I am free. What we have to explain is, how that comes.

We will find that we have these two impulsions in us. Our reason tells us that all our actions are caused, and at the same time, with every impulse we are asserting our freedom. The solution of the Vedanta is that there is freedom inside — that the soul is really free — but that

that soul's actions are percolating through body and mind, which are not free.

As soon as we react, we become slaves. A man blames me, and I immediately react in the form of anger. A little vibration which he created made me a slave. So we have to demonstrate our freedom.

*

All things in nature work according to law. Nothing is excepted. The mind as well as everything in external nature is governed and controlled by law.

Internal and external nature, mind and matter, are in time and space, and are bound by the law of causation.

The freedom of the mind is a delusion. How can the mind be free when it is controlled and bound by law?

The law of Karma is the law of causation.

We must become free. We are free; the work is to know it. We must give up all slavery, all bondage of whatever kind. We must not only give up our bondage to earth and everything and everybody on earth, but also to all ideas of heaven and happiness.

We are bound to earth by desire and also to God, heaven, and the angels. A slave is a slave whether to man, to God, or to angels.

The idea of heaven must pass away. The idea of heaven after death where the good live a life of eternal happiness is a vain dream, without a particle of meaning or sense in it.

Wherever there is happiness there must follow unhappiness sometime. Wherever there is pleasure there must be pain. This is absolutely certain, every action has its reaction somehow.

The idea of freedom is the only true idea of salvation — freedom from everything, the senses, whether of pleasure or pain, from good as well as evil.

More than this even, we must be free from death and to be free from death, we must be free from life. Life is but a dream of death. Where there is life, there will be death; so get away from life if you would be rid of death.

We are ever free if we would only believe it, only have faith enough. You are the soul, free and eternal, ever free ever blessed. Have faith enough and you will be free in a minute.

Everything in time, space, and causation is bound. The soul is beyond all time, all space, all causation. That which is bound is nature, not the soul.

Therefore proclaim your freedom and be what you are — ever free, ever blessed.

Time, space, and causation we call Maya.

*

The goal of all nature is freedom, and freedom is to be attained only by perfect unselfishness; every thought, word, or deed that is unselfish takes us towards the goal, and, as such, is called moral. That definition, you will find, holds good in every religion and every system of ethics.

FAITH IN GOD

A man must not only have faith but intellectual faith too. To make a man take up everything and believe it, would be to make him a lunatic.

I once had a book sent me, which said I must believe everything told in it. It said there was no soul, but that there were gods and goddesses in heaven, and a thread of light going from each of our heads to heaven!

How did the writer know all these things? She had been inspired, and wanted me to believe it too; and because I refused, she said, "You must be a very bad man; there is no hope for you!" This is fanaticism.

*

Never say man is weak. Wisdom-Yoga is no better than the others. Love is the ideal and requires no object. Love is God. So even through devotion we reach the subjective God. I am He!

How can one work, unless one loves city, country, animals, the universe? Reason leads to the finding of unity in variety. Let the atheist and the agnostic work for the social good. So God comes.

But this you must guard against: Do not disturb the faith of any. For you must know that religion is not in doctrines. Religion lies in being and becoming, in realisation.

All men are born idolaters. The lowest man is an animal. The highest man is perfect. And between these two, all have to think in sound and colour, in doctrine and ritual.

The test of having ceased to be an idolater is: "When you say 'I', does the body come into your thought or not? If it does, then you are still a worshipper of idols."

Religion is not intellectual jargon at all, but realisation. If you think about God, you are only a fool. The ignorant man, by prayer and devotion, can reach beyond the philosopher.

To know God, no philosophy is necessary. Our duty is not to disturb the faith of others. Religion is experience.

Above all and in all, be sincere; identification brings misery, because it brings desire. Thus the poor man sees gold, and identifies himself with the need of gold. Be the witness. Learn never to react .

*

There is no external test for inspiration, we know it ourselves; our guardian against mistake is negative — the voice of reason. All religion is going beyond reason, but reason is the only guide to get there.

Instinct is like ice, reason is the water, and inspiration is the subtlest form or vapour; one follows the other. Everywhere is this eternal sequence — unconsciousness, consciousness, intelligence — matter, body, mind — and to us it seems as if the chain began with the particular link we first lay hold of.

Arguments on both sides are of equal weight, and both are true. We must reach beyond both, to where there is neither the one nor the other. These successions are all Maya.

Religion is above reason, supernatural. Faith is not belief, it is the grasp on the Ultimate, an illumination. First hear, then reason and find out all that reason can give about the Atman; let the flood of reason flow over It, then take what remains.

If nothing remains, thank God you have escaped a superstition. When you have determined that nothing can take away the Atman, that It stands every test, hold fast to this and teach it to all. Truth cannot be partial; it is for the good of all.

Finally, in perfect rest and peace meditate upon It, concentrate your mind upon It, make yourself one with It. Then no speech is needed; silence will carry the truth.

Do not spend your energy in talking, but meditate in silence; and do not let the rush of the outside world disturb you. When your mind is in the highest state, you are unconscious of it. Accumulate power in silence and become a dynamo of spirituality.

What can a beggar give? Only a king can give, and he only when he wants nothing himself.

*

Work hard, be steady, and have faith in the Lord. Set to work.

You know the disease, you know the remedy, only have faith. Do not look up to the so-called rich and great; do not care for the heartless intellectual writers, and their cold-blooded newspaper articles.

ONENESS WITH GOD

Through freedom the sciences were built; and in them we have two sets of opinions, the one the materialistic and denouncing, and the other the positive and constructive. It is a most curious fact that in every society you find them.

Supposing there is an evil in society, you will find immediately one group rise up and denounce it in vindictive fashion, which sometimes degenerates into fanaticism. There are fanatics in every society, and women frequently join in these outcries, because of their impulsive nature.

Every fanatic who gets up and denounces something can secure a following. It is very easy to break down; a maniac can break anything he likes, but it would be hard for him to build up anything. These fanatics may do some good, according to their light, but much more harm. Because social institutions are not made in a day, and to change them means removing the cause.

Suppose there is an evil; denouncing it will not remove it, but you must go to work at the root. First find out the cause, then remove it, and the effect will be removed also. Mere outcry not produce any effect, unless indeed it produces misfortune.

*

There are others who had sympathy in their hearts and who understood the idea that we must go deep into the cause, these were the great saints. One fact you must remember, that all the great teachers of the world have declared that they came not to destroy but to fulfil.

Many times his has not been understood, and their forbearance has been thought to be an unworthy compromise with existing popular opinions. Even now, you occasionally hear that these prophets and great teachers were rather cowardly, and dared not say and do what they thought was right; but that was not so.

Fanatics little understand the infinite power of love in the hearts of these great sages who looked upon the inhabitants of this world as their children. They were the real fathers, the real gods, filled with infinite sympathy and patience for everyone; they were ready to bear and forbear. They knew how human society should grow, and patiently slowly, surely, went on applying their remedies, not by denouncing and frightening people, but by gently and kindly leading them upwards step by step.

Such were the writers of the Upanishads. They knew full well how the old ideas of God were not reconcilable with the advanced ethical ideas of the time; they knew full well that what the atheists were preaching contained a good deal of truth, nay, great nuggets of truth; but at the same time, they understood that those who wished to sever the thread that bound the beads, who wanted to build a new society in the air, would entirely fail.

We never build anew, we simply change places; we cannot have anything new, we only change the position of things. The seed grows into the tree, patiently and gently; we must direct our energies towards the truth and fulfil the truth that exists, not try to make new truths.

Thus, instead of denouncing these old ideas of God as unfit for modern times, the ancient sages began to seek out the reality that was in them. The result was the Vedanta philosophy, and out of the old deities, out of the monotheistic God, the Ruler of the universe, they found yet higher and higher ideas in what is called the Impersonal Absolute; they found oneness throughout the universe.

He who sees in this world of manifoldness that One running through all, in this world of death he who finds that One Infinite Life, and in this world of insentience and ignorance he who finds that One Light and Knowledge, unto him belongs eternal peace. Unto none else, unto none else.

*

The people of old knew that fire lived in the flint and in dry wood, but friction was necessary to call it out. So this fire of freedom and purity is the nature of every soul, and not a quality, because qualities can be acquired and therefore can be lost.

The soul is one with Freedom, and the soul is one with Existence, and the soul is one with Knowledge. The Sat-Chit-Ânanda — Existence Knowledge-Bliss Absolute — is the nature, the birthright of the Soul, and all the manifestations that we see are Its expressions, dimly or brightly manifesting Itself. Even death is but a manifestation of that Real Existence.

Birth and death, life and decay, degeneration and regeneration — are all manifestations of that Oneness. So, knowledge, however it manifests itself, either as ignorance or as learning, is but the manifestation of that same Chit, the essence of knowledge; the difference is only in degree, and not in kind.

The difference in knowledge between the lowest worm that crawls under our feet and the highest genius that the world may produce is only one of degree, and not of kind. The Vedantin thinker boldly says that the enjoyments in this life, even the most degraded joys, are but manifestations of that One Divine Bliss, the Essence of the Soul.

*

We believe in one God, the Father of us all, who is omnipresent and omnipotent, and who guides and preserves His children with infinite love. We believe in a Personal God as the Christians do, but we go further: we below that we are He!

That His personality is manifested in us, that God is in us, and that we are in God. We believe there is a germ of truth in all religions, and the Hindu bows down to them all; for in this world, truth is to be found not in subtraction but in addition.

We would offer God a bouquet of the most beautiful flowers of all the diverse faiths. We must love God for love's sake, not for the hope of reward. We must do our duty for duty's sake not for the hope of reward. We must worship the beautiful for beauty's sake, not for the hope of reward.

Thus in the purity of our hearts shall we see God. Sacrifices genuflexions, mumblings, and mutterings are not religion. They are only good if they stimulate us to the brave performance of beautiful and heroic deeds and lift our thoughts to the apprehension of the divine perfection

What good is it, if we acknowledge in our prayers that God is the Father of us all, and in our daily lives do not treat every man as our brother? Books are only made so that they may point the way to a higher life; but no good results unless the path is trodden with unflinching steps!

Every human personality may be compared to a glass globe. There is the same pure white light — an emission of the divine Being — in the centre of each, but the glass being of different colours and thickness, the rays assume diverse aspects in the transmission.

The equality and beauty of each central flame is the same, and the apparent inequality is only in the imperfection of the temporal instrument of its expression. As we rise higher and higher in the scale of being, the medium becomes more and more translucent.

*

What we want is not so much spirituality as a little of the bringing down of the Advaita into the material world. First bread and then religion. We stuff them too much with religion, when the poor fellows have been starving. No dogmas will satisfy the cravings of hunger.

There are two curses here: first our weakness, secondly, our hatred, our dried-up hearts.

You may talk doctrines by the millions, you may have sects by the hundreds of millions; ay, but it is nothing until you have the heart to feel. Feel for them as your Veda teaches you, till you find they are parts of your own bodies, till you realise that you and they, the poor and the rich, the saint and the sinner, are all parts of One Infinite Whole, which you call Brahman.

*

"He goes from death to death who sees the many here." See that One and be free.

How are we to see it? This mind, so deluded, so weak, so easily led, even this mind can be strong and may catch a glimpse of that knowledge, that Oneness, which saves us from dying again and again.

As rain falling upon a mountain flows in various streams down the sides of the mountain, so all the energies which you see here are from that one Unit. It has become manifold falling upon Maya. Do not run after the manifold; go towards the One.

"He is in all that moves; He is in all that is pure; He fills the universe; He is in the sacrifice; He is the guest in the house; He is in man, in water, in animals, in truth; He is the Great One. As fire coming into this world is manifesting itself in various forms, even so, that one Soul of the universe is manifesting Himself in all these various forms. As air coming into this universe manifests itself in various forms, even so, the One Soul of all souls, of all beings, is manifesting Himself in all forms."

This is true for you when you have understood this Unity, and not before Then is all optimism, because He is seen everywhere.

The question is that if all this be true that that Pure One — the Self, the Infinite — has entered all this, how is it that He suffers, how is it that He becomes miserable, impure?

He does not, says the Upanishad. "As the sun is the cause of the eyesight of every being, yet is not made defective by the defect in any eye, even so the Self of all is not affected by the miseries of the body, or by any misery that is around you."

I may have some disease and see everything yellow, but the sun is not affected by it.

"He is the One, the Creator of all, the Ruler of all, the Internal Soul of every being — He who makes His Oneness manifold. Thus sages who realise Him as the Soul of their souls, unto them belongs eternal peace; unto none else, unto none else. He who in this world of evanescence finds Him who never changes, he who in this universe of death finds that One Life, he who in this manifold finds that Oneness, and all those who realise Him as the Soul of their souls, to them belongs eternal peace; unto none else, unto none else. Where to find Him in the external world, where to find Him in the suns, and moons, and stars? There the sun cannot illumine, nor the moon, nor the stars, the flash of lightning cannot illumine the place; what to speak of this mortal fire? He shining, everything else shines. It is His light that they have borrowed, and He is shining through them."

Here is another beautiful simile. Those of you who have been in India and have seen how the banyan tree comes from one root and spreads itself far around, will understand this.

He is that banyan tree; He is the root of all and has branched out until He has become this universe, and however far He extends, every one of these trunks and branches is connected.

*

"He the Omnipresent, the One without a second, the One without a body, pure, the great poet of the universe, whose metre is the suns and stars, is giving to each what he deserves" (Isha Upanishad, 8, adapted).

*

"He, the One, who vibrates more quickly than mind, who attains to more speed than mind can ever do, whom even the gods reach not, nor thought grasps, He moving, everything moves. In Him all exists. He is moving. He is also immovable. He is near and He is far. He is inside everything. He is outside everything, interpenetrating everything. Whoever sees in every being that same Atman, and whoever sees everything in that Atman, he never goes far from that Atman. When all life and the whole universe are seen in this Atman, then alone man has attained the secret. There is no more delusion for him. Where is any more misery for him who sees this Oneness in the universe?"

*

The seer is really the Self, the pure one, the ever holy, the infinite, the immortal. This is the Self of man. And what are the instruments? The Chitta or mind-stuff, the Buddhi or determinative faculty, the Manas or mind, and the Indriyas or sense-organs.

These are the instruments for him to see the external world, and the identification of the Self with the instruments is what is called the ignorance of egoism. We say, "I am the mind," "I am thought," "I am angry," or "I am happy".

How can we be angry and how can we hate? We should identify ourselves with the Self that cannot change. If It is unchangeable, how can It be one moment happy, and one moment unhappy? It is formless, infinite, omnipresent.

What can change It? It is beyond all law. What can affect it? Nothing in the universe can produce an effect on It. Yet through ignorance, we identify ourselves with the mind-stuff, and think we feel pleasure or pain.

*

This Oneness of life, this Oneness of everything, is another great theme of the Vedanta,.

We shall see how it demonstrates that all our misery comes through ignorance, and this ignorance is the idea of manifoldness, this separation between man and man, between nation and nation, between earth and moon, between moon and sun. Out of this idea of separation between atom and atom comes all misery.

But the Vedanta says this separation does not exist, it is not real. It is merely apparent, on the surface. In the heart of things there is Unity still. If you go below the surface, you find that Unity between man and man, between races and races, high and low, rich and poor, gods and men, and men and animals.

If you go deep enough, all will be seen as only variations of the One, and he who has attained to this conception of Oneness has no more delusion. What can delude him? He knows the reality of everything, the secret of everything. Where is there any more misery for him? What does he desire?

He has traced the reality of everything to the Lord, the Centre, the Unity of everything, and that is Eternal Existence, Eternal Knowledge, Eternal Bliss. Neither death nor disease, nor sorrow, nor misery, nor discontent is there.

All is Perfect Union and Perfect Bliss. For whom should he mourn then? In the Reality, there is no death, there is no misery; in the Reality, there is no one to mourn for, no one to be sorry for. He has penetrated everything, the Pure One, the Formless, the Bodiless, the Stainless.

He the Knower, He the Great Poet, the Self-Existent, He who is giving to everyone what he deserves. They grope in darkness who worship this ignorant world, the world that is produced out of ignorance, thinking of it as Existence, and those who live their whole lives in this world, and never find anything better or higher, are groping in still greater darkness.

But he who knows the secret of nature, seeing That which is beyond nature through the help of nature, he crosses death, and through the help of That which is beyond nature, he enjoys Eternal Bliss.

"Thou sun, who hast covered the Truth with thy golden disc, do thou remove the veil, so that I may see the Truth that is within thee. I have known the Truth that is within thee, I have known what is the real meaning of thy rays and thy glory and have seen That which shines in thee; the Truth in thee I see, and That which is within thee is within me, and I am That."

*

If then we are beyond all law, we must be omniscient, ever-blessed; all knowledge must be in us and all power and blessedness. Certainly. You are the omniscient. omnipresent being of the universe.

But of such beings can there be many? Can there be a hundred thousand millions of omnipresent beings? Certainly not. Then, what becomes of us all? You are only one; there is only one such Self, and that One Self is you.

Standing behind this little nature is what we call the Soul. There is only One Being, One Existence, the ever-blessed, the omnipresent, the omniscient, the birthless, deathless.

"Through His control the sky expands, through His control the air breathes, through His control the sun shines, and through His control all live. He is the Reality in nature, He is the Soul of your soul, nay, more, you are He, you are one with Him."

Wherever there are two, there is fear, there is danger, there is conflict, there is strife. When it is all One, who is there to hate, who is there to struggle with? When it is all He, with whom can you fight? T

his explains the true nature of life; this explains the true nature of being. this is perfection, and this is God. As long as you see the many, you are under delusion.

"In this world of many he who sees the One, in this everchanging world he who sees Him who never changes, as the Soul of his own soul, as his own Self, he is free, he is blessed, he has reached the goal."

Therefore know that thou art He; thou art the God of this universe, "Tat Tvam Asi" (That thou art).

All these various ideas that I am a man or a woman, or sick or healthy, or strong or weak, or that I hate or I love, or have a little power, are but hallucinations. Away with them!

What makes you weak? What makes you fear? You are the One Being in the universe. What frightens you? Stand up then and be free.

Know that every thought and word that weakens you in this world is the only evil that exists. Whatever makes men weak and fear is the only evil that should be shunned.

What can frighten you? If the suns come down, and the moons crumble into dust, and systems after systems are hurled into annihilation, what is that to you?

Stand as a rock; you are indestructible. You are the Self, the God of the universe. Say — "I am Existence Absolute, Bliss Absolute, Knowledge Absolute, I am He," and like a lion breaking its cage, break your chain and be free for ever.

What frightens you, what holds you down? Only ignorance and delusion; nothing else can bind you. You are the Pure One, the Ever-blessed.

*

Faith in God and in one's own Self is virtue; doubt is sin. Knowledge of oneness is virtue; seeing diversity is sin. The different scriptures only show the means of attaining virtue.

*

Two forces seem to be working throughout nature. One of these is constantly differentiating, and the other is as constantly unifying; the one making more and more for separate individuals, the other, as it were, bringing the individuals into a mass, bringing out sameness in the midst of all this differentiation. It seems that the action of these two forces enters into every department of nature and of human life.

On the physical plane, we always find the two forces most distinctly at work, separating the individuals, making them more and more distinct from other individuals, and again making them into species and classes, and bringing out similarities of expressions, and form. The same holds good as regards the social life of man.

Since the time when society began, these two forces have been at work, differentiating and unifying. Their action appears in various forms, and is called by various names, in different places, and at different times. But the essence is present in all, one making for differentiation, and the other for sameness; the one making for caste, and the other breaking it down; one making for classes and privileges, and the other destroying them.

The whole universe seems to be the battle-ground of these two forces. On the one hand, it is urged, that though this unifying process exists, we ought to resist it with all our might, because it leads towards death, that perfect unity is perfect annihilation, and that when the differentiating process that is at work in this universe ceases, the universe comes to an end. It is differentiation that causes the phenomena that are before us; unification would reduce them all to a homogeneous and lifeless matter.

Such a thing, of course, mankind wants to avoid. The same argument is applied to all the things and facts that we see around us. It is urged that even in physical body and social classification, absolute sameness would produce natural death and social death. Absolute sameness of thought and feeling would produce mental decay and degeneration.

Sameness, therefore, is to be avoided. This has been the argument on the one side, and it has been urged in every country and in various times, with only a change of language.

Practically it is the same argument which is urged by the Brahmins of India, when they want to uphold the divisions and castes, when they want to uphold the privileges of a certain portion of the community, against everybody else. The destruction of caste, they declare, would lead to destruction of society, and boldly they produce the historical fact that theirs has been the longest-lived society.

So they, with some show of force, appeal to this argument. With some show of authority they declare that that alone which makes the individual live the longest life must certainly be better than that which produces shorter lives.

On the other hand, the idea of oneness has had its advocates throughout all times. From the days of the Upanishads, the Buddhas, and Christs, and all other great preachers of religion, down to our present day, in the new political aspirations, and in the claims of the oppressed and the downtrodden, and of all those who find themselves bereft of privileges — comes out the one assertion of this unity and sameness.

*

The rational West is earnestly bent upon seeking out the rationality, the raison d' être of all its philosophy and its ethics. And you all know well that ethics cannot be derived from the mere sanction of any personage, however great and divine he may have been.

Such an explanation of the authority of ethics appeals no more to the highest of the world's thinkers. They want something more than human sanction for ethical and moral codes to be binding, they want some eternal principle of truth as the sanction of ethics.

And where is that eternal sanction to be found except in the only Infinite Reality that exists in you and in me and in all, in the Self, in the Soul? The infinite oneness of the Soul is the eternal sanction of all morality, that you and I are not only brothers — every literature voicing man's struggle towards freedom has preached that for you — but that you and I are really one.

This is the dictate of Indian philosophy. This oneness is the rationale of all ethics and all spirituality. Europe wants it today just as much as our downtrodden masses do, and this great principle is even now unconsciously forming the basis of all the latest political and social aspirations that are coming up in England, in Germany, in France, and in America.

And mark it, my friends, that in and through all the literature voicing man's struggle towards freedom, towards universal freedom, again and again you find the Indian Vedantic ideals coming out prominently. In some cases the writers do not know the source of their inspiration, in some cases they try to appear very original, and a few there are, bold and grateful enough to mention the source and acknowledge their indebtedness to it.

*

It is from the idea of the manifold that the ideas of virtue and vice have evolved. The more a man advances towards oneness, the more ideas of "I" and "you" subside, ideas from which all these pairs of opposites such as virtue and vice have originated.

When the idea that So-and-so is different from me comes to the mind, all other ideas of distinction begin to manifest, while with the complete realisation of oneness, no more grief or illusion remains for man, " — For him who sees oneness, where is there any grief or any delusion?"

Sin may be said to be the feeling of every kind of weakness. From this weakness spring jealousy, malice, and so forth.

Hence weakness is sin. The Self within is always shining forth resplendent. Turning away from that people say "I", "I", "I", with their attention held up by this material body, this queer cage of flesh and bones. This is the root of all weakness. From that habit only, the relative outlook on life has emerged in this world. The absolute Truth lies beyond that duality.

*

Mohammed found that Christianity was straying out from the Semitic fold and his teachings were to show what Christianity ought to be as a Semitic religion, that it should hold to one God. The Aryan idea that "I and my Father are one" disgusted and terrified him.

In reality the conception of the Trinity was a great advance over the dualistic idea of Jehovah, who was for ever separate from man. The theory of incarnation is the first link in the chain of ideas leading to the recognition of the oneness of God and man.

God appearing first in one human form, then re-appearing at different times in other human forms, is at last recognised as being in every human form, or in all men. Monistic is the highest stage, monotheistic is a lower stage. Imagination will lead you to the highest even more rapidly and easily than reasoning.

*

In all religions we travel from a lesser to a higher truth, never from error to truth. There is a Oneness behind all creation, but minds are very various. 'That which exists is One, sages call It variously.'

What I mean is that one progresses from a smaller to a greater truth. The worst religions are only bad readings of the froth. One gets to understand bit by bit. Even devil-worship is but a perverted reading of the ever-true and immutable Brahman. Other phases have more or less of the truth in them. No form of religion possesses it entirely.

*

All that is meant by dying or being born is simply changes in the plane of vision. Neither do you move, nor does that move upon which you project your vision. You are the permanent, the unchangeable.

How can you come and go? It is impossible; you are omnipresent. The sky never moves, but the clouds move over the surface of the sky, and we may think that the sky itself moves, just as when you are in a railway train, you think the land is moving.

It is not so, but it is the train which is moving. You are where you are; these dreams, these various clouds move. One dream follows another without connection. There is no such thing as law or connection in this world, but we are thinking that there is a great deal of connection.

When this dream changes, another dream will seem quite as connected as this. When we dream, the things we see all seem to be connected; during the dream we never think they are incongruous; it is only when we wake that we see the want of connection.

When we wake from this dream of the world and compare it with the Reality, it will be found all incongruous nonsense, a mass of incongruity passing before us, we do not know whence or whither, but we know it will end; and this is called Maya, and is like masses of fleeting fleecy clouds.

They represent all this changing existence, and the sun itself, the unchanging, is you. When you look at that unchanging Existence from the outside, you call it God; and when you look at it from the inside, you call it yourself. It is but one.

There is no God separate from you, no God higher than you, the real "you". All the gods are little beings to you, all the ideas of God and Father in heaven are but your own reflection. God Himself is your image.

"God created man after His own image." That is wrong. Man creates God after his own image. That is right.

Throughout the universe we are creating gods after our own image. We create the god and fall down at his feet and worship him; and when this dream comes, we love it!

This is a good point to understand — that the sum and substance of this lecture is that there is but One Existence, and that One-Existence seen through different constitutions appears either as the earth, or heaven, or hell, or gods, or ghosts, or men, or demons, or world, or all these things.

But among these many, "He who sees that One in this ocean of death, he who sees that One Life in this floating universe, who realises that One who never changes, unto him belongs eternal peace; unto none else, unto none else."

*

"This earth is blissful ('sweet' is the literal translation) to all beings and all beings are sweet to this earth; they all help each other. And all the sweetness is the Atman, that effulgent, immortal One who is inside this earth."

Whose is this sweetness? How can there be any sweetness but He? That one sweetness is manifesting itself in various ways. Wherever there is any love, any sweetness in any human being, either in a saint or a sinner, either in an angel or a murderer, either in the body, mind, or the senses, it is He.

Physical enjoyments are but He, mental enjoyments are but He, spiritual enjoyments are but He. How can there be anything but He? How can there be twenty thousand gods and devils fighting with each other? Childish dreams!

Whatever is the lowest physical enjoyment is He, and the highest spiritual enjoyment is He. There is no sweetness but He. Thus says Yajnavalkya.

When you come to that state and look upon all things with the same eye, when you see even in the drunkard's pleasure in drink only that sweetness, then you have got the truth, and then alone you will know what happiness means, what peace means, what love means; and so long as toll make these vain distinctions, silly, childish, foolish superstitions, all sorts of misery will come.

But that immortal One, the effulgent One, He is inside the earth, it is all His sweetness, and the same sweetness is in the body.

This body is the earth, as it were, and inside all the powers of the body, all the enjoyments of the body, is He; the eyes see, the skin touches; what are all these enjoyments? That Self-effulgent One who is in the body, He is the Atman.

This world, so sweet to all beings, and every being so sweet to it, is but the Self-effulgent; the Immortal is the bliss in that world. In us also, He is that bliss. He is the Brahman.

"This air is so sweet to all beings, and all beings are so sweet to it. But He who is that Self-effulgent Immortal Being in the air — is also in this body. He is expressing Himself as the life of all beings. This sun is so sweet to all beings. All beings are so sweet to this sun. He who is the Self-effulgent Being in the sun, we reflect Him as the smaller light. What can be there but His reflection? He is in the body, and it is His reflection which makes us see the light. This moon is so sweet to all, and every one is so sweet to the moon, but that Self-effulgent and Immortal One who is the soul of that moon, He is in us expressing Himself as mind. This lightning is so beautiful, every one is so sweet to the lightning, but the Self-effulgent and Immortal One is the soul of this lightning, and is also in us, because all is that Brahman. The Atman, the Self, is the king of all beings."

These ideas are very helpful to men; they are for meditation. For instance, meditate on the earth; think of the earth and at the same time know that we have That which is in the earth, that both are the same. Identify the body with the earth, and identify the soul with the Soul behind. Identify the air with the soul that is in the air and that is in me. They are all one, manifested in different forms. To realise this unity is the end and aim of all meditation.

*

One principle the Vedanta philosophy lays down — and that, the Vedanta claims, is to be found in every religion in the world — is that man is divine, that all this which we see around us is the outcome of that consciousness of the divine.

Everything that is strong, and good, and powerful in human nature is the outcome of that divinity, and though potential in many, there is no difference between man and man essentially, all being alike divine. There is, as it were, an infinite ocean behind, and you and I are so many waves, coming out of that infinite ocean; and each one of us is trying his best to manifest that infinite outside.

So, potentially, each one of us has that infinite ocean of Existence, Knowledge, and Bliss as our birthright, our real nature; and the difference between us is caused by the greater or lesser power to manifest that divine.

Therefore the Vedanta lays down that each man should be treated not as what he manifests, but as what he stands for. Each human being stands for the divine, and, therefore, every teacher should be helpful, not by condemning man, but by helping him to call forth the divinity that is within him.

It also teaches that all the vast mass of energy that we see displayed in society and in every plane of action is really from inside out; and, therefore, what is called inspiration by other sects, the Vedantist begs the liberty to call the expiration of man.

Consciously or unconsciously, every man is trying to unfold that divinity. At the same time it does not quarrel with other sects; the Vedanta has no quarrel with those who do not understand this divinity of man.

Now, this idea, claims the Vedanta, is to be found in all religions, whether in India or outside of it; only, in some of them, the idea is expressed through mythology, and in others, through symbology. The Vedanta claims that there has not been one religious inspiration, one manifestation of the divine man, however great, but it has been the expression of that infinite oneness in human nature; and all that we call ethics and morality and doing good to others is also but the manifestation of this oneness.

There are moments when every man feels that he is one with the universe, and he rushes forth to express it, whether he knows it or not. This expression of oneness is what we call love and sympathy, and it is the basis of all our ethics and morality. This is summed up in the Vedanta philosophy by the celebrated aphorism, Tat Tvam Asi, "Thou art That".

To every man, this is taught: Thou art one with this Universal Being, and, as such, every soul that exists is your soul; and every body that exists is your body; and in hurting anyone, you hurt yourself, in loving anyone, you love yourself.

As soon as a current of hatred is thrown outside, whomsoever else it hurts, it also hurts yourself; and if love comes out from you, it is bound to come back to you. For I am the universe; this universe is my body. I am the Infinite, only I am not conscious of it now; but I am struggling to get this consciousness of the Infinite, and perfection will be reached when full consciousness of this Infinite comes.

LOVE FOR GOD

It is not the place that makes heaven or hell, but the mind. Love knows no fear, there can be no love where it is. In love of any sort external objects are only suggested by something within — it is one's own ideal projected, and God is the highest ideal that can be conceived of.

Hatred of the world does not drive good men from it, but the world slips away from the great and saintly. The world, the family and social life, are all training grounds, that is all.

When one realizes that God is love, it does not matter what his other attributes are, that is the only essential.

*

"Bhakti cannot be used to fulfil any desires, itself being the check to all desires." Narada gives these as the signs of love: "When all thoughts, all words, and all deeds are given up unto the Lord, and the least forgetfulness of God makes one intensely miserable, then love has begun."

"This is the highest form of love because therein is no desire for reciprocity, which desire is in all human love."

"A man who has gone beyond social and scriptural usage, he is a Sannyâsin. When the whole soul goes to God, when we take refuge only in God, then we know that we are about to get this love."

Obey the scriptures until you are strong enough to do without them; then go beyond them. Books are not an end-all. Verification is the only proof of religious truth.

Each must verify for himself; and no teacher who says, "I have seen, but you cannot", is to be trusted, only that one who says, "You can see too". All scriptures, all truths are Vedas in all times, in all countries; because these truths are to be seen , and any one may discover them.

"When the sun of Love begins to break on the horizon, we want to give up all our actions unto God; and when we forget Him for a moment, it grieves us greatly."

Let nothing stand between God and your love for Him. Love Him, love Him, love Him; and let the world say what it will. Love is of three sorts — one demands, but gives nothing; the second is exchange; and the third is love without thought of return — love like that of the moth for the light.

"Love is higher than work, than Yoga, than knowledge."

Work is merely a schooling for the doer; it can do no good to others. We must work out our own problem; the prophets only show us how to work. "What you think, you become ", so if you throw your burden on Jesus, you will have to think of Him and thus become like Him — you love Him.

"Extreme love and highest knowledge are one."

But theorising about God will not do; we must love and work. Give up the world and all worldly things, especially while the "plant" is tender. Day and night think of God and think of nothing else as far as possible. The daily necessary thoughts can all be thought through God. Eat to Him, drink to Him, sleep to Him, see Him in all. Talk of God to others; this is most beneficial.

Get the mercy of God and of His greatest children: these are the two chief ways to God. The company of these children of light is very hard to get; five minutes in their company will change a whole life; and if you really want it enough, one will come to you.

The presence of those who love God makes a place holy, "such is the glory of the children of the Lord". They are He; and when they speak, their words are scriptures. The place where they have been becomes filled with their vibrations, and those going there feel them and have a tendency to become holy also.

"To such lovers there is no distinction of caste, learning, beauty, birth, wealth, or occupation; because all are His."

Give up all evil company, especially at the beginning. Avoid worldly company, that will distract your mind. Give up all "me and mine ". To him who has nothing in the universe the Lord comes.

Cut the bondage of all worldly affections; go beyond laziness and all care as to what becomes of you. Never turn back to see the result of what you have done. Give all to the Lord and go on and think not of it.

The whole soul pours in a continuous current to God; there is no time to seek money, or name, or fame, no time to think of anything but God; then will come into our hearts that infinite, wonderful bliss of Love. All desires are but beads of glass.

Love of God increases every moment and is ever new, to be known only by feeling it. Love is the easiest of all, it waits for no logic, it is natural. We need no demonstration, no proof. Reasoning is limiting something by our own minds. We throw a net and catch something, and then say that we have demonstrated it; but never, never can we catch God in a net.

Love should be unrelated. Even when we love wrongly, it is of the true love, of the true bliss; the power is the same, use it as we may. Its very nature is peace and bliss. The murderer when he kisses his baby forgets for an instant all but love.

Give up all self, all egotism, get out of anger, lust, give all to God. "I am not, but Thou art; the old man is all gone, only Thou remainest." "I am Thou." Blame none; if evil comes, know the Lord is playing with you and be exceeding glad.

Love is beyond time and space, it is absolute.

*

We must not be extremely attached to anything excepting God. See everything, do everything, but be not attached. As soon as extreme attachment comes, a man loses himself, he is no more master of himself, he is a slave. If a woman is tremendously attached to a man, she becomes a slave to that man. There is no use in being a slave. There are higher things in this world than becoming a slave to a human being. Love and do good to everybody, but do not become a slave.

In the first place, attachment degenerates us, individually, and in the second place, makes us extremely selfish. Owing to this failing, we want to injure others to do good to those we love. A good many of the wicked deeds done in this world are really done through attachment to certain persons. So all attachment excepting that for good works should be avoided; but love should be given to everybody.

*

The natural state of this universe is attraction; and that is surely followed by an ultimate disunion. Even so, love is the natural impetus of union in the human heart; and though itself a great cause of misery, properly directed towards the proper object, it brings deliverance. The object of Bhakti is God. Love cannot be without a subject and an object. The object of love again must be at first a being who can reciprocate our love. Therefore the God of love must be in some sense a human God. He must be a God of love. Aside from the question whether such a God exists or not, it is a fact that to those who have love in their heart this Absolute appears as a God of love, as personal.

*

The lower forms of worship, which embody the idea of God as a judge or punisher or someone to be obeyed through fear, do not deserve to be called love, although they are forms of worship gradually expanding into higher forms. We pass on to the consideration of love itself.

So long as there is fear, it is not love. Love banishes all fear. A mother with her baby will face a tiger to save her child. The second angle is that love never asks, never begs. The third or the apex is that love loves for the sake of love itself. Even the idea of object vanishes. Love is the only form in which love is loved. This is the highest abstraction and the same as the Absolute.

*

(Love) can never be the means. The man who says, "I love you for such and such a thing", does not love. Love can never be the means; it must be the perfect end.

What is the end and aim of love? To love God, that is all. Why should one love God? [There is] no why, because it is not the means. When one can love, that is salvation, that is perfection, that is heaven. What more? What else can be the end? What can you have higher than love?

*

He who desires God will get Love, unto him God gives Himself. Love is always mutual, reflective. You may hate me, and if I want to love you, you repulse me. But if I persist, in a month or a year you are bound to love me. It is a well-known psychological phenomenon.

As the loving wife thinks of her departed husband, with the same love we must desire the Lord, and then we will find God, and all books and the various sciences would not be able to teach us anything. By reading books we become parrots; no one becomes learned by reading books. If a man reads but one word of love, he indeed becomes learned. So we want first to get that desire.

*

As soon as a man begins to believe there is a God, he becomes mad with longing to get to Him. Others may go their way, but as soon as a man is sure that there is a much higher life than that which he is leading here, as soon as he feels sure that the senses are not all, that this limited, material body is as nothing compared with the immortal, eternal, undying bliss of the Self, he becomes mad until he finds out this bliss for himself.

And this madness, this thirst, this mania, is what is called the "awakening" to religion, and when that has come, a man is beginning to be religious. But it takes a long time. All these forms and ceremonies, these prayers and pilgrimages, these books, bells, candles, and priests, are the preparations; they take off the impurities from the soul. And when the soul has become pure, it naturally wants to get to the mine of all purity, God Himself.

Just as a piece of iron, which had been covered with the dust of centuries, might be lying near a magnet all the time, and yet not be attracted by it, but as soon as the dust is cleared away, the iron is drawn by the magnet; so, when the human soul, covered with the dust of ages, impurities, wickednesses, and sins, after many births, becomes purified enough by these forms and ceremonies, by doing good to others, loving other beings, its natural spiritual attraction comes, it wakes up and struggles towards God.

Yet, all these forms and symbols are simply the beginning, not true love of God. Love we hear spoken of everywhere Everyone says, "Love God." Men do not know what it into love; if they did, they would not talk so glibly about it. Every man says he can love, and then, in no time, finds out that there is no love in his nature. Every woman says she can love and soon finds out that she cannot.

The world is full of the talk of love, but it is hard to love. Where is love? How do you know that there is love? The first test of love is that it knows no bargaining. So long as you see a man love another only to get something from him, you know that that is not love; it is shopkeeping. Wherever there is any question of buying and selling, it is not love. So, when a man prays to God, "Give me this, and give me that", it is not love. How can it be? I offer you a prayer, and you give me something in return; that is what it is, mere shopkeeping.

*

A certain great king went to hunt in a forest, and there he happened to meet a sage. He had a little conversation with him and became so pleased with him that he asked him to accept a present from him.

"No," said the sage, "I am perfectly satisfied with my condition; these trees give me enough fruit to eat; these beautiful pure streams supply me with all the water I want; I sleep in these caves. What do I care for your presents, though you be an emperor?"

The emperor said, "Just to purify me, to gratify me, come with me into the city and take some present."

At last the sage consented to go with the emperor, and he was taken into the emperor's palace, where there were gold, jewellery, marble, and most wonderful things. Wealth and power were manifest everywhere.

The emperor asked the sage to wait a minute, while he repeated his prayer, and he went into a corner and began to pray, "Lord, give me more wealth, more children, more territory."

In the meanwhile, the sage got up and began to walk away. The emperor saw him going and went after him. "Stay, Sir, you did not take my present and are going away."

The sage turned to him and said, "Beggar, I do not beg of beggars. What can you give? You have been begging yourself all the time."

That is not the language of love. What is the difference between love and shopkeeping, if you ask God to give you this, and give you that?

*

The first test of love is that it knows no bargaining. Love is always the giver, and never the taker.

Says the child of God, "If God wants, I give Him my everything, but I do not want anything of Him. I want nothing in this universe. I love Him, because I want to love Him, and I ask no favour in return. Who cares whether God is almighty or not? I do not want any power from Him nor any manifestation of His power. Sufficient for me that He is the God of love. I ask no more question."

The second test is that love knows no fear. So long as man thinks of God as a Being sitting above the clouds, with rewards in one hand and punishments in the other, there can be no love.

Can you frighten one into love? Does the lamb love the lion? The mouse, the cat? The slave, the master? Slaves sometimes simulate love, but is it love? Where do you ever see love in fear? It is always a sham. With love never comes the idea of fear.

Think of a young mother in the street: if a dog barks at her, she flees into the nearest house. The next day she is in the street with her child, and suppose a lion rushes upon the child, where will be her position? Just at the mouth of the lion, protecting her child. Love conquered all her fear.

So also in the love of God. Who cares whether God is a rewarder or a punisher? That is not the thought of a lover.

Think of a judge when he comes home, what does his wife see in him? Not a judge, or a rewarder or punisher, but her husband, her love. What do his children see in him? Their loving father, not the punisher or rewarder.

So the children of God never see in Him a punisher or a rewarder. It is only people who have never tasted of love that fear and quake. Cast off all fear — though these horrible ideas of God as a punisher or rewarder may have their use in savage minds. Some men, even the most intellectual, are spiritual savages, and these ideas may help them.

But to men who are spiritual, men who are approaching religion, in whom spiritual insight is awakened, such ideas are simply childish, simply foolish. Such men reject all ideas of fear.

The third is a still higher test. Love is always the highest ideal. When one has passed through the first two stages, when one has thrown off all shopkeeping, and cast off all fear, one then begins to realise that love is always the highest ideal. How many times in this world we see a beautiful woman loving an ugly man? How many times we see a handsome man loving an ugly woman! What is the attraction? Lookers-on only see the ugly man or the ugly woman, but not so the lover; to the lover the beloved is the most beautiful being that ever existed.

How is it? The woman who loves the ugly man takes, as it were, the ideal of beauty which is in her own mind, and projects it on this ugly man; and what she worships and loves is not the ugly man, but her own ideal. That man is, as it were, only the suggestion, and upon that suggestion she throws her own ideal, and covers it; and it becomes her object of worship.

Now, this applies in every case where we love. Many of us have very ordinary looking brothers or sisters; yet the very idea of their being brothers or sisters makes them beautiful to us.

*

No one in this world can really love anything but God. Man finds out that human love is all hollow. Men cannot love though they talk of it.

The wife says she loves her husband and kisses him; but as soon as he dies, the first thing she thinks about is the bank account, and what she shall do the next day. The husband loves the wife; but when she becomes sick and loses her beauty, or becomes haggard, or makes a mistake, he ceases to care for her. All the love of the world is hypocrisy and hollowness.

A finite subject cannot love, nor a finite object be loved. When the object of the love of a man is dying every moment, and his mind also is constantly changing as he grows, what eternal love can you expect to find in the world? There cannot be any real love but in God: why then all these loves? These are mere stages. There is a power behind impelling us forward, we do not know where to seek for the real object, but this love is sending us forward in search of it.

Again and again we find out our mistake. We grasp something, and find it slips through our fingers, and then we grasp something else. Thus on and on we go, till at last comes light; we come to God, the only One who loves. His love knows no change and is ever ready to take us in. How long would any of you bear with me if I injured you? He in whose mind is no anger, hatred, or envy, who never loses his balance, dies, or is born, who is he but God?

*

All the different kinds of love which we see in the world, and with which we are more or less playing merely, have God as the one goal; but unfortunately, man does not know the infinite ocean into which this mighty river of love is constantly flowing, and so, foolishly, he often tries to direct it to little dolls of human beings. The tremendous love for the child that is in human nature is not for the little doll of a child; if you bestow it blindly and exclusively on the child, you will suffer in consequence.

But through such suffering will come the awakening by which you are sure to find out that the love which is in you, if it is given to any human being, will sooner or later bring pain and sorrow as the result. Our love must, therefore, be given to the Highest One who never dies and never changes, to Him in the ocean of whose love there is neither ebb nor flow.

Love must get to its right destination; it must go unto Him who is really the infinite ocean of love. All rivers flow into the ocean. Even the drop of water coming down from the mountain side cannot stop its course after reaching a brook or a river, however big it may be; at last even that drop somehow does find its way to the ocean.

God is the one goal of all our passions and emotions. If you want to be angry, be angry with Him. Chide your Beloved, chide your Friend.

Whom else can you safely chide? Mortal man will not patiently put up with your anger; there will be a reaction. If you are angry with me, I am sure quickly to react, because I cannot patiently put up with your anger.

Say unto the Beloved, “Why do You not come to me; why do You leave me thus alone?”

Where is there any enjoyment but in Him? What enjoyment can there be in little clods of earth? It is the crystallised essence of infinite enjoyment that we have to seek, and that is in God.

Let all our passions and emotions go up unto Him. They are meant for Him, for if they miss their mark and go lower, they become vile; and when they go straight to the mark, to the Lord, even the lowest of them becomes transfigured. All the energies of the human body and mind, howsoever they may express themselves, have the Lord as their one goal, as their Ekâyana.

All loves and all passions of the human heart must go to God. He is the Beloved. Whom else can this heart love? He is the most beautiful, the most sublime, He is beauty itself, sublimity itself. Who in this universe is more beautiful than He? Who in this universe is more fit to become the husband than He? Who in this universe is fitter to be loved than He? So let Him be the husband, let Him be the Beloved.

*

The world presents to us manifold stages of love. We have first to clear the ground. Upon our view of life the whole theory of love will rest.

To think that this world is the aim and end of life is brutal and degenerating. Any man who starts in life with that idea degenerates himself. He will never rise higher, he will never catch this glimpse from behind, he will always be a slave to the senses. He will struggle for the dollar that will get him a few cakes to eat.

Better die than live that life. Slaves of this world, slaves of the senses, let us rouse ourselves; there is something higher than this sense-life.

Do you think that man, the Infinite Spirit was born to be a slave to his eyes, his nose, and his ears? There is an Infinite, Omniscient Spirit behind that can do everything, break every bond; and that Spirit we are, and we get that power through love. This is the ideal we must remember.

*

The tree receives support and shelter from the hedge that surrounds it when young; but unless the hedge is removed, the growth and strength of that tree will be hindered. Formal worship, as we have seen, is a necessary stage, but gradually by slow growth we outgrow it and come to a higher platform.

When love to God becomes perfect, we think no more of the qualities of God — that He is omnipotent, omnipresent, and all those big adjectives. We do not want anything of God, so we do not care to notice these qualities. Just all we want is love of God. But anthropomorphism still follows us. We cannot get away from our humanity, we cannot jump out of our bodies; so we must love God as we love one another.

There are five steps in human love.

1. The lowest, most commonplace, "peaceful" love, when we look up to our Father for all we want — protection, food, etc.

2. The love which makes us want to serve. Man wants to serve God

as his master, the longing to serve dominating every other feeling; and we are indifferent whether the master is good or bad, kind or unkind.

3. The love of a friend, the love of equals — companions, playmates. Man feels God to be his companion.

4. Motherly love. God is looked upon as a child. In India this is considered a higher love than the foregoing, because it has absolutely no element of fear.

5. The love of husband and wife; love for love's sake — God the perfect, beloved one.

It has been beautifully expressed: "Four eyes meet, a change begins to come into two souls; love comes in the middle between these two souls and makes them one."

When a man has this last and most perfect form of love, then all desires vanish, forms and doctrines and churches drop away, even the desire for freedom (the end and aim of all religions is freedom from birth and death and other things) is given up. The highest love is the love that is sexless, for it is perfect unity that is expressed in the highest love, and sex differentiates bodies.

It is therefore only in spirit that union is possible. The less we have of the physical idea, the more perfect will be our love; at last all physical thought will be forgotten, and the two souls will become one. We love, love always. Love comes and penetrates through the forms and sees beyond.

It has been said, "The lover sees Helen's beauty in an Ethiopian's brow." The Ethiopian is the suggestion and upon that suggestion the man throws his love.

As the oyster throws over the irritants, it finds in its shell, the substance that turns the irritants into beautiful pearls, so man throws out love, and it is always man's highest ideal that he loves, and the highest ideal is always selfless; so man loves love.

God is love, and we love God — or love love. We only see love, love cannot be expressed. "A dumb man eating butter" cannot tell you what butter is like. Butter is butter, and its qualities cannot be expressed to those who have not tasted it. Love for love's sake cannot be expressed to those who have not felt it.

Love may be symbolised by a triangle. The first angle is, love never begs, never asks for anything; the second, love knows no fear; the third and the apex, love for love's sake.

Through the power of love the senses become finer and higher. The perfect love is very rare in human relation, for human love is almost always interdependent and mutual. But God's love is a constant stream, nothing can hurt or disturb it.

When man loves God as his highest ideal, as no beggar, wanting nothing, then is love carried to the extreme of evolution, and it becomes a great power in the universe. It takes a long time to get to these things, and we have to begin by that which is nearest to our nature; some are born to service, some to be mothers in love. Anyhow, the result is with God. We must take advantage of nature.

*

Bhakti-Yoga: teaches how to love, without any ulterior motives, loving God and loving the good because it is good to do so, not for going to heaven, nor to get children, wealth, or anything else. It teaches them that love itself is the highest recompense of love --- that God Himself is love.

It teaches them to pay all kinds of tribute to God as the Creator, the Omnipresent, Omniscient, Almighty Ruler, the Father and the Mother. The highest phrase that can express Him, the highest idea that the human mind can conceive of Him, is that He is the God of Love. Wherever there is love, it is He.

"Wherever there is any love, it is He, the Lord is present there."

Where the husband kisses the wife, He is there in the kiss; where the mother kisses the child, He is there in the kiss; where friends clasp hands, He, the Lord, is present as the God of Love. When a great man loves and wishes to help mankind, He is there giving freely His bounty out of His love to mankind.

Wherever the heart expands, He is there manifested. This is what the Bhakti-Yoga teaches.

*

Thus sang the royal Hebrew sage, thus sang they of India. "O beloved, one kiss of Thy lips! Kissed by Thee, one's thirst for Thee increaseth for ever! All sorrows cease, one forgets the past, present, and future, and only thinks of Thee alone." That is the madness of the lover, when all desires have vanished.

"Who cares for salvation? Who cares to be saved? Who cares to be perfect even? Who cares for freedom?" — says the lover. "I do not want wealth, nor even health; I do not want beauty, I do not want intellect: let me be born again and again, amid all the evils that are in the world; I will not complain, but let me love Thee, and that for love's sake."

That is the madness of love which finds expression in these songs. The highest, most expressive, strongest, and most attractive human love is that between man and woman, and, therefore, that language was used in expressing the deepest devotion. The madness of this human love was the faintest echo of the mad love of the saints.

The true lovers of God want to become mad, inebriated with the love of God, to become "God-intoxicated men". They want to drink of the cup of love which has been prepared by the saints and sages of every religion, who have poured their heart's blood into it, and in which hare been concentrated all the hopes of those who have loved God without seeking reward, who wanted love for itself only.

The reward of love is love, and what a reward it is! It is the only thing that takes off all sorrows, the only cup, by the drinking of which this disease of the world vanishes Man becomes divinely mad and forgets that be is man.

*

Whatever occurs in our life, whether good or bad, is bringing us to Him. One man kills another because of some selfish purpose. But the motive behind is love, whether for himself or for any one else. Whether we do good or evil, the propeller is love. When a tiger kills a buffalo, it is because he or his cubs are hungry.

God is love personified. He is apparent in everything. Everybody is being drawn to Him whether he knows it or not. When a woman loves her husband, she does not understand that it is the divine in her husband that is the great attractive power.

The God of Love is the one thing to be worshipped. So long as we think of Him only as the Creator and Preserver, we can offer Him external worship, but when we get beyond all that and think Him to be Love Incarnate, seeing Him in all things and all things in Him, it is then that supreme Bhakti is attained.

*

Though the love of a mother is in some ways greater, yet the whole world takes the love of man and woman as the type (of the soul's relation to God). No other has such tremendous idealising power. The beloved actually becomes what he is imagined to be. This love transforms its object.

*

A great saint said, using the language of a girl, describing love: "Four eyes met. There were changes in two souls. And now I cannot tell whether he is a man and I am a woman, or he is a woman and I a man. This only I remember, two souls were. Love came, and there was one."

In the highest love, union is only of the spirit. All love of any other kind is quickly evanescent. Only the spiritual lasts, and this grows.

Love sees the Ideal. This is the third angle of the triangle. God has been Cause, Creator, Father. Love is the culmination. The mother regrets that her child is humpbacked, but when she has nursed him for a few days, she loves him and thinks him most beautiful. The lover sees the beauty of Helen in the brow of Ethiopia. We do not commonly realise what happens. The brow of Ethiopia is merely a suggestion: the man sees Helen. His ideal is thrown upon the suggestion and covers it, as the oyster makes sand into a pearl. God is this ideal, through which man may see all.

Hence we come to love love itself. This love cannot be expressed. No words can utter it. We are dumb about it.

The senses become very much heightened in love. Human love, we must remember, is mixed up with attributes. It is dependent, too, on the other's attitude. Indian languages have words to describe this interdependence of love. The lowest love is selfish; it consists in pleasure of being loved. We say in India, "One gives the cheek, the other kisses." Above this is mutual love. But this also ceases mutually. True love is all giving. We do not even want to see the other, or to do anything to express our feeling. It is enough to give. It is almost impossible to love a human being like this, but it is possible to love God.

THE EXTERNAL OF THE MAN

According to us, there are three things in the makeup of man. There is the body, there is the mind, and there is the soul.

First let us consider the body, which is the most external thing about man.

First, see how various are the differences with respect to the body. How many varieties of nose, face, hair, height, complexion, breadth, etc., there are!

The modern ethnologists hold that variety of complexion is due to intermixture of blood. Though the hot or cold climate of the place to a certain extent affects the complexion, no doubt, yet the main cause of its change is heredity. Even in the coldest parts of the world, people with dark complexions are seen, and again in the hottest countries white men are seen to live. The complexion of the aboriginal tribes of Canada, in America, and of the Eskimos of the Northern Polar regions, is not white. While islands, such as Borneo, Celebes, etc., situated in the equatorial regions are peopled by white aborigines.

According to the Hindu Shastras, the three Hindu castes, Brahmana, Kshatriya, and Vaishya, and the several nations outside India, to wit, Cheen, Hun, Darad, Pahlava, Yavana, and Khâsh are all Aryas. This Cheen of our Shastras is not the modern Chinaman. Besides, in those days, the Chinamen did not call themselves Cheen at all. There was a distinct, powerful nation, called Cheen, living in the north-eastern parts of Kashmir, and the Darads lived where are now seen the hill-tribes between India and Afghanistan. Some remnants of the ancient Cheen are yet to be found in very small numbers, and Daradisthan is yet in existence. In the Râjatarangini , the history of Kashmir, references are often made to the supremacy of the powerful Darad-Raj. An ancient tribe of Huns reigned for a long period in the north-western parts of India. The Tibetans now call themselves Hun, but this Hun is perhaps "Hune". The fact is, that the Huns referred to in Manu are not the modern Tibetans, but it is quite probable that the modern Tibetans are the product of a mixture of the ancient Aryan Huns and some other Mogul tribes that came to Tibet from Central Asia. According to Prjevalski and the Duc d' Orleans, the Russian and French travellers, there are still found in some parts of Tibet tribes with faces and eyes of the Aryan type. "Yavana" was the name given to the Greeks. There has been much dispute about the origin of this name. Some say that the name Yavana was first used to designate a tribe of Greeks inhabiting the place called "Ionia", and hence, in the Pâli writs of the Emperor Asoka, the Greeks are named

"Yonas", and afterwards from this "Yona" the Sanskrit word Yavana, was derived. Again, according to some of our Indian antiquarians, the word Yavana does not stand for the Greeks. But all these views are wrong. The original word is Yavana itself; for not only the Hindus but the ancient Egyptians and the Babylonians as well called the Greeks by that name. By the word Pahlava is meant the ancient Parsees, speaking the Pahlavi tongue. Even now, Khash denotes the semi-civilised Aryan tribes living in mountainous regions and in the Himalayas, and the word is still used in this sense. In that sense, the present Europeans are the descendants of the Khash; in other words, those Aryan tribes that were uncivilised in ancient days are all Khash.

In the opinion of modern savants, the Aryans had reddish-white complexion, black or red hair, straight noses, well-drawn eyes, etc.; and the formation of the skull varied a little according to the colour of the hair. Where the complexion is dark, there the change has come to pass owing to the mixture of the pure Aryan blood with black races. They hold that there are still some tribes to the west of the Himalayan borders who are of pure Aryan blood, and that the rest are all of mixed blood; otherwise, how could they be dark? But the European Pundits ought to know by this time that, in the southern parts of India, many children are born with red hair, which after two or three years changes into black, and that in the Himalayas many have red hair and blue or grey eyes.

Let the Pundits fight among themselves; it is the Hindus who have all along called themselves Aryas. Whether of pure or mixed blood, the Hindus are Aryas; there it rests. If the Europeans do not like us, Aryas, because we are dark, let them take another name for themselves — what is that to us?

Whether black or white, it does not matter; but of all the nations of the world, the Hindus are the handsomest and finest in feature. I am not bragging nor saying anything in exaggeration because they belong to my own nationality, but this fact is known all over the world. Where else can one find a higher percentage of fine-featured men and women than in India? Besides, it has to be taken into consideration how much more is required in our country to make us look handsome than in other countries, because our bodies are so much more exposed. In other countries, the attempt is always to make ugly persons appear beautiful under cover of elaborate dresses and clothes.

Of course, in point of health, the Westerners are far superior to us. In the West, men of forty years and women of fifty years are still young. This is, no doubt, because they take good food, dress well and live in a good climate, and above all, the secret is that they do not marry at an early age. Ask those few strong tribes among ourselves and see what their marriageable age is. Ask the hill tribes, such as, the Goorkhas, the Punjabis, the Jats, and the Afridis, what their marriageable age is. Then read your own Shastras — thirty is the age fixed for the Brahmana, twenty-five for the Kshatriya, and twenty for the Vaishya. In point of longevity and physical and mental strength, there is a great difference between the Westerners and ourselves. As soon as we attain to forty, our hope and physical and mental strength are on the decline. While, at that age, full of youthful vigour and hope, they have only made a start.

*

THE NATURE OF THE BODY

The Hindu believes that every soul is a circle whose circumference is nowhere, but whose centre is located in the body, and that death means the change of this centre from body to body. Nor is the soul bound by the conditions of matter. In its very essence it is free, unbounded, holy, pure, and perfect. But somehow or other it finds itself tied down to matter, and thinks of itself as matter.

*

Here I stand and if I shut my eyes, and try to conceive my existence, "I", "I", "I", what is the idea before me? The idea of a body. Am I, then, nothing but a combination of material substances? The Vedas declare, "No". I am a spirit living in a body. I am not the body. The body will die, but I shall not die. Here am I in this body; it will fall, but I shall go on living. I had also a past. The soul was not created, for creation means a combination which means a certain future dissolution. If then the soul was created, it must die. Some are born happy, enjoy perfect health, with beautiful body, mental vigour and all wants supplied. Others are born miserable, some are without hands or feet, others again are idiots and only drag on a wretched existence. Why, if they are all created, why does a just and merciful God create one happy and another unhappy, why is He so partial? Nor would it mend matters in the least to hold that those who are miserable in this life will be happy in a future one. Why should a man be miserable even here in the reign of a just and merciful God?

*

According to the Advaita philosophy, there is only one thing real in the universe, which it calls Brahman; everything else is unreal, manifested and manufactured out of Brahman by the power of Mâyâ. To reach back to that Brahman is our goal. We are, each one of us, that Brahman, that Reality, plus this Maya. If we can get rid of this Maya or ignorance, then we become what we really are. According to this philosophy, each man consists of three parts — the body, the internal organ or the mind, and behind that, what is called the Âtman, the Self. The body is the external coating and the mind is the internal coating of the Atman who is the real perceiver, the real enjoyer, the being in the body who is working the body by means of the internal organ or the mind.

The Âtman is the only existence in the human body which is immaterial. Because it is immaterial, it cannot be a compound, and because it is not a compound, it does not obey the law of cause and effect, and so it is immortal. That which is immortal can have no beginning because everything with a beginning must have an end. It also follows that it must be formless; there cannot be any fond without matter. Everything that has form must have a beginning and an end. We have none of us seen a form which had not a beginning and will not have an end. A form comes out of a combination of force and matter. This chair has a peculiar form, that is to say a certain quantity of matter is acted upon by a certain amount of force and made to assume a particular shape. The shape is the result of a combination of matter and force. The combination cannot be eternal; there must come to every combination a time when it will dissolve. So all forms have a beginning and an end. We know our body will perish; it had a beginning and it will have an end. But the Self having no form, cannot be bound by the law of beginning and end. It is existing from infinite time; just as time is eternal, so is the Self of man eternal. Secondly, it must be all-pervading. It is only form that is conditioned and limited by space; that which is formless cannot be confined in space. So, according to Advaita Vedanta, the Self, the Atman, in you, in me, in every one, is omnipresent. You are as much in the sun now as in this earth, as much in England as in America. But the Self acts through the mind and the body, and where they are, its action is visible.

*

Each work we do, each thought we think, produces an impression, called in Sanskrit Samskâra, upon the mind and the sum total of these impressions becomes the tremendous force which is called "character". The character of a man is what he has created for himself; it is the result of the mental and physical actions that he has done in his life. The sum total of the Samskaras is the force which gives a man the next direction after death. A man dies; the body falls away and goes back to the elements; but the Samskaras remain, adhering to the mind which, being made of fine material, does not dissolve, because the finer the material, the more persistent it is. But the mind also dissolves in the long run, and that is what we are struggling for. In this connection, the best illustration that comes to my mind is that of the whirlwind. Different currents of air coming from different directions meet and at the meeting-point become united and go on rotating; as they rotate, they form a body of dust, drawing in bits of paper, straw, etc., at one place, only to drop them and go on to another, and so go on rotating, raising and forming bodies out of the materials which are before them. Even so the forces, called Prâna in Sanskrit, come together and form the body and the mind out of matter, and move on until the body falls down, when they raise other materials to make another body, and when this falls, another rises, and thus the process goes on. Force cannot travel without matter. So when the body falls down, the mind-stuff remains, Prana in the form of Samskaras acting on it; and then it goes on to another point, raises up another whirl from fresh materials, and begins another motion; and so it travels from place to place until the force is all spent; and then it falls down, ended. So when the mind will end, be broken to pieces entirely, without leaving any Samskara, we shall be entirely free, and until that time we are in bondage; until then the Atman is covered by the whirl of the mind, and imagines it is being taken from place to place. When the whirl falls down, the Atman finds that It is all-pervading. It can go where It likes, is entirely free, and is able to manufacture any number of minds or bodies It likes; but until then It can go only with the whirl. This freedom is the goal towards which we are all moving.

*

All the forces that are working in this body have been produced out of food; we see that every day.

*

No man was ever born who could stop his body one moment from changing. Body is the name of a series of changes. "As in a river the masses of water are changing before you every moment, and new masses are coming, yet taking similar form, so is it with this body." Yet the body must be kept strong and healthy. It is the best instrument we have. Yet the body must be kept strong and healthy. It is the best instrument we have.

*

The misery that we suffer comes from ignorance, from non-discrimination between the real and the unreal. We all take the bad for the good, the dream for the reality. Soul is the only reality, and we have forgotten it. Body is an unreal dream, and we think we are all bodies. This non-discrimination is the cause of misery. It is caused by ignorance. When discrimination comes, it brings strength, and then alone can we avoid all these various ideas of body, heavens, and gods. This ignorance arises through differentiating by species, sign, and place. For instance, take a cow. The cow is differentiated from the dog by species. Even with the cows alone how do we make the distinction between one cow and another? By signs. If two objects are exactly similar, they can be distinguished if they are in different places. When objects are so mixed up that even these differential will not help us, the power of discrimination acquired by the above-mentioned practice will give us the ability to distinguish them. The highest philosophy of the Yogi is based upon this fact, that the Purusha is pure and perfect, and is the only "simple" that exists in this universe. The body and mind are compounds, and yet we are ever identifying ourselves with them This is the great mistake that the distinction has been lost. When this power of discrimination has been attained, man sees that everything in this world, mental and physical, is a compound, and, as such, cannot be the Purusha.

*

Body is the name of a stream of matter continuously changing.

*

God is the material cause of the universe. The body may be changed — may be young or old, strong or weak — but that does not affect the soul at all. It is the same eternal existence, manifesting through the body. Bodies come and go, but the soul does not change. Even so the whole universe is the body of God, and in that sense it is God. But the change in the universe does not affect God. Out of this material He creates the universe, and at the end of a cycle His body becomes finer, it contracts; at the beginning of another cycle it becomes expanded again, and out of it evolve all these different worlds.

*

Get rid of the bondage of body; we have become slaves to it and learnt to hug our chains and love our slavery; so much so that we long to perpetuate it, and go on with "body" "body" for ever. Do not cling to the idea of "body", do not look for a future existence in any way like this one; do not love or want the body, even of those dear to us.

*

There is but one temple — the body. It is the only temple that ever existed. In this body, He resides, the Lord of souls and the King of kings. We do not see that, so we make stone images of Him and build temples over them. Vedanta has been in India always, but India is full of these temples — and not only temples, but also caves containing carved images. "The fool, dwelling on the bank of the Gangâ, digs a well for water!" Such are we! Living in the midst of God — we must go and make images. We project Him in the form of the image, while all the time He exists in the temple of our body. We are lunatics, and this is the great delusion.

*

In this universe there is one continuous substance on every plane of existence. Physically this universe is one: there is no difference between the sun and you. The scientist will tell you it is only a fiction to say the contrary. There is no real difference between the table and me; the table is one point in the mass of matter, and I another point.

Each form represents, as it were, one whirlpool in the infinite ocean of matter, of which not one is constant. Just as in a rushing stream there may be millions of whirlpools, the water in each of which is different every moment, turning round and round for a few seconds, and then passing out, replaced by a fresh quantity, so the whole universe is one constantly changing mass of matter, in which all forms of existence are so many whirlpools. A mass of matter enters into one whirlpool, say a human body, stays there for a period, becomes changed, and goes out into another, say an animal body this time, from which again after a few years, it enters into another whirlpool, called a lump of mineral. It is a constant change. Not one body is constant. There is no such thing as my body, or your body, except in words. Of the one huge mass of matter, one point is called a moon, another a sun, another a man, another the earth, another a plant, another a mineral. Not one is constant, but everything is changing, matter eternally concreting and disintegrating. So it is with the mind. Matter is represented by the ether; when the action of Prana is most subtle, this very ether, in the finer state of vibration, will represent the mind and there it will be still one unbroken mass. If you can simply get to that subtle vibration, you will see and feel that the whole universe is composed of subtle vibrations.

*

It is the want that creates the body. It is the light that has bored the holes, as it were, in your head, called the eyes. If the light had not existed, you would have had no eyes. It is sound that had made the ears. The object of perception existed first, before you made the organ. In a few hundred thousand years or earlier, we may have other organs to perceive electricity and other things. There is no desire for a peaceful mind. Desire will not come unless there is something outside to fulfil it. The outside something just bores a hole in the body, as it were, and tries to get into the mind. So, when the desire will arise to have a peaceful, quiet life, that shall come where everything shall be propitious for the development of the mind — you may take that as my experience. It may come after thousands of lives, but it must come. Hold on to that, the desire. You cannot have the strong desire if its object was not outside for you already.

*

No two persons have the same mind or the same body.

*

Every child born into the world is born with a certain accumulated experience. The idea of independence which possesses us shows there is something in us besides mind and body. The body and mind are dependent. The soul that animates us is an independent factor that creates this wish for freedom.

*

All the forces and forms that we see are combinations. This form before us is a composition of several component parts, and so every force that we see is similarly composite. If you take the scientific idea of force, and call it the sum total, the resultant of several forces, what becomes of your individuality? Everything that is a compound must sooner or later go back to its component parts. Whatever in this universe is the result of the combination of matter or force must sooner or later go back to its components. Whatever is the result of certain causes must die, must be destroyed. It gets broken up, dispersed, and resolved back into its components. Soul is not a force; neither is it thought. It is the manufacturer of thought, but not thought itself; it is the manufacturer of the body, but not the body. Why so? We see that the body cannot be the soul. Why not? Because it is not intelligent. A corpse is not intelligent, nor a piece of meat in a butcher's shop. What do we mean by intelligence? Reactive power.

*

The name of the energy in the universe is Prâna, which is the force residing in these elements. Mind is the great instrument for using the Prana. Mind is material. Behind the mind is Âtman which takes hold of the Prana. Prana is the driving power of the world, and can be seen in every manifestation of life. The body is mortal and the mind is mortal; both, being compounds, must die. Behind all is the Atman which never dies. The Atman is pure intelligence controlling and directing Prana. But the intelligence we see around us is always imperfect.

*

The body is our enemy, and yet is our friend.

*

The body is subject to the law of growth and decay, what grows must of necessity decay.

*

The body must be properly taken care of. The people who torture their flesh are demoniacal.

*

The less the thought of the body, the better. For it is the body that drags us down. It is attachment, identification, which makes us miserable. That is the secret: To think that I am the spirit and not the body, and that the whole of this universe with all its relations, with all its good and all its evil, is but as a series of paintings — scenes on a canvas — of which I am the witness.

*

The organs are the horses, the mind is the rein, the intellect is the charioteer, the soul is the rider, and the body is the chariot. The master of the household, the King, the Self of man, is sitting in this chariot. If the horses are very strong and do not obey the rein, if the charioteer, the intellect, does not know how to control the horses, then the chariot will come to grief. But if the organs, the horses, are well controlled, and if the rein, the mind, is well held in the hands of the charioteer, the intellect, the chariot reaches the goal.

*

The root of evil is in the illusion that we are bodies. This, if any, is the original sin.

*

There are the altars, but here is the greatest of altars, the living, conscious human body, and to worship at this altar is far higher than the worship of any dead symbols.

*

When there is real purification of the body, external and internal, there arises neglect of the body, and the idea of keeping it nice vanishes. A face which others call most beautiful will appear to the Yogi as merely animal, if there is not intelligence behind it. What the world calls a very common face he regards as heavenly, if the spirit shines behind it. This thirst after body is the great bane of human life. So the first sign of the establishment of purity is that you do not care to think you are a body. It is only when purity comes that we get rid of the body idea.

*

We see every day that the cause of our pain or pleasure is always our joining ourselves with the body. If I were perfectly certain that I am not this body, I should take no notice of heat and cold, or anything of the kind. This body is a combination. It is only a fiction to say that I have one body, you another, and the sun another. The whole universe is one ocean of matter, and you are the name of a little particle, and I of another, and the sun of another. We know that this matter is continuously changing. What is forming the sun one day, the next day may form the matter of our bodies.

*

Through ignorance we have joined ourselves with a particular body, and thus opened ourselves to misery. This idea of body is a simple superstition. It is superstition that makes us happy or unhappy. It is superstition caused by ignorance that makes us feel heat and cold, pain and pleasure. It is our business to rise above this superstition, and the Yogi shows us how we can do this. It has been demonstrated that, under certain mental conditions, a man may be burned, yet he will feel no pain. The difficulty is that this sudden upheaval of the mind comes like a whirlwind one minute, and goes away the next. If, however, we gain it through Yoga, we shall permanently attain to the separation of Self from the body.

*

This body is not I.

*

There are several obstructions to the practice of Yoga. The first obstruction is an unhealthy body: if the body is not in a fit state, the practice will be obstructed. Therefore we have to keep the body in good health; we have to take care of what we eat and drink, and what we do. Always use a mental effort, what is usually called "Christian Science," to keep the body strong. That is all — nothing further of the body. We must not forget that health is only a means to an end. If health were the end, we would be like animals; animals rarely become unhealthy.

*

When the forces that hold it together go away, the body must fall.

EDUCATION

You consider a man as educated if only he can pass some examinations and deliver good lectures. The education which does not help the common mass of people to equip themselves for the struggle for life, which does not bring out strength of character, a spirit of philanthropy, and the courage of a lion — is it worth the name?

Real education is that which enables one to stand on one's own legs. The education that you are receiving now in schools and colleges is only making you a race of dyspeptics. You are working like machines merely, and living a jelly-fish existence.

The peasant, the shoemaker, the sweeper, and such other lower classes of India have much greater capacity for work and self-reliance than you. They have been silently working through long ages and producing the entire wealth of the land, without a word of complaint.

Very soon they will get above you in position. Gradually capital is drifting into their hands, and they are not so much troubled with wants as you are. Modern education has changed your fashion, but new avenues of wealth lie yet undiscovered for want of the inventive genius.

You have so long oppressed these forbearing masses; now is the time for their retribution. And you will become extinct in your vain search for employment, making it the be-all and end-all of your life.

*

Coming to great leaders of mankind, we always find that it was the personality of the man that counted. Now, take all the great authors of the past, the great thinkers. Really speaking, how many thoughts have they thought?

Take all the writings that have been left to us by the past leaders of mankind; take each one of their books and appraise them. The real thoughts, new and genuine, that have been thought in this world up to this time, amount to only a handful. Read in their books the thoughts they have left to us.

The authors do not appear to be giants to us, and yet we know that they were great giants in their days. What made them so? Not simply the thoughts they thought, neither the books they wrote, nor the speeches they made, it was something else that is now gone, that is their personality.

As I have already remarked, the personality of the man is two-thirds, and his intellect, his words, are but one-third. It is the real man, the personality of the man, that runs through us. Our actions are but effects. Actions must come when the man is there; the effect is bound to follow the cause.

The ideal of all education, all training, should be this man-making. But, instead of that, we are always trying to polish up the outside. What use in polishing up the outside when there is no inside? The end and aim of all training is to make the man grow. The man who influences, who throws his magic, as it were, upon his fellow-beings, is a dynamo of power, and when that man is ready, he can do anything and everything he likes; that personality put upon anything will make it work.

*

Learning has no place in religion; for the majority learning is a block in the way. A man may have read all the libraries in the world and many not be religious at all, and another, who cannot perhaps write his own name, senses religion and realises it.

The whole of religion is our own inner perception. When I use the words "man-making religion", I do not mean books, nor dogmas, nor theories. I mean the man who has realised, has fully perceived, something of that infinite presence in his own heart.

The man at whose feet I sat all my life — and it is only a few ideas of his that try to teach — could [hardly] write his name at all. All my life I have not seen another man like that, and I have travelled all over the world.

When I think of that man, I feel like a fool, because I want to read books and he never did. He never wanted to lick the plates after other people had eaten. That is why he was his own book. All my life I am repeating what Jack said and John said, and never say anything myself.

Mind you, there is no value in learning. You are all mistaken in learning. The only value of knowledge is in the strengthening, the disciplining, of the mind. By all this eternal swallowing it is a wonder that we are not all dyspeptics.

Let us stop, and burn all the books, and get hold of ourselves and think. You all talk [about] and get distracted over losing your "individuality". You are losing it every moment of your lives by this eternal swallowing.

If any one of you believes what I teach, I will be sorry. I will only be too glad if I can excite in you the power of thinking for yourselves. My ambition is to talk to men and women, not to sheep. By men and women, I mean individuals. You are not little babies to drag all the filthy rags from the street and bind them up into a doll!

"This is a place for learning! That man is placed in the university! He knows all about what Mr. Blank said!" But Mr. Blank said nothing! If I had the choice I would say to the professor, "Get out! You are nobody! " Remember this individualism at any cost! Think wrong if you will, no matter whether you get truth or not. The whole point is to discipline the mind. That truth which you swallow from others will not be yours. You cannot teach truth from my mouth; neither can you learn truth from my mouth. None can teach another. You have to realise truth and work it out for yourself according to your own nature. All must struggle to be individuals — strong, standing on your own feet, thinking your own thoughts, realising your own Self. No use swallowing doctrines others pass on — standing up together like soldiers in jail, sitting down together, all eating the same food, all nodding their heads at the same time. Variation is the sign of life. Sameness is the sign of death.

*

Mere book-learning won't do. We want that education by which character is formed, strength of mind is increased, the intellect is expanded, and by which one can stand on one's own feet.

*

What is education? Is it book-learning? No. Is it diverse knowledge? Not even that. The training by which the current and expression of will are brought under control and become fruitful is called education. Now consider, is that education as a result of which the will, being continuously choked by force through generations, is well-nigh killed out; is that education under whose sway even the old ideas, let alone the new ones, are disappearing one by one; is that education which is slowly making man a machine? It is more blessed, in my opinion, even to go wrong, impelled by one's free will and intelligence than to be good as an automaton.

*

All the wealth of the world cannot help one little Indian village if the people are not taught to help themselves. Our work should be mainly educational , both moral and intellectual.

*

Educate and raise the masses, and thus alone a nation is possible. Our reformers do not see where the wound is, they want to save the nation by marrying the widows; do you think that a nation is saved by the number of husbands its widows get? Nor is our religion to blame, for an idol more or less makes no difference.

The whole defect is here: The real nation who live in cottage have forgotten their manhood, their individuality. Trodden under the foot of the Hindu, Mussulman, or Christian, they have come to think that they are born to be trodden under the foot of everybody who has money enough in his pocket. They are to be given back their lost individuality. They are to be educated.

Whether idols will remain or not, whether widows will have husbands enough or not, whether caste is good or bad, I do not bother myself with such questions. Everyone must work out his own salvation. Our duty is to put the chemicals together, the crystallisation will come through God's laws. Let us put ideas into their heads, and they will do the rest.

Now this means educating the masses. Here are these difficulties. A pauper government cannot, will not, do anything; so no help from that quarter.

*

Education is not filling the mind with a lot of facts. Perfecting the instrument and getting complete mastery of my own mind [is the ideal of education]. Education is the manifestation of the perfection already in man.

*

Life is a series of fights and disillusionments. The secret of life is not enjoyment, but education through experience. But, alas, we are called off the moment we begin really to learn. That seems to be a potent argument for a future existence. Everywhere it is better to have a whirlwind come over the work. That clears the atmosphere and gives us a true insight into the nature of things. It is begun anew, but on adamantine foundations.

*

Even the most educated people of other countries turn up their noses at an angle of forty-five degrees and call our religion idolatry. I have seen that; and they never stopped to think what a mass of superstition there was in their own heads. It is still so everywhere, this tremendous sectarianism, the low narrowness of the mind. The thing which a man has is the only thing worth having; the only life worth living is his own little life of dollar-worship and mammon-worship; the only little possession worth having is his own property, and nothing else. If he can manufacture a little clay nonsense or invent a machine, that is to be admired beyond the greatest possessions. That is the case over the whole world in spite of education and learning. But education has yet to be in the world, and civilisation — civilisation has begun nowhere yet. Ninety-nine decimal nine per cent of the human race are more or less savages even now. We may read of these things in books, and we hear of toleration in religion and all that, but very little of it is there yet in the world; take my experience for that. Ninety-nine per cent do not even think of it. There is tremendous religious persecution yet in every country in which I have been, and the same old objections are raised against learning anything new.

*

How can there be any progress of the country without the spread of education, the dawning of knowledge?

*

If the mountain does not come to Mohammed, Mohammed must go to the mountain. If the poor cannot come to education, education must reach them at the plough, in the factory, everywhere. If the poor boy cannot come to education, education must go to him.

*

On one side, new India is saying, "If we only adopt Western ideas, Western language, Western food, Western dress, and Western manners, we shall be as strong and powerful as the Western nations"; on the other, old India is saying, "Fools! By imitation, other's ideas never become one's own; nothing, unless earned, is your own. Does the ass in the lion's skin become the lion?"

On one side, new India is saving, "What the Western nations do is surely good, otherwise how did they become so great?" On the other side, old India is saying, "The flash of lightning is intensely bright, but only for a moment; look out, boys, it is dazzling your eyes. Beware! "

Have we not then to learn anything from the West? Must we not needs try and exert ourselves for better things? Are we perfect? Is our society entirely spotless, without any flaw. There are many things to learn, he must struggle for new and higher things till we die — struggle is the end of human life. Shri Ramakrishna used to say, "As long as I live, so long do I learn." That man or that society which has nothing to learn is already in the jaws of death. Yes, learn we must many things from the West: but there are fears as well.

*

I am a man of action. Simply advice upon advice is being given —

this one says this, that one says that; again that man threatens, and this one frightens! This life is not, in my view, such a sweet thing that I would long to live through so much care and caution and fear. Money, life, friends, and relatives, and the love of men and myself — if one wants to enter into work fully assured beforehand of all these — if one has to be so much ridden with fear, then one will get just what Gurudeva used to say, "The crow thinks itself very clever but . . ." (The crow thinks itself very clever, but it cannot help eating filth.) — well, he will get that. After all, what is the purpose behind all these — money and wealth, Maths and institutions, preaching and lecturing? There is only one purpose in the whole of life — education. Otherwise what is the use of men and women, land and wealth?

*

You cannot teach a child any more than you can grow a plant. All you can do is on the negative side—you can only help. It is a manifestation from within; it develops its own nature—you can only take away obstructions.

*

CONCENTRATION

To me the very essence of education is concentration of mind, not the collecting of facts. If I had to do my education over again, and had any voice in the matter, I would not study facts at all. I would develop the power of concentration and detachment, and then with a perfect instrument I could collect facts at will. Side by side, in the child, should be developed the power of concentration and detachment.

*

All knowledge that we have, either of the external or internal world, is obtained through only one method — by the concentration of the mind. No knowledge can be had of any science unless we can concentrate our minds upon the subject. The astronomer concentrates his mind through the telescope and so on. If you want to study your own mind, it will be the same process. You will have to concentrate your mind and turn it back upon itself. The difference in this world between mind and mind is simply the fact of concentration. One, more concentrated than the other, gets more knowledge.

*

Concentration is the essence of all knowledge, nothing can be done without it. Ninety per cent of thought force is wasted by the ordinary human being, and therefore he is constantly committing blunders; the trained man or mind never makes a mistake. Concentration is restraining the mind into smaller and smaller limits.

When the mind is concentrated and turned backward on itself, all within us will be our servants, not our masters. The Greeks applied their concentration to the external world, and the result was perfection in art, literature, etc. The Hindu concentrated on the internal world, upon the unseen realms in the Self, and developed the science of Yoga.

Yoga is controlling the senses, will and mind. The benefit of its study is that we learn to control instead of being controlled.

Mind seems to be layer on layer. Our real goal is to cross all these intervening strata of our being and find God. The end and aim of Yoga is to realise God.

To do this we must go beyond relative knowledge, go beyond the sense-world. The world is awake to the senses, the children of the Lord are asleep on that plane. The world is asleep to the Eternal, the children of the Lord are awake in that realm. These are the sons of God.

There is but one way to control the senses — to see Him who is the Reality in the universe. Then and only then can we really conquer our senses.

*

The more this power of concentration, the more knowledge is acquired, because this is the one and only method of acquiring knowledge. Even the lowest shoeblack, if he gives more concentration, will black shoes better; the cook with concentration will cook a meal all the better. In making money, or in worshipping God, or in doing anything, the stronger the power of concentration, the better will that thing be done. This is the one call, the one knock, which opens the gates of nature, and lets out floods of light. This, the power of concentration, is the only key to the treasure-house of knowledge.

*

How are we to know that the mind has become concentrated? Because the idea of time will vanish. The more time passes unnoticed the more concentrated we are. In common life we see that when we are interested in a book we do not note the time at all; and when we leave the book, we are often surprised to find how many hours have passed. All time will have the tendency to come and stand in the one present. So the definition is given: When the past and present come and stand in one, the mind is said to be concentrated.

*

We read many books, but that does not bring us knowledge. We may read all the Bibles in the world, but that will not give us religion. Theoretical religion is easy enough to get, any one may get that. What we want is practical religion.

The Christian idea of a practical religion is in doing good works — worldly utility.

What good is utility? Judged from a utilitarian standpoint, religion is a failure. Every hospital is a prayer that more people may come there. What is meant by charity? Charity is not fundamental. It is really helping on the misery of the world, not eradicating it. One looks for name and fame and covers his efforts to obtain them with the enamel of charity and good works. He is working for himself under the pretext of working for others. Every so-called charity is an encouragement of the very evil it claims to operate against.

Men and women go to balls and dance all night in honour of some hospital or other charitable institution then go home, behave like beasts, and bring devils into the world to fill jails, insane asylums, and hospitals. So it goes on, and it is called good works — building hospital etc. The ideal of good works is to lessen, or eradicate, the misery of the world. The Yogi says, all misery comes from not being able to control the mind. The Yogi's ideal is freedom from nature. Conquest of nature is his standard of work. The Yogi says that all power is in the soul, and by the controlling of the mind and body one conquers nature by the power of the soul.

*

How has all the knowledge in the world been gained but by the concentration of the powers of the mind? The world is ready to give up its secrets if we only know how to knock, how to give it the necessary blow. The strength and force of the blow come through concentration. There is no limit to the power of the human mind. The more concentrated it is, the more power is brought to bear on one point; that is the secret.

*

It is impossible to find God outside of ourselves. Our own souls contribute all the divinity that is outside of us. We are the greatest temple. The objectification is only a faint imitation of what we see within ourselves.

Concentration of the powers of the mind is our only instrument to help us see God. If you know one soul (your own), you know all souls, past, present, and to come. The will concentrates the mind, certain things excite and control this will, such as reason, love, devotion, breathing. The concentrated mind is a lamp that shows us every corner of the soul.

*

The main difference between men and the animals is the difference in their power of concentration. All success in any line of work is the result of this. Everybody knows something about concentration. We see its results every day. High achievements in art, music, etc., are the results of concentration. An animal has very little power of concentration. Those who have trained animals find much difficulty in the fact that the animal is constantly forgetting what is told him. He cannot concentrate his mind long upon anything at a time. Herein is the difference between man and the animals — man has the greater power of concentration. The difference in heir power of concentration also constitutes the difference between man and man. Compare the lowest with the highest man. The difference is in the degree of concentration. This is the only difference.

Everybody's mind becomes concentrated at times. We all concentrate upon those things we love, and we love those things upon which we concentrate our minds. What mother is there that does not love the face of her homeliest child? That face is to her the most beautiful in the world. She loves it because she concentrates her mind on it; and if every one could concentrate his mind on that same face, every one would love it. It would be to all the most beautiful face. We all concentrate our minds upon those things we love. When we hear beautiful music, our minds become fastened upon it, and we cannot take them away. Those who concentrate their minds upon what you call classical music do not like common music, and vice versa. Music in which the notes follow each other in rapid succession holds the mind readily. A child loves lively music, because the rapidity of the notes gives the mind no chance to wander. A man who likes common music dislikes classical music, because it is more complicated and requires a greater degree of concentration to follow it.

The great trouble with such concentrations is that we do not control the mind; it controls us. Something outside of ourselves, as it were, draws the mind into it and holds it as long as it chooses. We hear melodious tones or see a beautiful painting, and the mind is held fast! We cannot take it away.

If I speak to you well upon a subject you like, your mind becomes concentrated upon what I am saying. I draw your mind away from yourself and hold it upon the subject in spite of yourself. Thus our attention is held, our minds are concentrated upon various things, in spite of ourselves. We cannot help it.

Now the question is: Can this concentration be developed, and can we become masters of it? The Yogis say, yes. The Yogis say that we can get perfect control of the mind. On the ethical side there is danger in the development of the power of concentration — the danger of concentrating the mind upon an object and then being unable to detach it at will. This state causes great suffering. Almost all our suffering is caused by our not having the power of detachment. So along with the development of concentration we must develop the power of detachment. We must learn not only to attach the mind to one thing exclusively, but also to detach it at a moment's notice and place it upon something else. These two should be developed together to make it safe.

This is the systematic development of the mind. To me the very essence of education is concentration of mind, not the collecting of facts. If I had to do my education over again, and had any voice in the matter, I would not study facts at all. I would develop the power of concentration and detachment, and then with a perfect instrument I could collect facts at will. Side by side, in the child, should be developed the power of concentration and detachment.

*

In the lives of all great men, past and present, we find this tremendous power of concentration. Those are men of genius, you say. The science of Yoga tells us that we are all geniuses if we try hard to be. Some will come into this life better fitted and will do it quicker perhaps. We can all do the same. The same power is in everyone. The subject of the present lecture is how to concentrate the mind in order to study the mind itself. Yogis have laid down certain rules and this night I am going to give you a sketch of some of these rules.

PRACTICE OF CONCENTRATION

Concentration, of course, comes from various sources. Through the senses you can get concentration. Some get it when they hear beautiful music, others when they see beautiful scenery. Some get concentrated by lying upon beds of spikes, sharp iron spikes, others by sitting upon sharp pebbles. These are extraordinary cases [using] most unscientific procedure. Scientific procedure is gradually training the mind.

One gets concentrated by holding his arm up. Torture gives him the concentration he wants. But all these are extraordinary.

Universal methods have been organised according to different philosophers. Some say the state we want to attain is superconsciousness of the mind — going beyond the limitations the body has made for us. The value of ethics to the Yogi lies in that it makes the mind pure. The purer the mind, the easier it is to control it. The mind takes every thought that rises and works it out. The grosser the mind, the more difficult [it is] to control [it]. The immoral man will never be able to concentrate his mind to study psychology. He may get a little control as he begins, get a little power of hearing. and even those powers will go from him. The difficulty is that if you study closely, you see how [the] extraordinary power arrived at was not attained by regular scientific training. The men who, by the power of magic, control serpents will be killed by serpents. The man who attains any extraordinary powers will in the long run succumb to those powers. There are millions [who] receive power through all sorts of ways in India. The vast majority of them die raving lunatics. Quite a number commit suicide, the mind [being] unbalanced.

The study must be put on the safe side: scientific, slow, peaceful. The first requisite is to be moral. Such a man wants the gods to come down, and they will come down and manifest themselves to him. That is our psychology and philosophy in essence, [to be] perfectly moral. Just think what that means! No injury, perfect purity, perfect austerity! These are absolutely necessary. Just think, if a man can attain all these in perfection! What more do you want? If he is free from all enmity towards any being, all animals will give up their enmity [in his presence]. The Yogis lay down very strict laws so that one cannot pass off for a charitable man without being charitable.

*

The law of laws is concentration. First, concentrate all the nerve energies and all power lodged in the cells of the body into one force and direct it at will. Then bring the mind, which is thinner matter, into one centre. The mind has layer after layer. When the nerve force concentrated is made to pass through the spinal column, one layer of the mind is open. When it is concentrated in one bone [plexus, or "lotus"], another part of the world is open. So from world to world it goes until it touches the pineal gland in the centre of the brain. This is the seat of conservation of potential energy, the source of both activity and passivity.

*

No one method can suit all. Different methods are not steps necessary to be taken one after another. Ceremonials are the lowest form; next God external, and after that God internal. In some cases gradation may be needed, but in many only one way is required. It would be the height of folly to say to everyone, "You must pass through Karma and Bhakti before you can reach Jnana."

Stick to your reason until you reach something higher; and you will know it to be higher, because it will not jar with reason. The stage beyond consciousness is inspiration (Samâdhi); but never mistake hysterical trances for the real thing.

It is a terrible thing to claim this inspiration falsely, to mistake instinct for inspiration. There is no external test for inspiration, we know it ourselves; our guardian against mistake is negative — the voice of reason. All religion is going beyond reason, but reason is the only guide to get there.

Instinct is like ice, reason is the water, and inspiration is the subtlest form or vapour; one follows the other. Everywhere is this eternal sequence — unconsciousness, consciousness, intelligence — matter, body, mind — and to us it seems as if the chain began with the particular link we first lay hold of. Arguments on both sides are of equal weight, and both are true. We must reach beyond both, to where there is neither the one nor the other. These successions are all Maya.

*

t is easy to concentrate the mind on external things, the mind naturally goes outwards; but not so in the case of religion, or psychology, or metaphysics, where the subject and the object, are one. The object is internal, the mind itself is the object, and it is necessary to study the mind itself — mind studying mind. We know that there is the power of the mind called reflection. I am talking to you. At the same time I am standing aside, as it were, a second person, and knowing and hearing what I am talking. You work and think at the same time, while a portion of your mind stands by and sees what you are thinking. The powers of the mind should be concentrated and turned back upon itself, and as the darkest places reveal their secrets before the penetrating rays of the sun, so will this concentrated mind penetrate its own innermost secrets. Thus will we come to the basis of belief, the real genuine religion. We will perceive for ourselves whether we have souls, whether life is of five minutes or of eternity, whether there is a God in the universe or more. It will all be revealed to us. This is what Raja-Yoga proposes to teach. The goal of all its teaching is how to concentrate the minds, then, how to discover the innermost recesses of our own minds, then, how to generalise their contents and form our own conclusions from them. It, therefore, never asks the question what our religion is, whether we are Deists or Atheists, whether Christians, Jews, or Buddhists. We are human beings; that is sufficient. Every human being has the right and the power to seek for religion. Every human being has the right to ask the reason, why, and to have his question answered by himself, if he only takes the trouble.

So far, then, we see that in the study of this Raja-Yoga no faith or belief is necessary. Believe nothing until you find it out for yourself; that is what it teaches us.

*

Do you mean to say that the facts of our awakened state require any dreams or imaginings to prove them? Certainly not. This study of Raja-Yoga takes a long time and constant practice. A part of this practice is physical, but in the main it is mental. As we proceed we shall find how intimately the mind is connected with the body. If we believe that the mind is simply a finer part of the body, and that mind acts upon the body, then it stands to reason that the body must react upon the mind. If the body is sick, the mind becomes sick also. If the body is healthy, the mind remains healthy and strong. When one is angry, the mind becomes disturbed. Similarly when the mind is disturbed, the body also becomes disturbed. With the majority of mankind the mind is greatly under the control of the body, their mind being very little developed. The vast mass of humanity is very little removed from the animals. Not only so, but in many instances, the power of control in them is little higher than that of the lower animals. We have very little command of our minds. Therefore to bring that command about, to get that control over body and mind, we must take certain physical helps. When the body is sufficiently controlled, we can attempt the manipulation of the mind. By manipulating the mind, we shall be able to bring it under our control, make it work as we like, and compel it to concentrate its powers as we desire.

MAN MAKING EDUCATION

(Conversation with Priya Nath Sen)

Q. Why, what is the defect in the present university system?

Swamiji: It is almost wholly one of defects. Why, it is nothing but a perfect machine for turning out clerks. I would even thank my stars if that were all. But no! See how men are becoming destitute of Shraddhâ and faith. They assert that the Gita is only an interpolation, and that the Vedas are but rustic songs! They like to master every detail concerning things and nations outside of India, but if you ask them, they do not know even the names of their own forefathers up to the seventh generation, not to speak of the fourteenth!

Q. But what does that matter? What if they do not know the names of their forefathers?

Swamiji: Don't think so. A nation that has no history of its own has nothing in this world. Do you believe that one who has such faith and pride as to feel, "I come of noble descent", can ever turn out to be bad? How could that be? That faith in himself would curb his actions and feelings, so much so that he would rather die than commit wrong. So a national history keeps a nation well-restrained and does not allow it to sink so low. Oh, I know you will say, "But we have not such a history!" No, there is not any, according to those who think like you. Neither is there any, according to your big university scholars; and so also think those who, having travelled through the West in one great rush, come back dressed in European style and assert, "We have nothing, we are barbarians." Of course, we have no history exactly like that of other countries. Suppose we take rice, and the Englishmen do not. Would you for that reason imagine that they all die of starvation, and are going to be exterminated? They live quite well on what they can easily procure or produce in their own country and what is suited to them. Similarly, we have our own history exactly as it ought to have been for us. Will that history be made extinct by shutting your eyes and crying, "Alas! we have no history!" Those who have eyes to see, find a luminous history there, and on the strength of that they know the nation is still alive. But that history has to be rewritten. It should be restated and suited to the understanding and ways of thinking which our men have acquired in the present age through Western education.

Q. How has that to be done?

Swamiji: That is too big a subject for a talk now. However, to bring that about, the old institution of "living with the Guru" and similar systems of imparting education are needed. What we want are Western science coupled with Vedanta, Brahmacharya as the guiding motto, and also Shraddhâ and faith in one's own self. Another thing that we want is the abolition of that system which aims at educating our boys in the same manner as that of the man who battered his ass, being advised that it could thereby be turned into a horse.

Q. What do you mean by that?

Swamiji: You see, no one can teach anybody. The teacher spoils everything by thinking that he is teaching. Thus Vedanta says that within man is all knowledge—even in a boy it is so—and it requires only an awakening, and that much is the work of a teacher. We have to do only so much for the boys that they may learn to apply their own intellect to the proper use of their hands, legs, ears, eyes, etc., and finally everything will become easy. But the root is religion. Religion is as the rice, and everything else, like the curries. Taking only curries causes indigestion, and so is the case with taking rice alone. Our pedagogues are making parrots of our boys and ruining their brains by cramming a lot of subjects into them. Looking from one standpoint, you should rather be grateful to the Viceroy for his proposal of reforming the university system, which means practically abolishing higher education; the country will, at least, feel some relief by having breathing time. Goodness gracious! What a fuss and fury about graduating, and after a few days all cools down! And after all that, what is it they learn but that what religion and customs we have are all bad, and what the Westerners have are all good! At last, they cannot keep the wolf from the door! What does it matter if this higher education remains or goes? It would be better if the people got a little technical education, so that they might find work and earn their bread, instead of dawdling about and crying for service.

*

If I can get some unmarried graduates, I may try to send them over to Japan and make arrangements for their technical education there, so that when they come back, they may turn their knowledge to the best account for India. What a good thing that would be!

In my opinion, if all our rich and educated men once go and see Japan, their eyes will be opened. There, in Japan, you find a fine assimilation of knowledge, and not its indigestion, as we have here.

They have taken everything from the Europeans, but they remain Japanese all the same, and have not turned European; while in our country, the terrible mania of becoming Westernised has seized upon us like a plague.

*

What we need, you know, is to study, independent of foreign control, different branches of the knowledge that is our own, and with it the English language and Western science; we need technical education and all else that may develop industries So that men, instead of seeking for service, may earn enough to provide for themselves, and save something against a rainy day.

DISADVANTAGE OF CURRENT EDUCATION SYSTEM

"The education that you are getting now has some good points, but it has a tremendous disadvantage which is so great that the good things are all weighed down. In the first place it is not a man-making education, it is merely and entirely a negative education. A negative education or any training that is based on negation, is worse than death. The child is taken to school, and the first thing he learns is that his father is a fool, the second thing that his grandfather is a lunatic, the third thing that all his teachers are hypocrites, the fourth that all the sacred books are lies! By the time he is sixteen he is a mass of negation, lifeless and boneless. And the result is that fifty years of such education has not produced one original man in the three Presidencies. Every man of originality that has been produced has been educated elsewhere, and not in this country, or they have gone to the old universities once more to cleanse themselves of superstitions. Education is not the amount of information that is put into your brain and runs riot there, undigested, all your life. We must have life-building, man-making, character-making assimilation of ideas. If you have assimilated five ideas and made them your life and character, you have more education than any man who has got by heart a whole library यथा खरश्चन्दनभारवाही भारस्य वेत्ता न तु चन्दनस्य। — "The ass carrying its load of sandalwood knows only the weight and not the value of the sandalwood." If education is identical with information, the libraries are the greatest sages in the world, and encyclopaedias are the Rishis. The ideal, therefore, is that we must have the whole education of our country, spiritual and secular, in our own hands, and it must be on national lines, through national methods as far as practical."

EDUCATION AND PERFECTION

Religion is the manifestation of the Divinity already in man. Therefore, the only duty of the teacher in both cases is to remove all obstructions from the way. Hands off! as I always say, and everything will be right. That is, our duty is to clear the way. The Lord does the rest.

*

The child is taken to school, and the first thing he learns is that his father is a fool, the second thing that his grandfather is a lunatic, the third thing that all his teachers are hypocrites, the fourth that all the sacred books are lies! By the time he is sixteen he is a mass of negation, lifeless and boneless. And the result is that fifty years of such education has not produced one original man in the three Presidencies.

*

We have wept long enough. No more weeping, but stand on your feet and be men. It is a man-making religion that we want. It is man-making theories that we want. It is man-making education all roundthat we want.

*

In the first place it is not a man-making education, it is merely and entirely a negative education. A negative education or any training that is based on negation, is worse than death.

*

What is education? Is it book-learning? No. Is it diverse knowledge? Not even that. The training by which the current and expression of will are brought under control and become fruitful is called education. Now consider, is that education as a result of which the will, being continuously choked by force through generations, is well-nigh killed out; is that education under whose sway even the old ideas, let alone the new ones, are disappearing one by one; is that education which is slowly making man a machine? It is more blessed, in my opinion, even to go wrong, impelled by one's free will and intelligence than to be good as an automaton. Again, can that be called society which is formed by an aggregate of men who are like lumps of clay, like lifeless machines, like heaped up pebbles? How can such society fare well? Were good possible, then instead of being slaves for hundreds of years, we would have been the greatest nation on earth, and this soil of India, instead of being a mine of stupidity, would have been the eternal fountain-head of learning.

*

All perfection is there already in the soul. But this perfection has been covered up by nature; layer after layer of nature is covering this purity of the soul.

*

Every individual has in himself perfection. It lies within the dark recesses of his physical being.

*

"Children of immortal bliss" — what a sweet, what a hopeful name! Allow me to call you, brethren, by that sweet name — heirs of immortal bliss — yea, the Hindu refuses to call you sinners. Ye are the Children of God, the sharers of immortal bliss, holy and perfect beings. Ye divinities on earth — sinners! It is a sin to call a man so; it is a standing libel on human nature. Come up, O lions, and shake off the delusion that you are sheep; you are souls immortal, spirits free, blest and eternal; ye are not matter, ye are not bodies; matter is your servant, not you the servant of matter.

*

Perfection is man's nature, only it is barred in and prevented from taking its proper course. Exactly here education should work to remove the barrier, the obstacle, the cloud, so that one becomes able to realise his perfect real nature.

*

The one who does not have faith in himself (his divine nature) is an atheist. Thus, education has the responsibility to introduce man/child with his divinity.

SANSKRIT EDUCATION

My idea is first of all to bring out the gems of spirituality that are stored up in our books and in the possession of a few only, hidden, as it were, in monasteries and in forests — to bring them out; to bring the knowledge out of them, not only from the hands where it is hidden, but from the still more inaccessible chest, the language in which it is preserved, the incrustation of centuries of Sanskrit words. In one word, I want to make them popular. I want to bring out these ideas and let them be the common property of all, of every man in India, whether he knows the Sanskrit language or not. The great difficulty in the way is the Sanskrit language — the glorious language of ours; and this difficulty cannot be removed until — if it is possible — the whole of our nation are good Sanskrit scholars. You will understand the difficulty when I tell you that I have been studying this language all my life, and yet every new book is new to me. How much more difficult would it then be for people who never had time to study the language thoroughly! Therefore the ideas must be taught in the language of the people; at the same time, Sanskrit education must go on along with it, because the very sound of Sanskrit words gives a prestige and a power and a strength to the race. The attempts of the great Ramanuja and of Chaitanya and of Kabir to raise the lower classes of India show that marvellous results were attained during the lifetime of those great prophets; yet the later failures have to be explained, and cause shown why the effect of their teachings stopped almost within a century of the passing away of these great Masters. The secret is here. They raised the lower classes; they had all the wish that these should come up, but they did not apply their energies to the spreading of the Sanskrit language among the masses. Even the great Buddha made one false step when he stopped the Sanskrit language from being studied by the masses. He wanted rapid and immediate results, and translated and preached in the language of the day, Pâli. That was grand; he spoke in the language of the people, and the people understood him. That was great; it spread the ideas quickly and made them reach far and wide. But along with that, Sanskrit ought to have spread. Knowledge came, but the prestige was not there, culture was not there. It is culture that withstands shocks, not a simple mass of knowledge. You can put a mass of knowledge into the world, but that will not do it much good. There must come culture into the blood. We all know in modern times of nations which have masses of knowledge, but what of them? They are like tigers, they are like savages, because culture is not there. Knowledge is only skin-deep, as civilisation is, and a little scratch brings out the old savage. Such things happen; this is the danger. Teach the masses in the vernaculars, give them ideas; they will get information, but something more is necessary; give them culture. Until you give them that, there can be no permanence in the raised condition of the masses. There will be another caste created, having the advantage of the Sanskrit language, which will quickly get above the rest and rule them all the same. The only safety, I tell you men who belong to the lower castes, the only way to raise your condition is to study Sanskrit, and this fighting and writing and frothing against the higher castes is in vain, it does no good, and it creates fight and quarrel, and this race, unfortunately already divided, is going to be divided more and more. The only way to bring about the levelling of caste is to appropriate the culture, the education which is the strength of the higher castes. That done, you have what you want.

EDUCATION IS THE SOLUTION

From the day when education and culture etc. began to spread gradually from patricians to plebeians, grew the distinction between the modern civilisation as of Western countries, and the ancient civilisation as of India, Egypt, Rome, etc. I see it before my eyes, a nation is advanced in proportion as education and intelligence spread among the masses.

The chief cause of India's ruin has been the monopolising of the whole education and intelligence of the land, by dint of pride and royal authority, among a handful of men. If we are to rise again, we shall have to do it in the same way, i.e. by spreading education among the masses.

A great fuss has been made for half a century about social reform. Travelling through various places of India these last ten years, I observed the country full of social reform associations. But I did not find one association for them by sucking whose blood the people known as "gentlemen" have become and continue to be gentlemen!

How many sepoys were brought by the Mussulmans? How many Englishmen are there? Where, except in India, can be had millions of men who will cut the throats of their own fathers and brothers for six rupees? Sixty millions of Mussulmans in seven hundred years of Mohammedan rule, and two millions of Christians in one hundred years of Christian rule — what makes it so?

Why has originality entirely forsaken the country? Why are our deft-fingered artisans daily becoming extinct, unable to compete with the Europeans? By what power again has the German labourer succeeded in shaking the many-century-grounded firm footing of the English labourer?

*

Education, education, education alone! Travelling through many cities of Europe and observing in them the comforts and education of even the poor people, there was brought to my mind the state of our own poor people, and I used to shed tears.

What made the difference? Education was the answer I got.

Through education comes faith in one's own Self, and through faith in one's own Self the inherent Brahman is waking up in them, while the Brahman in us is gradually becoming dormant. In New York I used to observe the Irish colonists come — downtrodden, haggard-looking, destitute of all possessions at home, penniless, and wooden-headed — with their only belongings, a stick and a bundle of rags hanging at the end of it, fright in their steps, alarm in their eyes.

A different spectacle in six months — the man walks upright, his attire is changed! In his eyes and steps there is no more sign of fright. What is the cause?

Our Vedanta says that that Irishman was kept surrounded by contempt in his own country — the whole of nature was telling him with one voice, "Pat, you have no more hope, you are born a slave and will remain so."

Having been thus told from his birth, Pat believed in it and hypnotised himself that he was very low, and the Brahman in him shrank away. While no sooner had he landed in America than he heard the shout going up on all sides, "Pat, you are a man as we are. It is man who has done all, a man like you and me can do everything: have courage!"

Pat raised his head and saw that it was so, the Brahman within woke up. Nature herself spoke, as it were, "Arise, awake, and stop not till the goal is reached" (Katha Upanishad, I. ii. 4.)

*

Likewise the education that our boys receive is very negative. The schoolboy learns nothing, but has everything of his own broken down — want of Shraddhâ is the result. The Shraddha which is the keynote of the Veda and the Vedanta — the Shraddha which emboldened Nachiketâ to face Yama and question him, through which Shraddha this world moves the annihilation of that Shraddha! — "The ignorant, the man devoid of Shraddha, the doubting self runs to ruin."

Therefore are we so near destruction. The remedy now is the spread of education.

*

All other kinds of knowledge are but non-knowledge in comparison with Self-knowledge.

By Self-knowledge, I do not mean thereby, matted hair, staff, Kamandalu, and mountain caves which the word suggests. What do I mean then? Cannot the knowledge, by which is attained even freedom from the bondage of worldly existence, bring ordinary material prosperity? Certainly it can.

Freedom, dispassion, renunciation all these are the very highest ideals, but—"Even a little of this Dharma saves one from the great fear (of birth and death)."

*

Secondly, along with this, education has to be imparted.

That is easy to say, but how to reduce it into practice? There are thousands of unselfish, kind-hearted men in our country who has renounced everything. In the same way as they travel about and give religious instructions without any remuneration, so at least half of them can be trained as teachers or bearers of such education as we need most.

For that, we want first of all a centre in the capital of each Presidency, from whence to spread slowly throughout the whole of India. Two centres have recently been started in Madras and Calcutta; there is hope of more soon.

Then, the greater part of the education to the poor should be given orally, time is not yet ripe for schools. Gradually in these main centres will be taught agriculture, industry, etc., and workshops will be established for the furtherance of arts. To sell the manufactures of those workshops in Europe and America, associations will be started like those already in existence.

It will be necessary to start centres for women, exactly like those for men. But you are aware how difficult that is in this country.

Again, "The snake which bites must take out its own poison" — and that this is going to be is my firm conviction; the money required for these works would have to come from the West. And for that reason, our religion should be preached in Europe and America.

*

We have had a negative education all along from our boyhood. We have only learnt that we are nobodies. Seldom are we given to understand that great men were ever born in our country. Nothing positive has been taught to us. We do not even know how to use our hands and feet!

We master all the facts and figures concerning the ancestors of the English, but we are sadly unmindful about our own. We have learnt only weakness. Being a conquered race, we have brought ourselves to believe that we are weak and have no independence in anything.

The faith in our own selves must be reawakened, and, then only, all the problems which face our country will gradually be solved by ourselves.

TRUTH

MEDITATING ON THE ATMAN

As the tortoise tucks its feet and head inside the shell, and you may kill it and break it in pieces, and yet it will not come out, even so the character of that man who has control over his motives and organs is unchangeably established. He controls his own inner forces, and nothing can draw them out against his will.

By this continuous reflex of good thoughts, good impressions moving over the surface of the mind, the tendency for doing good becomes strong. And as the result we feel able to control the Indriyas (the sense-organs, the nerve-centres).

Thus alone will character be established, then alone a man gets to truth. Such a man is safe for ever; he cannot do any evil. You may place him in any company, there will be no danger for him.

*

If I teach you that your nature is evil, that you should go home and sit in sackcloth and ashes and weep your lives out because you took certain false steps, it will not help you, but will weaken you all the more, and I shall be showing you the road to more evil than good. If this room is full of darkness for thousands of years and you come in and begin to weep and wail, "Oh the darkness", will the darkness vanish? Strike a match and light comes in a moment.

What good will it do you to think all your lives, "Oh, I have done evil, I have made many mistakes"? It requires no ghost to tell us that.

Bring in the light and the evil goes in a moment. Build up your character, and manifest your real nature, the Effulgent, the Resplendent, the Ever-Pure, and call It up in everyone that you see.

I wish that everyone of us had come to such a state that even in the vilest of human beings we could see the Real Self within, and instead of condemning them, say, "Rise thou effulgent one, rise thou who art always pure, rise thou birthless and deathless, rise almighty, and manifest thy true nature. These little manifestations do not befit thee."

This is the highest prayer that the Advaita teaches. This is the one prayer, to remember our true nature, the God who is always within us, thinking of it always as infinite, almighty, ever-good, ever-beneficent, selfless, bereft of all limitations.

And because that nature is selfless, it is strong and fearless; for only to selfishness comes fear. He who has nothing to desire for himself, whom does he fear, and what can frighten him? What fear has death for him? What fear has evil for him?

So if we are Advaitists, we must think from this moment that our old self is dead and gone. The old Mr., Mrs., and Miss So-and-so are gone, they were mere superstitions, and what remains is the ever-pure, the ever-strong, the almighty, the all-knowing — that alone remains for us, and then all fear vanishes from us.

Who can injure us, the omnipresent? All weakness has vanished from us, and our only work is to arouse this knowledge in our fellow beings. We see that they too are the same pure self, only they do not know it; we must teach them, we must help them to rouse up their infinite nature.

This is what I feel to be absolutely necessary all over the world. These doctrines are old, older than many mountains possibly. All truth is eternal. Truth is nobody's property; no race, no individual can lay any exclusive claim to it. Truth is the nature of all souls. Who can lay an, special claim to it?

But it has to be made practical, to be made simple (for the highest truths are always simple), so that it may penetrate every pore of human society, and become the property of the highest intellects and the commonest minds, of the man, woman, and child at the same time. All these ratiocinations of logic, all these bundles of metaphysics, all these theologies and ceremonies may have been good in their own time, but let us try to make things simpler and bring about the golden days when every man will be a worshipper, and the Reality in every man will be the object of worship.

*

The idea of duty varies much among different nations. In one country, if a man does not do certain things, people will say he has acted wrongly; while if he does those very things in another country, people will say that he did not act rightly — and yet we know that there must be some universal idea of duty. In the same way, one class of society thinks that certain things are among its duty, while another class thinks quite the opposite and would be horrified if it had to do those things.

Two ways are left open to us — the way of the ignorant, who think that there is only one way to truth and that all the rest are wrong, and the way of the wise, who admit that, according to our mental constitution or the different planes of existence in which we are, duty and morality may vary.

The important thing is to know that there are gradations of duty and of morality — that the duty of one state of life, in one set of circumstances, will not and cannot be that of another.

*

Unity in variety is the plan of creation. However men and women may vary individually, there is unity in the background. The different individual characters and classes of men and women are natural variations in creation.

Hence, we ought not to judge them by the same standard or put the same ideal before them. Such a course creates only an unnatural struggle, and the result is that man begins to hate himself and is hindered from becoming religious and good. Our duty is to encourage every one in his struggle to live up to his own highest ideal, and strive at the same time to make the ideal as near as possible to the truth.

*

Let us work without desire for name or fame or rule over others. Let us be free from the triple bonds of lust, greed of gain, and anger. And this truth is with us!

*

We all understand that desires are wrong, but what is meant by giving up desires? How could life go on? It would be the same suicidal advice, killing the desire and the man too. The solution is this. Not that you should not have property, not that you should not have things which are necessary and things which are even luxuries.

Have all that you want, and more, only know the truth and realise it. Wealth does not belong to anybody. Have no idea of proprietorship, possessorship. You are nobody, nor am I, nor anyone else.

All belongs to the Lord, because the opening verse told us to put the Lord in everything. God is in the wealth that you enjoy. He is in the desire that rises in your mind. He is in the things you buy to satisfy your desire; He is in your beautiful attire, in your beautiful ornaments. This is the line of thought.

All will be metamorphosed as soon as you begin to see things in that light. If you put God in your every movement, in your conversation, in your form, in everything, the whole scene changes, and the world, instead of appearing as one of woe and misery, will become a heaven.

"The kingdom of heaven is within you," says Jesus; so says the Vedanta, and every great teacher. "He that hath eyes to see, let him see, and he that hath ears to hear, let him hear." The Vedanta proves that the truth for which we have been searching all this time is present, and was all the time with us.

In our ignorance, we thought we had lost it, and went about the world crying and weeping, struggling to find the truth, while all along it was dwelling in our own hearts. There alone can we find it.

If we understand the giving up of the world in its old, crude sense, then it would come to this: that we must not work, that we must be idle, sitting like lumps of earth, neither thinking nor doing anything, but must become fatalists, driven about by every circumstance, ordered about by the laws of nature, drifting from place to place.

That would be the result. But that is not what is meant. We must work. Ordinary mankind, driven everywhere by false desire, what do they know of work? The man propelled by his own feelings and his own senses, what does he know about work? He works, who is not propelled by his own desires, by any selfishness whatsoever. He works, who has no ulterior motive in view. He works, who has nothing to gain from work.

*

Many want pleasure [as] the goal. For that pleasure they seek only the senses. On the higher planes much pleasure is to be sought. Then on spiritual planes. Then in himself — God within him. The man whose pleasure is outside of [himself] becomes unhappy when that outside thing goes.

You cannot depend for this pleasure upon anything in this universe. If all my pleasures are in myself, I must have pleasure all the time because I can never lose my Self. Mother, father, child, wife, body, wealth — everything I can lose except my self. All desire is contained in the Self. This is individuality which never changes, and this is perfect.

And how to get it? They find what the great souls of this world — all great men and women — found. They all had the one truth, that this false individuality must go.

So this ego — the less there is of it, the nearer I am to that which I really am: the universal body. The less I think of my own individual mind, the nearer I am to that universal mind. The less I think of my own soul, the nearer I am to the universal soul.

We live in one body. We have some pain, some pleasure. Just for this little pleasure we have by living in this body, we are ready to kill everything in the universe to preserve ourselves.

If we had two bodies, would not that be much better? So on and on to bliss. I am in everybody. Through all hands I work; through all feet I walk. I speak through every mouth; I live in every body. Infinite my bodies, infinite my minds. I lived in Jesus of Nazareth, in Buddha, in Mohammed — in all the great and good of the past, of the present. I am going to live in all that [may] come afterwards. Is that theory [No, it is the truth.]

If you can realise this, how infinitely more pleasurable that will be. What an ecstasy of joy! Which one body is so great that we need here anything [of] the bodyAfter living in all the bodies of others, all the bodies there are in this world, what becomes of us? [We become one with the Infinite. And] that is the goal. That is the only way. One [man] says, "If I know the truth, I shall be melted away like butter." I wish people would be, but they are too tough to be melted so quickly!

*

The Jivanmukta ('the living free' or one who knows) alone is able to give real love, real charity, real truth, and it is truth alone that makes us free. Desire makes slaves of us, it is an insatiable tyrant and gives its victims no rest; but the Jivanmukta has conquered all desire by rising to the knowledge that he is the One and there is nothing left to wish for.

The mind brings before us all our delusions — body, sex, creed, caste, bondage; so we have to tell the truth to the mind incessantly, until it is made to realise it. Our real nature is all bliss, and all the pleasure we know is but a reflection, an atom, of that bliss we get from touching our real nature.

That is beyond both pleasure and pain. It is the "witness" of the universe, the unchanging reader before whom turn the leaves of the book of life.

Through practice comes Yoga, through Yoga comes knowledge, through knowledge love, and through love bliss.

*

The moment you think creed and form and ceremony the "be-all" and "end-all", then you are in bondage. Take part in them to help others, but take care they do not become a bondage. Religion is one, but its application must be various. Let each one, therefore, give his message; but find not the defects in other religions.

You must come out from all form if you would see the Light. Drink deep of the nectar of the knowledge of God. The man who realises.

"I am He", though clad in rags, is happy. Go forth into the Eternal and come back with eternal energy. The slave goes out to search for truth; he comes back free.

*

Slavery is slavery. The chain of gold is quite as bad as the chain of iron. Is there a way out?

It is only the question of memory [of your true nature], not salvation by work. Do you get salvation? You are [already] free.

Go on saying, "I am free". Never mind if the next moment delusion comes and says, "I am bound." Dehypnotise the whole thing.

[This truth] is first to be heard. Hear it first. Think on it day and night. Fill the mind [with it] day and night: "I am It. I am the Lord of the universe. Never was there any delusion. "

Meditate upon it with all the strength of the mind till you actually see these walls, houses, everything, melt away — [until] body, everything, vanishes. "I will stand alone. I am the One."

Struggle on! "Who cares! We want to be free; [we] do not want any powers. Worlds we renounce; heavens we renounce; hells we renounce. What do I care about all these powers, and this and that! What do I care if the mind is controlled or uncontrolled! Let it run on. What of that! I am not the mind, Let it go on!"

*

There was never a human race which did not have a religion and worship some sort of God or gods. Whether the God or gods existed or not is no question; but what is the analysis of this psychological phenomenon? Why is all the world trying to find, or seeking for, a God? Why?

Because in spite of all this bondage, in spite of nature and this tremendous energy of law grinding us down, never allowing us to turn to any side — wherever we go, whatever we want to do, we are thwarted by this law, which is everywhere — in spite of all this, the human soul never forgets its freedom and is ever seeking it.

The search for freedom is the search of all religions; whether they know it or not, whether they can formulate it well or ill, the idea is there. Even the lowest man, the most ignorant, seeks for something which has power over nature's laws. He wants to see a demon, a ghost, a god — somebody who can subdue nature, for whom nature is not almighty, for whom there is no law.

"Oh, for somebody who can break the law!" That is the cry coming from the human heart. We are always seeking for someone who breaks the law. The rushing engine speeds along the railway track; the little worm crawls out of its way. We at once say, "The engine is dead matter, a machine; and the worm is alive," because the worm attempted to break the law.

The engine, with all its power and might, can never break the law. It is made to go in any direction man wants, and it cannot do otherwise; but the worm, small and little though it was, attempted to break the law and avoid the danger. It tried to assert itself against law, assert its freedom; and there was the sign of the future God in it.

Everywhere we see this assertion of freedom, this freedom of the soul. It is reflected in every religion in the shape of God or gods; but it is all external yet — for those who only see the gods outside.

Man decided that he was nothing. He was afraid that he could never be free; so he went to seek for someone outside of nature who was free. Then he thought that there were many and many such free beings, and gradually he merged them all into one God of gods and Lord of lords.

Even that did not satisfy him. He came a little closer to truth, a little nearer; and then gradually found that whatever he was, he was in some way connected with the God of gods and Lord of lords; that he, though he thought himself bound and low and weak, was somehow connected with that God of gods.

Then visions came to him; thought arose and knowledge advanced. And he began to come nearer and nearer to that God, and at last found out that God and all the gods, this whole psychological phenomenon connected with the search for an all-powerful free soul, was but a reflection of his own idea of himself.

And then at last he discovered that it was not only true that "God made man after His own image", but that it was also true that man made God after his own image. That brought out the idea of divine freedom. The Divine Being was always within, the nearest of the near. Him we had ever been seeking outside, and at last found that He is in the heart of our hearts.

You may know the story of the man who mistook his own heartbeat for somebody knocking at the door, and went to the door and opened it, but found nobody there, so he went back. Again he seemed to hear a knocking at the door, but nobody was there. Then he understood that it was his own heartbeat, and he had misinterpreted it as a knocking at the door.

Similarly, man after his search finds out that this infinite freedom that he was placing in imagination all the time in the nature outside is the internal subject, the eternal Soul of souls; this Reality, he himself.

Thus at last he comes to recognise this marvellous duality of existence: the subject, infinite and finite in one — the Infinite Being is also the same finite soul. The Infinite is caught, as it were, in the meshes of the intellect and apparently manifests as finite beings, but the reality remains unchanged.

This is, therefore, true knowledge: that the Soul of our souls, the Reality that is within us, is That which is unchangeable, eternal, ever-blessed, ever-free. This is the only solid ground for us to stand upon.

This, then, is the end of all death, the advent of all immortality, the end of all misery. And he who sees that One among the many, that One unchangeable in the universe of change, he who sees Him as the Soul of his soul, unto him belongs eternal peace — unto none else.

*

Consciousness is a bondage. The argument from design claims that intelligence precedes form; but if intelligence is the cause of anything, it itself is in its turn an effect. It is Maya. God creates us, and we create God, and this is Maya.

The circle is unbroken; mind creates body, and body creates mind; the egg brings the chicken, the chicken the egg; the tree the seed, the seed the tree. The world is neither entirely differentiated nor yet entirely homogeneous. Man is free and must rise above both sides. Both are right in their place; but to reach truth, "isness", we must transcend all that we now know of existence, will, consciousness, doing, going, knowing.

There is no real individuality of the Jiva (separate soul); eventually it, as a compound, will go to pieces. Only that which is beyond further analysis is "simple", and that alone is truth, freedom, immortality, bliss.

*

The pure heart is the best mirror for the reflection of truth, so all these disciplines are for the purification of the heart. And as soon as it is pure, all truths flash upon it in a minute; all truth in the universe will manifest in your heart, if you are sufficiently pure.

It is the heart that reaches the goal. Follow the heart. A pure heart sees beyond the intellect; it gets inspired; it knows things that reason can never know, and whenever there is conflict between the pure heart and the intellect, always side with the pure heart, even if you think what your heart is doing is unreasonable. When it is desirous of doing good to others, your brain may tell you that it is not politic to do so, but follow your heart, and you will find that you make less mistakes than by following your intellect.

*

The essential truth is realisation. Know that to be the goal. Each distinct creed is but a way to the Truth.

The test of progress is the amount of renunciation that one has attained. Where you find the attraction for lust and wealth considerably diminished, to whatever creed he may belong, know that his inner spirit is awakening. The door of Self-realisation has surely opened for him.

On the contrary, if you observe a thousand outward rules and quote a thousand scriptural texts, still, if it has not brought the spirit of renunciation in you, know that your life is in vain. Be earnest over this realisation and set your heart on it. Well, you have read enough of scriptures. But tell me, of what avail has it been? Some perhaps thinking of money have become millionaires, whereas you have become a Pundit by thinking of scriptures. But both are bondages. Attain the supreme knowledge and go beyond Vidyâ and Avidyâ, relative knowledge and ignorance.

*

Experience is the only source of knowledge. Experience is the only teacher we have. We may talk and reason all our lives, but we shall not understand a word of truth, until we experience it ourselves.

You cannot satisfy my curiosity to see a country by showing me a map; I must have actual experience. Maps can only create curiosity in us to get more perfect knowledge. Beyond that, they have no value whatever.

Clinging to books only degenerates the human mind. Was there ever a more horrible blasphemy than the statement that all the knowledge of God is confined to this or that book? How dare men call God infinite, and yet try to compress Him within the covers of a little book!

Millions of people have been killed because they did not believe what the books said, because they would not see all the knowledge of God within the covers of a book. Of course this killing and murdering has gone by, but the world is still tremendously bound up in a belief in books.

*

To believe blindly is to degenerate the human soul. Be an atheist if you want, but do not believe in anything unquestioningly. Why degrade the soul to the level of animals? You not only hurt yourselves thereby, but you injure society, and make danger for those that come after you. Stand up and reason out, having no blind faith. Religion is a question of being and becoming, not of believing. This is religion, and when you have attained to that you have religion. Before that you are no better than the animals. "Do not believe in what you have heard," says the great Buddha, "do not believe in doctrines because they have been handed down to you through generations; do not believe in anything because it is followed blindly by many; do not believe because some old sage makes a statement; do not believe in truths to which you have become attached by habit; do not believe merely on the authority of your teachers and elders. Have deliberation and analyse, and when the result agrees with reason and conduces to the good of one and all, accept it and live up to it."

*

Religion is above reason, supernatural. Faith is not belief, it is the grasp on the Ultimate, an illumination. First hear, then reason and find out all that reason can give about the Atman; let the flood of reason flow over It, then take what remains. If nothing remains, thank God you have escaped a superstition. When you have determined that nothing can take away the Atman, that It stands every test, hold fast to this and teach it to all. Truth cannot be partial; it is for the good of all.

Finally, in perfect rest and peace meditate upon It, concentrate your mind upon It, make yourself one with It. Then no speech is needed; silence will carry the truth. Do not spend your energy in talking, but meditate in silence; and do not let the rush of the outside world disturb you. When your mind is in the highest state, you are unconscious of it. Accumulate power in silence and become a dynamo of spirituality.

What can a beggar give? Only a king can give, and he only when he wants nothing himself.

*

The progress of the world means more enjoyment and more misery too. This mixture of life and death, good and evil, knowledge and ignorance is what is called Maya — or the universal phenomenon.

You may go on for eternity inside this net, seeking for happiness — you find much, and much evil too. To have good and no evil is childish nonsense.

Two ways are left open — one by giving up all hope to take up the world as it is and bear the pangs and pains in the hope of a crumb of happiness now and then. The other, to give up the search for pleasure, knowing it to be pain in another form, and seek for truth — and those that dare try for truth succeed in finding that truth as ever present — present in themselves.

Then we also discover how the same truth is manifesting itself both in our relative error and knowledge — we find also that the same truth is bliss which again is manifesting itself as good and evil, and with it also we find real existence which is manifesting itself as both death and life.

*

He who thinks himself free, free he becomes; he who thinks himself bound, bound he remains — this popular saying is true: 'As one thinks, so one becomes'." He alone who is always awake to the idea of freedom, becomes free; he who thinks he is bound, endures life after life in the state of bondage. It is a fact.

This truth holds good both in spiritual and temporal matters. Those who are always down-hearted and dispirited in this life can do no work; from life to life they come and go wailing and moaning. "The earth is enjoyed by heroes" — this is the unfailing truth.

*

God is life; God is truth… everything else than God is nothing — here today, gone tomorrow.

*

There is no real individuality of the Jiva (separate soul); eventually it, as a compound, will go to pieces. Only that which is beyond further analysis is "simple", and that alone is truth, freedom, immortality, bliss. All struggles for the preservation of this illusive individuality are really vices. All struggles to lose this individuality are virtues. Everything in the universe is trying to break down this individuality, either consciously or unconsciously. All morality is based upon the destruction of separateness or false individuality, because that is the cause of all sin.

*

Knowledge can never be created; it can only be discovered; and every man who makes a great discovery is inspired. Only, when it is a spiritual truth he brings, we call him a prophet; and when it is on the physical plane, we call him a scientific man, and we attribute more importance to the former, although the source of all truth is one.

Brahman is the essence, the reality of all knowledge, and that all manifestations as knower, knowing, and known are mere imaginings in Brahman. Ramanuja attributes consciousness to God; the real monists attribute nothing, not even existence in any meaning that we can attach to it. Ramanuja declares that God is the essence of conscious knowledge. Undifferentiated consciousness, when differentiated, becomes the world.

*

All religions, without one exception, hold that man is a degeneration of what he was, whether they clothe this in mythological words, or in the clear language of philosophy, or in the beautiful expressions of poetry. This is the one fact that comes out of every scripture and of every mythology that the man that is, is a degeneration of what he was. This is the kernel of truth within the story of Adam's fall in the Jewish scripture. This is again and again repeated in the scriptures of the Hindus; the dream of a period which they call the Age of Truth, when no man died unless he wished to die, when he could keep his body as long as he liked, and his mind was pure and strong. There was no evil and no misery; and the present age is a corruption of that state of perfection.

*

A proper psychology is essential to the understanding of religion. To reach Truth by reason alone is impossible, because imperfect reason cannot study its own fundamental basis. Therefore the only way to study the mind is to get at facts, and then intellect will arrange them and deduce the principles. The intellect has to build the house; but it cannot do so without bricks and it cannot make bricks. Jnana-Yoga is the surest way of arriving at facts.

*

Be pure, give up superstition and see the wonderful harmony of nature. Superstition gets the better of religion. All the religions are good, since the essentials are the same. In every religion there is the essential truth and the non-essential casket in which this jewel lies.

Circumstances change; the receptacle is different; but the central truth remains. The essentials being the same, the educated people of every community retain the essentials.

Each man should have the perfect exercise of his individuality, but these individualities form a perfect whole. This marvelous condition is already in existence. Each creed has something to add to the wonderful structure.

*

We believe in one God, the Father of us all, who is omnipresent and omnipotent, and who guides and preserves His children with infinite love. We believe in a Personal God as the Christians do, but we go further: we below that we are He! That His personality is manifested in us, that God is in us, and that we are in God We believe there is a germ of truth in all religions, and the Hindu bows down to them all; for in this world, truth is to be found not in subtraction but in addition.

We would offer God a bouquet of the most beautiful flowers of all the diverse faiths. We must love God for love's sake, not for the hope of reward. We must do our duty for duty's sake not for the hope of reward. We must worship the beautiful for beauty's sake, not for the hope of reward.

Thus in the purity of our hearts shall we see God. Sacrifices genuflexions, mumblings, and mutterings are not religion. They are only good if they stimulate us to the brave performance of beautiful and heroic deeds and lift our thoughts to the apprehension of the divine perfection

What good is it, if we acknowledge in our prayers that God is the Father of us all, and in our daily lives do not treat every man as our brother? Books are only made so that they may point the way to a higher life; but no good results unless the path is trodden with unflinching steps! Every human personality may be compared to a glass globe.

There is the same pure white light — an emission of the divine Being — in the centre of each, but the glass being of different colours and thickness, the rays assume diverse aspects in the transmission. The equality and beauty of each central flame is the same, and the apparent inequality is only in the imperfection of the temporal instrument of its expression. As we rise higher and higher in the scale of being, the medium becomes more and more translucent.

EVIL

There is an idea other forms of worship are not errors. This is one of the great points to be remembered, that those who worship God through ceremonials and forms, however crude we may think them to be, are not in error. It is the journey from truth to truth, from lower truth to higher truth. Darkness is less light; evil is less good; impurity is less purity.

*

It must always be borne in mind that we should see others with eyes of love, with sympathy, knowing that they are going along the same path that we have trodden. If you are free, you must know that all will be so sooner or later, and if you are free, how can you see the impermanent? If you are really pure, how do you see the impure? For what is within, is without. We cannot see impurity without having it inside ourselves. This is one of the practical sides of Vedanta, and I hope that we shall all try to carry it into our lives.

*

One cannot divide the rights of the universe. To talk of "right" implies limitation. It is not "right" but "responsibility". Each is responsible for the evil anywhere in the world. No one can separate himself from his brother. All that unites with the universal is virtue; all that separates is sin. You are a part of the Infinite. This is your nature. Hence you are your brother's keeper.

The first end of life is knowledge; the second end of life is happiness. Knowledge and happiness lead to freedom. But not one can attain liberty until every being (ant or dog) has liberty. Not one can be happy until all are happy. When you hurt anyone you hurt yourself, for you and your brother are one. He is indeed a Yogi who sees himself in the whole universe and the whole universe in himself. Self-sacrifice, not self-assertion, is the law of the highest universe. The world is so evil because Jesus' teaching, "Resist not evil", has never been tried. Selflessness alone will solve the problem. Religion comes with intense self-sacrifice.

*

Every desire is fraught with evil, whether the desire itself be good or evil. It is like a dog jumping for a piece of meat which is ever receding from his reach, and dying a dog's death at last. Do not be like that. Cut off all desire.

*

Friendship, mercy, gladness, and indifference, being thought of in regard to subjects, happy, unhappy, good, and evil respectively, pacify the mind.

We must have these four sorts of ideas. We must have friendship for all; we must be merciful towards those that are in misery; when people are happy, we ought to be happy; and to the wicked we must be indifferent.

So with all subjects that come before us. If the subject is a good one, we shall feel friendly towards it; if the subject of thought is one that is miserable, we must be merciful towards it. If it is good, we must be glad; if it is evil, we must be indifferent. These attitudes of the mind towards the different subjects that come before it will make the mind peaceful. Most of our difficulties in our daily lives come from being unable to hold our minds in this way.

For instance, if a man does evil to us, instantly we want to react evil, and every reaction of evil shows that we are not able to hold the mind down; it comes out in waves towards the object, and we lose our power. Every reaction in the form of hatred or evil is so much loss to the mind; and every evil thought or deed of hatred, or any thought of reaction, if it is controlled, will be laid in our favour.

It is not that we lose by thus restraining ourselves; we are gaining infinitely more than we suspect. Each time we suppress hatred, or a feeling of anger, it is so much good energy stored up in our favour; that piece of energy will be converted into the higher powers.

*

Evil changes in form but remains the same in quality. In ancient times force ruled, today it is cunning. Misery in India is not so bad as in America, because the poor man here sees the greater contrast to his own bad condition.

Good and evil are inextricably combined, and one cannot be had without the other. The sum total of energy in this universe is like a lake, every wave inevitably leads to a corresponding depression. The sum total is absolutely the same; so to make one man happy is to make another unhappy. External happiness is material and the supply is fixed; so that not one grain can be had by one person without taking from another. Only bliss beyond the material world can be had without loss to any. Material happiness is but a transformation of material sorrow.

Never think, you can make the world better and happier. The bullock in the oil-mill never reaches the wisp of hay tied in front of him, he only grinds out the oil. So we chase the will-o'-the-wisp of happiness that always eludes us, and we only grind nature's mill, then die, merely to begin again. If we could get rid of evil, we should never catch a glimpse of anything higher; we would be satisfied and never struggle to get free. When man finds that all search for happiness in matter is nonsense, then religion begins. All human knowledge is but a part of religion.

*

In the religion of Persia, there was the idea of Satan, but in India, no conception of Satan. Later books began to realise this new idea. Evil exists, and there is no shirking the fact. The universe is a fact; and if a fact, it is a huge composite of good and evil. Whoever rules must rule over good and evil. If that power makes us live, the same makes us die. Laughter and tears are kin, and there are more tears than laughter in this world. Who made flowers, who made the Himalayas? — a very good God. Who made my sins and weaknesses? — Karma, Satan, self. The result is a lame, one-legged universe, and naturally the God of the universe, a one-legged God.

*

The view of the absolute separation of good and evil, two cut and dried and separate existences, makes us brutes of unsympathetic hearts. The good woman jumps aside from the streetwalker. Why? She may be infinitely better than you in some respects. This view brings eternal jealousy and hatred in the world, eternal barrier between man and man, between the good man and the comparatively less good or evil man. Such brutal view is pure evil, more evil than evil itself. Good and evil are not separate existences, but there is an evolution of good, and what is less good we call evil.

*

Six hundred years before Christ, the priesthood of India exercised great influence over the minds of the people, and between the upper and nether millstone of intellectuality and learning the people were ground. Buddhism, which is the religion of more than two-third of the human family, was not founded as an entirely new religion, but rather as a reformation which carried off the corruption of the times.

Buddha seems to have been the only prophet who did everything for others and absolutely nothing for himself. He gave up his home and all the enjoyments of life to spend his days in search of the medicine for the terrible disease of human misery. In an age when men and priests were discussing the essence of the deity, he discovered what people had overlooked, that misery existed.

The cause of evil is our desire to be superior to others and our selfishness. The moment that the world becomes unselfish all evil will vanish. So long as society tries to cure evil by laws and institutions, evil will not be cured. The world has tried this method ineffectually for thousands of years. Force against force never cures, and the only cure for evil is unselfishness. We need to teach people to obey the laws rather than to make more laws. Buddhism was the first missionary religion of the world but it was one of the teachings of Buddhism not to antagonize any other religion. Sects weaken their power for good by making war on each other."

*

Good can never be done without doing evil. We cannot breathe a breath without killing thousands of poor little animals. National prosperity is another name for death and degradation to millions of other races. So is individual prosperity the beggaring of many. The world is evil — and will ever remain so. It is its nature, and cannot be changed.

*

It is all very well to say everything is right, but that is apt to degenerate into a sort of *laissez-faire*. I believe that the world is evil — made more hideous with a few dashes of good.

All our works have only this value, that they awaken some to the reality of this horror — and [those] flee for refuge to some place beyond, which is called God, or Christ, or Brahma, or Buddha, etc. Names do not make much difference.

*

Suppose I am doing an evil act, my mind is in a certain state of vibration, and all minds in the universe, which are in a similar state, have the possibility of being affected by the vibration of my mind. So, when I am doing a good action, my mind is in another state of vibration; and all minds similarly strung have the possibility of being affected by my mind; and this power of mind upon mind is more or less according as the force of the tension is greater or less.

*

Following this simile further, it is quite possible that, just as light waves may travel for millions of years before they reach any object, so thought waves may also travel hundreds of years before they meet an object with which they vibrate in unison.

It is quite possible, therefore, that this atmosphere of ours is full of such thought pulsations, both good and evil. Every thought projected from every brain goes on pulsating, as it were, until it meets a fit object that will receive it. Any mind which is open to receive some of these impulses will take them immediately.

So, when a man is doing evil actions, he has brought his mind to a certain state of tension and all the waves which correspond to that state of tension, and which may be said to be already in the atmosphere, will struggle to enter into his mind. That is why an evil-doer generally goes on doing more and more evil. His actions become intensified. Such also will be the case with the doer of good; he will open himself to all the good waves that are in the atmosphere, and his good actions also will become intensified.

We run, therefore, a twofold danger in doing evil: first, we open ourselves to all the evil influences surrounding us; secondly, we create evil which affects others, may be hundreds of years hence. In doing evil we injure ourselves and others also. In doing good we do good to ourselves and to others as well; and, like all other forces in man, these forces of good and evil also gather strength from outside.

*

According to Karma-Yoga, the action one has done cannot be destroyed until it has borne its fruit; no power in nature can stop it from yielding its results. If I do an evil action, I must suffer for it; there is no power in this universe to stop or stay it. Similarly, if I do a good action, there is no power in the universe which can stop its bearing good results. The cause must have its effect; nothing can prevent or restrain this.

*

In every country the evils exist not with, but against, religion.

*

A good many of the wicked deeds done in this world are really done through attachment to certain persons. So all attachment excepting that for good works should be avoided; but love should be given to everybody. Then as to jealousy. There should be no jealousy in regard to objects of the senses; jealousy is the root of all evil, and a most difficult thing to conquer.

*

Creation is not a "making" of something, it is the struggle to regain the equilibrium, as when atoms of cork are thrown to the bottom of a pail of water and rush to rise to the top, singly or in clusters. Life is and must be accompanied by *evil*. A little evil is the source of life; the little wickedness that is in the world is very good; for when the balance is regained, the world will end, because sameness and destruction are one. When this world goes, good and evil go with it; but when we can transcend this world, we get rid of both good and evil and have bliss.

There is no possibility of ever having pleasure without pain, good without evil; for living itself is just the lost equilibrium. What we want is freedom, not life, nor pleasure, nor good. Creation is infinite, without beginning and without end — the ever-moving ripple in an infinite lake. There are yet unreached depths and others where the equilibrium has been regained; but the ripple is always progressing, the struggle to regain the balance is eternal. Life and death are only different names for the same fact, the two sides of the one coin. Both are Maya, the inexplicable state of striving at one time to live, and a moment later to die.

*

In this universe where nothing is lost, where we live in the midst of death in *life*, every thought that is thought, in public or in private, in crowded thoroughfares or in the deep recesses of primeval forests, lives. They are continuously trying to become self-embodied, and until they have embodied themselves, they will struggle for expression, and any amount of repression cannot kill them. Nothing can be destroyed — those thoughts that caused evil in the past are also seeking embodiment, to be filtered through repeated expression and, at last, transfigured into perfect good.

*

An objective heaven or millennium has existence only in the fancy — but a subjective one is already in existence. The musk-deer, after vain search for the cause of the scent of the musk, at last will have to find it in himself.

Objective society will always be a mixture of good and evil — objective life will always be followed by its shadow death, and the longer the life, the longer will also be the shadow. It is only when the sun is on our own head that there is no shadow. When God and good and everything else is in us, there is no evil. In objective life, however, every bullet has its billet — evil goes with every good as its shadow. Every improvement is coupled with an equal degradation. The reason being that good and evil are not two things but one, the difference being only in manifestation — one of degree, not kind.

*

The evils that are in the world are caused by none else but ourselves. We have caused all this evil; and just as we constantly see misery resulting from evil actions, so can we also see that much of the existing misery in the world is the effect of the past wickedness of man.

Man alone, therefore, according to this theory, is responsible. God is not to blame. He, the eternally merciful Father, is not to blame at all. "We reap what we sow."

*

Good can never be done without doing evil. We cannot breathe a breath without killing thousands of poor little animals. National prosperity is another name for death and degradation to millions of other races. So is individual prosperity the beggaring of many. The world is evil — and will ever remain so. It is its nature, and cannot be changed — "Which one of you by taking thought . . ." etc

*

Why is there evil? The only way you can solve [the problem] is [by saying that God is] the cause of both good and evil. The great difficulty in the theory of the Personal God is that if you say He is only good and not evil, you will be caught in the trap of your own argument. How do you know there is [a] God? You say [that He is] the Father of this universe, and you say He is good; and because there is [also] evil in the world, God must be evil. The same difficulty!

There is no good, and there is no evil. God is all there is . How do you know what is good? You feel [it]. [How do you know what is evil? If evil comes, you feel it. We know good and evil by our feelings. There is not one man who feels only good, happy feelings. There is not one who feels only unhappy feelings.

*

PATH TO OVERCOMING EVIL

Those of you who have studied the Gita will remember the memorable passages: "He who looks upon the learned Brahmin, upon the cow, the elephant, the dog, or the outcast with the same eye, he indeed is the sage, and the wise man."

"Even in this life he has conquered relative existence whose mind is firmly fixed on this sameness, for the Lord is one and the same to all, and the Lord is pure; therefore those who have this sameness for all, and are pure, are said to be living in God."

This is the gist of Vedantic morality — this sameness for all. We have seen that it is the subjective world that rules the objective. Change the subject, and the object is bound to change; purify yourself, and the world is bound to be purified.

This one thing requires to be taught now more than ever before. We are becoming more and more busy about our neighbours, and less and less about ourselves. The world will change if we change; if we are pure, the world will become pure.

The question is why I should see evil in others. I cannot see evil unless I be evil. I cannot be miserable unless I am weak. Things that used to make me miserable when I was a child, do not do so now. The subject changed, so the object was bound to change; so says the Vedanta. All these things which we call causes of misery and evil, we shall laugh at when we arrive at that wonderful state of equality, that sameness.

This is what is called in Vedanta attaining to freedom. The sign of approaching that freedom is more and more of this sameness and equality. In misery and happiness the same, in success and defeat the same — such a mind is nearing that state of freedom.

The mind cannot be easily conquered. Minds that rise into waves at the approach of every little thing at the slightest provocation or danger, in what a state they must be! What to talk of greatness or spirituality, when these changes come over the mind? This unstable condition of the mind must be changed.

We must ask ourselves how far we can be acted upon by the external world, and how far we can stand on our own feet, in spite of all the forces outside us. When we have succeeded in preventing all the forces in the world from throwing us off our balance, then alone we have attained to freedom, and not before. That is salvation.

STAY ACTIVE

The faculty of organization is entirely absent in our nature, but this has to be infused. The great secret is— absence of jealousy, the indomitable perseverance and the undying faith in himself.

The faculty of organisation is entirely absent in our nature, but this has to be infused. The great secret is — absence of jealousy. Be always ready to concede to the opinions of your brethren, and try always to conciliate. That is the whole secret.

Fight on bravely! Life is short! Give it up to a great cause. We must not join any sect, but we must sympathise and work with each. . . . Work, work — conquer all by your love!

*

If a man feeds me every day of my life, in the long run I shall lose the use of my hands. Spiritual death is the result of following each other like a flock of sheep. Death is the result of inaction. Be active; and wherever there is activity, there must be difference.

Difference is the sauce of life; it is the beauty, it is the art of everything. Difference makes all beautiful here. It is variety that is the source of life, the sign of life. Why should we be afraid of it?

*

Discriminate within yourself between the real and the unreal. Have you not read the Vedanta? Even when you sleep, keep the sword of discrimination at the head of your bed, so that covetousness cannot approach you even in dream. Practising such strength, renunciation will gradually come, and then you will see the portals of heaven are wide open to you.

*

Everything is conscious which rebels against nature: there, consciousness is manifested. Just try to kill a little ant, even it will once resist to save its life. Where there is struggle, where there is rebellion, there is the sign of life, there consciousness is manifested.

*

I find in travelling in various countries that beneath the surface differences that we find in dress and food and little details of manners, man is man all the world over; the same wonderful human nature is everywhere represented. Yet there are certain characteristics, and in a few words, I would like to sum up all my experiences here. In this land of America, no question is asked about a man's peculiarities. If a man is a man, that is enough, and they take him into their hearts, and that is one thing I have never seen in any other country in the world.

*

According to Vedanta philosophy, man is divine, that all this which we see around us is the outcome of that consciousness of the divine. Everything that is strong, and good, and powerful in human nature is the outcome of that divinity, and though potential in many, there is no difference between man and man essentially, all being alike divine.

There is, as it were, an infinite ocean behind, and you and I are so many waves, coming out of that infinite ocean; and each one of us is trying his best to manifest that infinite outside. So, potentially, each one of us has that infinite ocean of Existence, Knowledge, and Bliss as our birthright, our real nature; and the difference between us is caused by the greater or lesser power to manifest that divine.

Therefore the Vedanta lays down that each man should be treated not as what he manifests, but as what he stands for. Each human being stands for the divine, and, therefore, every teacher should be helpful, not by condemning man, but by helping him to call forth the divinity that is within him.

It also teaches that all the vast mass of energy that we see displayed in society and in every plane of action is really from inside out; and, therefore, what is called inspiration by other sects, the Vedantist begs the liberty to call the expiration of man.

At the same time it does not quarrel with other sects; the Vedanta has no quarrel with those who do not understand this divinity of man. Consciously or unconsciously, every man is trying to unfold that divinity. Man is higher than all animals, than all angels; none is greater than man.

Man is like an infinite spring, coiled up in a small box, and that spring is trying to unfold itself; and all the social phenomena that we see the result of this trying to unfold. All the competitions and struggles and evils that we see around us are neither the causes of these unfoldments, nor the effects. As one of our great philosophers says — in the case of the irrigation of a field, the tank is somewhere upon a higher level, and the water is trying to rush into the field, and is barred by a gate.

But as soon as the gate is opened, the water rushes in by its own nature; and if there is dust and dirt in the way, the water rolls over them. But dust and dirt are neither the result nor the cause of this unfolding of the divine nature of man. They are coexistent circumstances, and, therefore, can be remedied.

*

Man according to the Vedanta philosophy, is the greatest being that is in the universe, and this world of work the best place in it, because only herein is the greatest and the best chance for him to become perfect. Angels or gods, whatever you may call them, have all to become men, if they want to become perfect. This is the great centre, the wonderful poise, and the wonderful opportunity — this human life.

*

Men can never be united unless there is a bond of common interest. You can never unite people merely by getting up meetings, societies, and lectures if their interests be not one and the same.

*

"Naked came I out of my mother's womb, and naked shall I return thither; the Lord gave and the Lord hath taken away; blessed be the name of the Lord." Thus said the old Jewish saint when suffering the greatest calamities that could befall man, and he erred not. Herein lies the whole secret of Existence.

Waves may roll over the surface and tempest rage, but deep down there is the stratum of infinite calmness, infinite peace, and infinite bliss. "Blessed are they that mourn, for they shall be comforted."

And why? Because it is during these moments of visitations when the heart is wrung by hands which never stop for the father's cries or the mother's wail, when under the load of sorrow, dejection, and despair, the world seems to be cut off from under our feet, and when the whole horizon seems to be nothing but an impenetrable sheet of misery and utter despair — that the internal eyes open, light flashes all of a sudden, the dream vanishes, and intuitively we come face to face with the grandest mystery in nature — Existence.

Yes, then it is — when the load would be sufficient to sink a lot of frail vessels — that the man of genius, of strength, the hero, sees that infinite, absolute, ever-blissful Existence per se, that infinite being who is called and worshipped under different names in different climes. Then it is, the shackles that bind the soul down to this hole of misery break, as it were, for a time, and unfettered it rises and rises until it reaches the throne of the Lord, "Where the wicked cease from troubling and the weary are at rest".

Cease not, brother, to send up petitions day and night, cease not to say day and night — THY WILL BE DONE.

*

Nightmares always begin pleasantly — only at the worst point [the] dream is broken — so death breaks [the] dream of life.

*

Our great defect in life is that we are so much drawn to the ideal, the goal is so much more enchanting, so much more alluring, so much bigger in our mental horizon, that we lose sight of the details altogether.

*

The essence of Vedanta is that there is but one Being and that every soul is that Being in full, not a part of that Being.

All the sun is reflected in each dew-drop. Appearing in time, space and causality, this Being is man, as we know him, but behind all appearance is the one Reality. Unselfishness is the denial of the lower or apparent self. We have to free ourselves from this miserable dream that we are these bodies.

We must know the truth, "I am He". We are not drops to fall into the ocean and be lost; each one is the whole , infinite ocean, and will know it when released from the fetters of illusion. Infinity cannot be divided, the "One without a second" can have no second, all is that One. This knowledge will come to all, but we should struggle to attain it now, because until we have it, we cannot really give mankind the best help.

*

The life of every man is, in a manner, the life of the past. It comes to him through heredity, through surroundings, through education, through his own reincarnation — the past of the race.

In a manner, the past of the earth, the past of the whole world is there, upon every soul. What are we, in the present, but a result, an effect, in the hands of that infinite past? What are we but floating waveless in the eternal current of events, irresistibly moved forward and onward and incapable of rest?

But you and I are only little things, bubbles. There are always some giant waves in the ocean of affairs, and in you and me the life of the past race has been embodied only a little; but there are giants who embody, as it were, almost the whole of the past and who stretch out their hands for the future.

These are the sign-posts here and there which point to the march of humanity; these are verily gigantic, their shadows covering the earth — they stand undying, eternal! As it has been said by the same Messenger, "No man hath seen God at any time, but through the Son." And that is true.

And where shall we see God but in the Son? It is true that you and I, and the poorest of us, the meanest even, embody that God, even reflect that God. The vibration of light is everywhere, omnipresent; but we have to strike the light of the lamp before we can see the light. The Omnipresent God of the universe cannot be seen until He is reflected by these giant lamps of the earth — The Prophets, the man-Gods, the Incarnations, the embodiments of God.

*

Try to expand. Remember the only sign of life is motion and growth. You must send the passed resolution to Dr. J. H. Barrows. . . . . . Keep on steadily. So far we have done wonderful things. Onward, brave souls, we will gain! Organise and found societies and go to work, that is the only way.

The first manifest effect of life is expansion. You must expand if you want to live. The moment you have ceased to expand, death is upon you, danger is ahead.

*

Thc most practical man would call life neither good nor evil.

*

The whole life is a succession of dreams. My ambition is to be a conscious dreamer, that is all.

*

This I have seen in life—those who are overcautious about themselves fall into dangers at every step; those who are afraid of losing honour and respect, get only disgrace; and those who are always afraid of loss, always loses.

*

No doubt, a householder having many other duties to perform, cannot as fully attain to this sameness; yet this should be also their ideal, for it is the ideal of all societies, of all mankind, all animals, and all nature, to attain to this sameness. But alas! they think inequality is the way to attain equality as if they could come to right by doing wrong!

This is the bane of human nature, the curse upon mankind, the root of all misery — this inequality. This is the source of all bondage, physical, mental, and spiritual.

*

This world is the great gymnasium where we come to make ourselves strong.

*

Three things are necessary to make every man great, every nation great: 1. Conviction of the powers of goodness, 2. Absence of jealousy and suspicion, 3) Helping all who are trying to be end and do good.

*

Unity in variety is the plan of creation, individuality in universality. Each cell has its part in bringing about consciousness. Man is individual and at the same time universal. It is while realising our individual nature that we realise even our national and universal nature. Each is an infinite circle whose centre is everywhere and circumference nowhere. By practice one can feel universal Selfhood which is the essence of Hinduism. He who sees in every being his own Self is a Pandita (sage).

*

We find that man, as it were, is always surrounded by something greater than himself, and he is trying to grasp the meaning of this. Man will ever [seek] the highest ideal.

He knows that it exists and that religion is the search after the highest ideal. At first all his searches were in the external plane — placed in heaven, in different places — just according to [his grasp] of the total nature of man.

[Later,] man began to look at himself a little closer and began to find out that the real "me" was not the "me" that he stands for ordinarily. As he appears to the senses is not the same as he really is. He began to [search] inside of himself, and found out that . . . the same ideal he [had placed] outside of himself is all the time within; what he was worshipping outside was his own real inner nature. The difference between dualism and monism is that when the ideal is put outside [of oneself], it is dualism. When God is [sought] within, it is monism.

*

Whichever way we turn in trying to understand things in their reality, if we analyse far enough, we find that at last we come to a peculiar state of things, seemingly a contradiction: something which our reason cannot grasp and yet is a fact. We take up something — we know it is finite; but as soon as we begin to analyse it, it leads us beyond our reason, and we never find an end to all its qualities, its possibilities, its powers, its relations. It has become infinite. Take even a common flower, that is finite enough; but who is there that can say he knows all about the flower? There is no possibility of anyone's getting to the end of the knowledge about that one flower. The flower has become infinite — the flower which was finite to begin with. Take a grain of sand. Analyse it. We start with the assumption that it is finite, and at last we find that it is not, it is infinite; all the same, we have looked upon it as finite. The flower is similarly treated as a finite something.

So with all our thoughts and experiences, physical and mental. We begin, we may think, on a small scale, and grasp them as little things; but very soon they elude our knowledge and plunge into the abyss of the infinite. And the greatest and the first thing perceived is ourselves. We are also in the same dilemma about existence. We exist. We see we are finite beings. We live and die. Our horizon is narrow. We are here, limited, confronted by the universe all around. Nature can crush us out of existence in a moment. Our little bodies are just held together, ready to go to pieces at a moment's notice. We know that. In the region of action how powerless we are! Our will is being thwarted at every turn. So many things we want to do, and how few we can do! There is no limit to our willing. We can will everything, want everything, we can desire to go to the dogstar. But how few of our desires can be accomplished! The body will not allow it. Well, nature is against the accomplishment of our will. We are weak. What is true of the flower, of the grain of sand, of the physical world, and of every thought, is a hundredfold more true of ourselves. We are also in the same dilemma of existence, being finite and infinite at the same time. We are like waves in the ocean; the wave is the ocean and yet not the ocean. There is not any part of the wave of which you cannot say, "It is the ocean." The name "ocean" applies to the wave and equally to every other part of the ocean, and yet it is separate from the ocean. So in this infinite ocean of existence, we are like wavelets. At the same time, when we want really to grasp ourselves, we cannot — we have become the infinite.

We seem to be walking in dreams. Dreams are all right in a dream-mind; but as soon as you want to grasp one of them, it is gone. Why? Not that it was false, but because it is beyond the power of reason, the power of the intellect to comprehend it. Everything in this life is so vast that the intellect is nothing in comparison with it. It refuses to be bound by the laws of the intellect! It laughs at the bondage the intellect wants to spread around it. And a thousandfold more so is this the case with the human soul. "We ourselves" — this is the greatest mystery of the universe.

*

When we are healthy and young, we think that all the wealth of the world will be ours, and when later we get kicked about by society like footballs and get older, we sit in a corner and croak and throw cold water on the enthusiasm of others. Few men know that with pleasure there is pain, and with pain, pleasure; and as pain is disgusting, so is pleasure, as it is the twin brother of pain. It is derogatory to the glory of man that he should be going after pain, and equally derogatory, that he should be going after pleasure. Both should be turned aside by men whose reason is balanced. Why will not men seek freedom from being played upon? This moment we are whipped, and when we begin to weep, nature gives us a dollar; again we are whipped, and when we weep, nature gives us a piece of ginger-bread, and we begin to laugh again.

The sage wants liberty; he finds that sense-objects are all vain and that there is no end to pleasures and pains. How many rich people in the world want to find fresh pleasures! All pleasures are old, and they want new ones. Do you not see how many foolish things they are inventing every day, just to titillate the nerves for a moment, and that done, how there comes a reaction? The majority of people are just like a flock of sheep. If the leading sheep falls into a ditch, all the rest follow and break their necks. In the same way, what one leading member of a society does, all the others do, without thinking what they are doing. When a man begins to see the vanity of worldly things, he will feel he ought not to be thus played upon or borne along by nature. That is slavery. If a man has a few kind words said to him, he begins to smile, and when he hears a few harsh words, he begins to weep. He is a slave to a bit of bread, to a breath of air; a slave to dress, a slave to patriotism, to country, to name, and to fame. He is thus in the midst of slavery and the real man has become buried within, through his bondage. What you call man is a slave. When one realises all this slavery, then comes the desire to be free; an intense desire comes. If a piece of burning charcoal be placed on a man's head, see how he struggles to throw it off. Similar will be the struggles for freedom of a man who really understands that he is a slave of nature.

*

Each soul is a star, and all stars are set in that infinite azure, that eternal sky, the Lord. There is the root, the reality, the real individuality of each and all. Religion began with the search after some of these stars that had passed beyond our horizon, and ended in finding them all in God, and ourselves in the same place. The whole secret is, then, that your father has given up the old garment he was wearing and is standing where he was through all eternity. Will he manifest another such garment in this or any other world?

I sincerely pray that he may not, until he does so in full consciousness. I pray that none may be dragged anywhither by the unseen power of his own past actions. I pray that all may be free, that is to say, may know that they are free. And if they are to dream again, let us pray that their dreams be all of peace and bliss.

*

From the highest to the lowest and most wicked man, in the greatest of; human beings and the lowest of crawling worms under our feet, is the soul, pure and perfect, infinite and ever-blessed. In the worm that soul is manifesting only an infinitesimal part of its power and purity, and in the greatest man it is manifesting most of it. The difference consists in the degree of manifestation, but not in the essence. Through all beings exists the same pure and perfect soul.

The idea of heaven is thought to be a low idea. It arises from the desire for a place of enjoyment. We foolishly want to limit the whole universe with our present experience.

Children think that the whole universe is full of children. Madmen think the whole universe a lunatic asylum, and so on. So those to whom this world is but sense-enjoyment, whose whole life is in eating and feasting, with very little difference between them and brute beasts—such are naturally found to conceive of places where they will have more enjoyments, because this life is short.

Their desire for enjoyment is infinite, so they are bound to think of places where they will have unobstructed enjoyment of the senses; and we see, as we go on, that those who want to go to such places will have to go; they will dream, and when this dream is over, they will be in another dream where there is plenty of sense-enjoyment; and when that dream breaks, they will have to think of something else. Thus they will be driving about from dream to dream.

*

The eternal, the infinite, the omnipresent, the omniscient is a principle, not a person. You, I, and everyone are but embodiments of that principle, and the more of this infinite principle is embodied in a person, the greater is he, and all in the end will be the perfect embodiment of that and thus all will be one as they are now essentially. This is all there is of religion, and the practice is through this feeling of oneness that is love. All old fogy forms are mere old superstitions. Now, why struggle to keep them alive? Why give thirsty people ditch-water to drink whilst the river of life and truth flows by? This is only human selfishness, nothing else.

Life is short — time is flying — that place and people where one's ideas work best should be the country and the people for everyone. Ay, for a dozen bold hearts, large, noble, and sincere!

*

This is the time to decide your future — while you possess the energy of youth, not when you are worn out and jaded, but in the freshness and vigour of youth. Work — this is the time; for the freshest, the untouched, and unsmelled flowers alone are to be laid at the feet of the Lord, and such He receives.

Rouse yourselves, therefore, or life is short. There are greater works to be done than aspiring to become lawyers and picking quarrels and such things. A far greater work is this sacrifice of yourselves for the benefit of your race, for the welfare of humanity. What is in this life?

*

This life is short, the vanities of the world are transient, but they alone live who live for others, the rest are more dead than alive.

*

Truce to foolish talk; talk of the Lord. Life is too short to be spent in talking about frauds and cranks.

*

From time immemorial India has been the mine of precious ideas to human society; giving birth to high ideas herself, she has freely distributed them broadcast over the whole world. The English are in India today, to gather those higher ideals, to acquire a knowledge of the Vedanta, to penetrate into the deep mysteries of that eternal religion which is yours. Give those in valuable gems in exchange for what you receive from them. The Lord took me to their country to remove this opprobrium of the beggar that is attributed by them to us. It is not right to go to England for the purpose of begging only. Why should they always give us alms? Does anyone do so for ever? It is not the law of nature to be always taking gifts with outstretched hands like beggars. To give and take is the law of nature. Any individual or class or nation that does not obey this law never prospers in life. We also must follow that law.

*

Man says, "I live." He knows not that it is [the fear of] death that makes him cling slavishly to life. He says "I enjoy." He never dreams that nature has enslaved him.

Nature grinds all of us. Keep count of the ounce of pleasure you get.

In the long run, nature did her work through you, and when you die your body will make other plants grow. Yet we think all the time that we are getting pleasure ourselves. Thus the wheel goes round.

*

God is cruel and not cruel. He is all being and not being at the same time. Hence He is all contradictions. Nature also is nothing but a mass of contradictions.

*

Nature's justice is uniformly stern and unrelenting.

*

The idea that the goal is far off, far beyond nature, attracting us all towards it, has to be brought nearer and nearer, without degrading or degenerating it. The God of heaven becomes the God in nature, and the God in nature becomes the God who is nature, and the God who is nature becomes the God within this temple of the body, and the God dwelling in the temple of the body at last becomes the temple itself, becomes the soul and man — and there it reaches the last words it can teach. He whom the sages have been seeking in all these places is in our own hearts; the voice that you heard was right, says the Vedanta, but the direction you gave to the voice was wrong. That ideal of freedom that you perceived was correct, but you projected it outside yourself, and that was your mistake. Bring it nearer and nearer, until you find that it was all the time within you, it was the Self of your own self. That freedom was your own nature, and this Maya never bound you. Nature never has power over you. Like a frightened child you were dreaming that it was throttling you, and the release from this fear is the goal: not only to see it intellectually, but to perceive it, actualise it, much more definitely than we perceive this world.

*

The law of Karma means the law of causation, of inevitable cause and sequence. Wheresoever there is a cause, there an effect must be produced; this necessity cannot be resisted, and this law of Karma, according to our philosophy, is true throughout the whole universe. Whatever we see, or feel, or do, whatever action there is anywhere in the universe, while being the effect of past work on the one hand, becomes, on the other, a cause in its turn, and produces its own effect. It is necessary, together with this, to consider what is meant by the word "law". By law is meant the tendency of a series to repeat itself. When we see one event followed by another, or sometimes happening simultaneously with another, we expect this sequence or co-existence to recur. Our old logicians and philosophers of the Nyâyâ school call this law by the name of Vyâpti. According to them, all our ideas of law are due to association. A series of phenomena becomes associated with things in our mind in a sort of invariable order, so that whatever we perceive at any time is immediately referred to other facts in the mind. Any one idea or, according to our psychology, any one wave that is produced in the mind-stuff, Chitta, must always give rise to many similar waves. This is the psychological idea of association, and causation is only an aspect of this grand pervasive principle of association. This pervasiveness of association is what is, in Sanskrit, called Vyâpti. In the external world the idea of law is the same as in the internal — the expectation that a particular phenomenon will be followed by another, and that the series will repeat itself.

Really speaking, therefore, law does not exist in nature. Practically it is an error to say that gravitation exists in the earth, or that there is any law existing objectively anywhere in nature. Law is the method, the manner in which our mind grasps a series of phenomena; it is all in the mind. Certain phenomena, happening one after another or together, and followed by the conviction of the regularity of their recurrence — thus enabling our minds to grasp the method of the whole series — constitute what we call law.

*

Such questions as, "Why did God create the universe?" "Why did the All-perfect create the imperfect?" etc., can never be answered, because such questions are logical absurdities. Reason exists in nature; beyond nature it has no existence.

God is omnipotent, hence to ask why He did so and so is to limit Him; for it implies that there is a purpose in His creating the universe. If He has a purpose, it must be a means to an end, and this would mean that He could not have the end without the means. The questions, why and wherefore, can only be asked of something which depends upon something else.

*

The oriental ideal is as necessary for the progress of the human race as is the occidental, and I think it is more necessary. Machines never made mankind happy and never will make. He who is trying to make us believe this will claim that happiness is in the machine; but it is always in the mind. That man alone who is the lord of his mind can become happy, and none else.

And what, after all, is this power of machinery? Why should a man who can send a current of electricity through a wire be called a very great man and a very intelligent man? Does not nature do a million times more than that every moment? Why not then fall down and worship nature? What avails it if you have power over the whole of the world, if you have mastered every atom in the universe? That will not make you happy unless you have the power of happiness in yourself, until you have conquered yourself. Man is born to conquer nature, it is true, but the Occidental means by "nature" only physical or external nature. It is true that external nature is majestic, with its mountains, and oceans, and rivers, and with its infinite powers and varieties. Yet there is a more majestic internal nature of man, higher than the sun, moon, and stars, higher than this earth of ours, higher than the physical universe, transcending these little lives of ours; and it affords another field of study.

There the Orientals excel, just as the Occidentals excel in the other. Therefore it is fitting that, whenever there is a spiritual adjustment, it should come from the Orient. It is also fitting that when the Oriental wants to learn about machine-making, he should sit at the feet of the Occidental and learn from him. When the Occident wants to learn about the spirit, about God, about the soul, about the meaning and the mystery of this universe, he must sit at the feet of the Orient to learn.

*

The external and internal natures are not two different things; they are really one. Nature is the sum total of all phenomena. "Nature" means all that is, all that moves.

*

The more you fly from nature, the more she follows you; and if you do not care for her at all, she becomes your slave.

*

The whole of nature is bound by the law of causation and is in time and space. We cannot see anything outside of space, yet we do not know space. We cannot perceive anything outside of time, yet we do not know time. We cannot understand anything except in terms of causality, yet we do not know what causation is. These three things — time, space, and causality — are in and through every phenomena, but they are not phenomena. They are as it were the forms or moulds in which everything must be cast before it can be apprehended. Matter is substance plus time, space, and causation. Mind is substance plus time, space and causation.

This fact can be expressed in another way. Everything is substance plus name and form. Name and form come and go, but substance remains ever the same. Substance, form, and name make this pitcher.

When it is broken, you do not call it pitcher any more, nor do you see its pitcher form. Its name and form vanish, but its substance remains. All the differentiation in substance is made by name and form. There are not real, because they vanish. What we call nature is not the substance, unchanging and indestructible. Nature is time, space and causation. Nature is name and form. Nature is Mâyâ. Maya means name and form, into which everything is cast. Maya is not real. We could not destroy it or change it if it were real. The substance is the noumenon, Maya is phenomena. There is the real "me" which nothing can destroy, and there is the phenomenal "me" which is continually changing and disappearing.

*

There are scholars who from the ancient Aryan literature show that religion originated in nature worship. Although in India we find proofs of ancestor worship everywhere, yet in the oldest records there is no trace of it whatsoever. In the Rig-Veda Samhitâ, the most ancient record of the Aryan race, we do not find any trace of it. Modern scholars think, it is the worship of nature that they find there. The human mind seems to struggle to get a peep behind the scenes. The dawn, the evening, the hurricane, the stupendous and gigantic forces of nature, its beauties, these have exercised the human mind, and it aspires to go beyond, to understand something about them. In the struggle they endow these phenomena with personal attributes, giving them souls and bodies, sometimes beautiful, sometimes transcendent. Every attempt ends by these phenomena becoming abstractions whether personalised or not. So also it is found with the ancient Greeks; their whole mythology is simply this abstracted nature worship. So also with the ancient Germans, the Scandinavians, and all the other Aryan races. Thus, on this side, too, a very strong case has been made out, that religion has its origin in the personification of the powers of nature.

These two views, though they seem to be contradictory, can be reconciled on a third basis, which, to my mind, is the real germ of religion, and that I propose to call the struggle to transcend the limitations of the senses. Either, man goes to seek for the spirits of his ancestors, the spirits of the dead, that is, he wants to get a glimpse of what there is after the body is dissolved, or, he desires to understand the power working behind the stupendous phenomena of nature. Whichever of these is the case, one thing is certain, that he tries to transcend the limitations of the senses. He cannot remain satisfied with his senses; he wants to go beyond them. The explanation need not be mysterious. To me it seems very natural that the first glimpse of religion should come through dreams. The first idea of immortality man may well get through dreams. Is that not a most wonderful state? And we know that children and untutored minds find very little difference between dreaming and their awakened state. What can be more natural than that they find, as natural logic, that even during the sleep state when the body is apparently dead, the mind goes on with all its intricate workings? What wonder that men will at once come to the conclusion that when this body is dissolved for ever, the same working will go on? This, to my mind, would be a more natural explanation of the supernatural, and through this dream idea the human mind rises to higher and higher conceptions. Of course, in time, the vast majority of mankind found out that these dreams are not verified by their waking states, and that during the dream state it is not that man has a fresh existence, but simply that he recapitulates the experiences of the awakened state.

But by this time the search had begun, and the search was inward, arid man continued inquiring more deeply into the different stages of the mind and discovered higher states than either the waking or the dreaming. This state of things we find in all the organised religions of the world, called either ecstasy or inspiration. In all organised religions, their founders, prophets, and messengers are declared to have gone into states of mind that were neither waking nor sleeping, in which they came face to face with a new series of facts relating to what is called the spiritual kingdom. They realised things there much more intensely than we realise facts around us in our waking state.

*

All the religions of the world have been built upon that one universal and adamantine foundation of all our knowledge — direct experience. The teachers all saw God; they all saw their own souls, they saw their future, they saw their eternity, and what they saw they preached. Only there is this difference that by most of these religions especially in modern times, a peculiar claim is made, namely, that these experiences are impossible at the present day; they were only possible with a few men, who were the first founders of the religions that subsequently bore their names. At the present time these experiences have become obsolete, and, therefore, we have now to take religion on belief. This I entirely deny. If there has been one experience in this world in any particular branch of knowledge, it absolutely follows that that experience has been possible millions of times before, and will be repeated eternally. Uniformity is the rigorous law of nature; what once happened can happen always.

*

Man's free agency is established in the soul, and the soul, realising itself to be free, is always asserting the fact in spite of the mind's bondage: "I am free! I am what I am! I am what I am!" This is our freedom. The soul — ever free, boundless, eternal — through aeons and aeons is manifesting itself more and more through its instrument, the mind.

What relation then does man bear to nature? From the lowest form of life to man, the soul is manifesting itself through nature. The highest manifestation of the soul is involved in the lowest form of manifest life and is working itself outward through the process called evolution.

The whole process of evolution is the soul's struggle to manifest itself. It is a constant struggle against nature. It is a struggle against nature, and not conformity to nature that makes man what he is. We hear a great deal about living in harmony with nature, of being in tune with nature. This is a mistake. This table, this pitcher, the minerals, a tree, are all in harmony with nature. Perfect harmony there, no discord. To be in harmony with nature means stagnation, death. How did man build this house? By being in harmony with nature? No. By fighting against nature. It is the constant struggle against nature that constitutes human progress, not conformity with it.

THE END OF ALL BONDAGE

There was never a human race which did not have a religion and worship some sort of God or gods. Whether the God or gods existed or not is no question; but what is the analysis of this psychological phenomenon?

Why is all the world trying to find, or seeking for, a God? Why?

Because in spite of all this bondage, in spite of nature and this tremendous energy of law grinding us down, never allowing us to turn to any side — wherever we go, whatever we want to do, we are thwarted by this law, which is everywhere — in spite of all this, the human soul never forgets its freedom and is ever seeking it. The search for freedom is the search of all religions; whether they know it or not, whether they can formulate it well or ill, the idea is there.

Even the lowest man, the most ignorant, seeks for something which has power over nature's laws. He wants to see a demon, a ghost, a god — somebody who can subdue nature, for whom nature is not almighty, for whom there is no law.

"Oh, for somebody who can break the law!" That is the cry coming from the human heart. We are always seeking for someone who breaks the law.

The rushing engine speeds along the railway track; the little worm crawls out of its way. We at once say, "The engine is dead matter, a machine; and the worm is alive," because the worm attempted to break the law. The engine, with all its power and might, can never break the law. It is made to go in any direction man wants, and it cannot do otherwise; but the worm, small and little though it was, attempted to break the law and avoid the danger. It tried to assert itself against law, assert its freedom; and there was the sign of the future God in it.

Everywhere we see this assertion of freedom, this freedom of the soul. It is reflected in every religion in the shape of God or gods; but it is all external yet — for those who only see the gods outside.

Man decided that he was nothing. He was afraid that he could never be free; so he went to seek for someone outside of nature who was free. Then he thought that there were many and many such free beings, and gradually he merged them all into one God of gods and Lord of lords.

Even that did not satisfy him. He came a little closer to truth, a little nearer; and then gradually found that whatever he was, he was in some way connected with the God of gods and Lord of lords; that he, though he thought himself bound and low and weak, was somehow connected with that God of gods.

Then visions came to him; thought arose and knowledge advanced. And he began to come nearer and nearer to that God, and at last found out that God and all the gods, this whole psychological phenomenon connected with the search for an all-powerful free soul, was but a reflection of his own idea of himself.

And then at last he discovered that it was not only true that "God made man after His own image", but that it was also true that man made God after his own image. That brought out the idea of divine freedom. The Divine Being was always within, the nearest of the near.

Him we had ever been seeking outside, and at last found that He is in the heart of our hearts. You may know the story of the man who mistook his own heartbeat for somebody knocking at the door, and went to the door and opened it, but found nobody there, so he went back.

Again he seemed to hear a knocking at the door, but nobody was there. Then he understood that it was his own heartbeat, and he had misinterpreted it as a knocking at the door.

Similarly, man after his search finds out that this infinite freedom that he was placing in imagination all the time in the nature outside is the internal subject, the eternal Soul of souls; this Reality, he himself.

Thus at last he comes to recognise this marvellous duality of existence: the subject, infinite and finite in one — the Infinite Being is also the same finite soul. The Infinite is caught, as it were, in the meshes of the intellect and apparently manifests as finite beings, but the reality remains unchanged.

This is, therefore, true knowledge: that the Soul of our souls, the Reality that is within us, is That which is unchangeable, eternal, ever-blessed, ever-free. This is the only solid ground for us to stand upon.

This, then, is the end of all death, the advent of all immortality, the end of all misery. And he who sees that One among the many, that One unchangeable in the universe of change, he who sees Him as the Soul of his soul, unto him belongs eternal peace — unto none else.